P9-DIZ-084

4-4

THEOLOGICAL INVESTIGATIONS

Volume XII

Also in this series

THEOLOGICAL INVESTIGATIONS

Vol. I
God, Christ, Mary and Grace

Vol. II
Man in the Church

Vol. III
Theology of the Spiritual Life

Vol. IV
More Recent Writings

Vol. V
Later Writings

Vol. VI
Concerning Vatican Council II

Vol. VII
Further Theology of the Spiritual Life 1

Vol. VIII
Further Theology of the Spiritual Life 2

Vol. IX
Writings of 1965–67 1

Vol. X
Writings of 1965–67 2

Vol. XI
Confrontations 1

THEOLOGICAL
INVESTIGATIONS

VOLUME XII
CONFRONTATIONS 2

by
KARL RAHNER

Translated by
DAVID BOURKE

A Crossroad Book
THE SEABURY PRESS • NEW YORK

1974
THE SEABURY PRESS
815 Second Avenue
New York, N.Y. 10017

A Translation of the second part of
SCHRIFTEN ZUR THEOLOGIE, IX
published by
Verlagsanstalt Benziger & Co. AG., Einsiedeln

This Translation
© Darton, Longman & Todd Ltd. 1974
First published 1974

All rights reserved. No part of this book may be
used or reproduced in any manner whatsoever without
the permission of The Seabury Press, except for
brief quotations in critical reviews and articles.

Library of Congress Catalog Card Number: 61-8189
ISBN: 0-8164-1179-4
Printed in the United States of America

CONTENTS

PART ONE *Ecclesiology*

1 THE TEACHING OFFICE OF THE CHURCH IN THE
PRESENT-DAY CRISIS OF AUTHORITY   3

2 THE POINT OF DEPARTURE IN THEOLOGY FOR
DETERMINING THE NATURE OF THE PRIESTLY
OFFICE   31

3 THEOLOGICAL REFLECTIONS ON THE PRIESTLY IMAGE
OF TODAY AND TOMORROW   39

4 ON THE DIACONATE   61

5 OBSERVATIONS ON THE FACTOR OF THE
CHARISMATIC IN THE CHURCH   81

6 SCHISM IN THE CATHOLIC CHURCH?   98

7 HERESIES IN THE CHURCH TODAY?   116

8 CONCERNING OUR ASSENT TO THE CHURCH AS SHE
EXISTS IN THE CONCRETE   142

9 ANONYMOUS CHRISTIANITY AND THE MISSIONARY
TASK OF THE CHURCH   161

PART TWO *Church and Society*

10 THE QUESTION OF THE FUTURE   181

11 PERSPECTIVES FOR THE FUTURE OF THE CHURCH   202

CONTENTS

12 ON THE STRUCTURE OF THE PEOPLE OF THE
   CHURCH TODAY   218

13 THE FUNCTION OF THE CHURCH AS A CRITIC OF
   SOCIETY   229

LIST OF SOURCES   250

INDEX OF PERSONS   253

INDEX OF SUBJECTS   255

PART ONE

Ecclesiology

I

THE TEACHING OFFICE OF THE
CHURCH IN THE PRESENT-DAY CRISIS
OF AUTHORITY

A THEOLOGICAL consideration of the Church's office to teach or magisterium[1] and the authority which, on a Catholic understanding of the Church, is to be attached to this, is not perhaps in any direct sense a suitable theme for ecumenical discussion or in controversial theology. And in fact our present consideration will indeed, to a large extent, take the form of a *quaestio disputata* internal to the Catholic body. But surely it is permissible to present even a consideration of this kind in the present context. First because even in a Protestant Church, despite all differences of opinion between Protestant and Catholic Christians precisely on the question of ecclesiastical authority, the subject of an official function to teach cannot altogether be evaded from the outset, as is shown, for instance, from the fact that instructional techniques have been raised as an issue for discussion.[2] Second because any further development in the theology of the Church's official teaching function, even within the Catholic body and on the basis of specifically Catholic principles may perhaps be able to bring us nearer to an ecumenical agreement. I propose, therefore, to put forward certain considerations concerning the authority of the Church's magisterium on a Catholic understanding of the Church. It is obvious that in view of the brevity of the time available these considerations will once more be very fragmentary in character, and our choice of subject-matter must necessarily appear somewhat arbitrary. Our aim, therefore, in these considerations of ours is not once again to present, or even to justify, the universal Catholic doctrine with regard to the official teaching function of the Church as this has once more been set

[1] Cf. also the article under this heading in *LTK* VI (2nd ed. 1961), 884-890, and 'Magisterium' *Sacramentum Mundi* 3 (New York and London, 1969), pp. 351-358.
[2] A survey and summary on this point is to be found in H. Hohlbein and W. Maurer, 'Lehrzuchtverfahren', *RGG* IV (3rd ed., 1960), 281-286.

3

forth in the Second Vatican Council (and, moreover, abstracting from the question of the collegiality of those in whom this official teaching function is vested, without any notable advances by comparison with the First Vatican Council). Our present aim is rather to lay bare certain problems inherent in this doctrine which have not been reflected upon, and so to provide a stimulus for a further development of this doctrine which may then perhaps even have better prospects of success in coping with the present-day crisis which threatens the teaching authority of the Church.

Let us begin by re-stating in contemporary terms the formal model which is customarily used in presentations of the teaching authority of the Church's official representatives. The following statement may perhaps achieve this:

As the absolute teacher and the prophet *par excellence* Jesus Christ delivered to the apostles a quite specific body of teaching. In doing so he also equipped these apostles with a quite specific formal authority deriving from himself and supplementary to the actual content of this doctrinal message which he handed down to them. It equips the apostles and authorises them to stand before their fellow men and claim the allegiance of their faith for the content of their message. It also equips them to preserve that message itself undistorted, to interpret it, and to explicitate it. The assistance of the Spirit of Christ promised to them guarantees that they shall make a right use of this formal authority to teach, and their use of it is 'infallibly' preserved from error in those cases in which the exercise of this teaching authority is accompanied by a claim to an absolute assent of faith on the part of those to whom their message is addressed, in other words in those cases in which the fulness of their authority is brought to bear. This teaching authority of the apostles has been handed down to the college of bishops under the pope.

This absolute authority can be exercised both in the ordinary proclamation of Christian doctrine and also in an act of the 'extraordinary magisterium', i.e. in the form of a definition on the part of a Council or of the pope. However in very many cases in which the authoritative magisterium is exercised it is not brought to bear with this absolute force, and the obligation which it lays upon the faithful is not the assent of their faith properly so called, but merely a qualified assent, for in such exercises of the official teaching authority of the Church the doctrine that is stated, though authentic, is not in itself irreformable. Rather it is a doctrine that is formulated as conscientiously as possible by the teaching authority to protect the essential and proper substance of the faith.

With the proviso that in the following considerations this conceptual model will have to be slightly expanded or more precisely defined in this or that respect, I believe that the terms in which I have just presented this conceptual model do justice to the essential tenor of the established ecclesiology of the Church with regard to her own teaching office.[3] But the very fact that it has been stated in such formal and abstract terms means that very much in it still remains unclarified and obscure. And it is with these elements that we shall be concerned in what follows. In this we are abstracting altogether from the questions (in themselves fundamental) of whether, how, and how far this conception of the teaching authority attached to the office of bishop can be justified on the basis of scripture as a whole, and we are abstracting even more from the still more difficult question of how, and to what extent a doctrinal authority of this kind can be traced back to a resolve of the pre-Easter Jesus himself. Here we are considering only the problems inherent in this conceptual model.

In considering this conceptual model of what is meant by the teaching authority of the official Church the first point that we notice is the absence of any reference to the Church as such. To state the matter more precisely: the Church as 'hearing' and believing is merely that which is addressed, that to which this authority is directed. Now in the Second Vatican Council statements are to be found at various points (though no specific presentation of these can be undertaken here) in which an attempt has been made to overcome this one-sided state of affairs in which the official teachers do all the speaking, and their point of view alone is expressed, while the Church of the faithful listening to them is in the position merely of an addressee obediently accepting the Church's teaching authority as vested in her bishops. The fact that sporadic attempts were made to overcome this situation in the Second Vatican Council should be neither doubted nor under-estimated, But I believe that initiatives of this kind have, after all, remained precisely at the level of initiatives and no more, and have therefore had hardly any practical effect in the life of the Church and in the manner in which her teaching is presented and listened to.[4]

The first point to bear in mind is that on any showing the apostles can

[3] The tendency referred to here is to be discerned in all the classical treatises of theology. Cf. e.g. *PSJ* I (Madrid, 4th ed., 1958), 503–993, where the authority of the official Church is treated of almost to the exclusion of all else.

[4] In this connection chapters II and IV of the Constitution 'Lumen Gentium' are significant. Here an infallibility of faith is attributed to the people of God as a whole, as also to the people of the Church as the recipients of teaching in particular. The Council itself has not attempted to carry this further by relating what it says in these chapters to the statements in chapter III, where it is the hierarchical structure of the Church that is being dealt with.

only be the bearers of a teaching authority of this kind to the extent that they themselves are believers and hearers. This is not merely because the unbeliever could have no reason and no motive for laying claim to or applying any such formal authority, nor merely because in fact in our case (in other cases it might conceivably be different) the exercise of such authority necessarily claims the allegiance of faith from the official bearers of this teaching authority themselves. This means that any officially appointed teacher who refused the allegiance of his faith would thereby himself be denying his own authority in the very act of laying claim to it. For this authority vested in him is at the same time an element in his own message. When an apostle preaches he bears witness precisely to his experience of Jesus' Resurrection, and it is quite impossible to separate this experience from his own *faith* in the Resurrection of Jesus.

Furthermore he always preaches as a member of a community of believers which asserts its claims openly in virtue of the fact that it also presents itself as the genuine continuation and perfection of the Old Testament community which was constituted by faith in the promises of God, those promises which have been fulfilled in Jesus. The apostolic preaching was always that of a member of the Old Testament community of the faith. It assumed as its starting-point the faith and the professed creed of Israel. It used this as the basis for its argument. In other words it proceeded from the faith of a Church which did not presuppose as infallible any teaching office which was institutional in the proper sense of the term. The preaching of the individual apostle, therefore, is not merely addressed to the believing community, but also proceeds from it. It bears witness to a faith which has already been brought into being by God alone in Jesus Christ, and it is only on this basis (this is a point which we shall have to consider more fully at a later stage) that it can also justify its own formal authority.[5]

The fact that the authority of the officially appointed teachers in the Church derives from the Church herself as a whole becomes still clearer

[5] This connection is in fact one which was clearly recognized in the ancient Church as well. On this cf. the extremely instructive study by G. Ludwig, *Die Primatsworte Mt 16:18-19 in der altkirchlichen Exegese* (Munster, 1952), and also K. Adam, 'Cyprians Kommentar zu Mt 16:18', *Gesammelte Aufsätze* (Augsburg, 1936), pp. 80–123; M. Lods, 'Le "Tu es Petrus" dans l'exégèse patristique', *Eglise et Théologie* 21/62 (1958), pp. 15–34; A. M. La Bonnardière, 'Tu es Petrus. La péricope Mt. 16:13–23 dans l'oeuvre de Saint Augustin', *Irénikon* 34 (1961), pp. 451–499. And in addition to these: B. Botte, H. Marot etc. (edd.), *Das Konzil und die Konzile* (Stuttgart, 1962); Y. Congar, ed., *L'Épiscopat et l'Église universelle*, Unam Sanctam 39 (Paris, 1962); *idem*, *L'Ecclésiologie du Haut Moyen Age* (Paris, 1968), pp. 138 ff.

when we consider the bearers of this authority in post-apostolic times. We are making it impossible for ourselves to achieve any insight into this truth that the authority of the official teachers in the Church derives from the Church as a whole if we suppose that we can conceive of a derived authority of this kind merely as corresponding to a popular and democratic form of government. On this interpretation the 'people' of the. Church in this sense would be the juridical subject of power extending the authority which it possesses as such to certain specific individuals as a decision of the people's own will. But to reject the conceptual model of a 'democracy' precisely of *this* sort is far from making it completely impossible to conceive of any way in which the authority of the Church can be derived from the believing Church as a whole. On any fully Catholic understanding of the Church the believing Church is not merely constituted as such by the factor of teaching authority. On the contrary for authority of this sort to be able to exist at all a believing Church has already to be in existence as its necessary prior condition.[6]

The basic principles leading to this insight are already to be found in the established ecclesiology of the seminaries. Thus for instance even in the First Vatican Council the nature and extent of the pope's authority to teach, especially with regard to its 'infallibility', are determined by the standards of the teaching authority actually exercised in the Church in general (DS 3074). But since there cannot be several supreme teaching authorities in the Church this relationship which the pope's authority to teach bears to that of the Church in general is not only a relationship of mere *equality* between two entities which are really distinct. Rather the pope's authority to teach them in a real sense be derived, at least from the *active* teaching authority of the Church as a whole. The truth that we are seeking to express in this way is simply that the derivation of an authority from Christ need not from the outset be incompatible with a derivation of this same authority from the Church. Rather both kinds of derivation can constitute two sides of a single objective situation, because ultimately speaking the derivation of a specific office from Christ is nothing else than an element in the derivation of the Church as a whole from Christ.[7]

---

[6] The author has pointed out a connection which is – mutatis mutandis – similiar in other contexts. Cf. K. Rahner and J. Ratzinger, *Revelation and Tradition,* Quaestiones Disputatae 17 (Freiburg, 1966). See also H. Fries, 'Lehramt als Dienst am Glauben', *Catholica* 23 (1969), pp. 154–186.

[7] On this cf. the extremely enlightening studies on the history of dogma in O. Rousseau, J. J. von Allmen et al. (edd.), *L'infaillibilité de l'Eglise,* Collection Irénikon (Chevetogne, 1963), esp. pp. 147 ff.

In the Second Vatican Council too (Lumen Gentium No. 25) the teaching authority of the pope and bishops is regarded as deriving univocally from Christ and aimed at the Church rather than deriving from it. In this way it is emphazised that it is not primarily in virtue of the agreement of the Church that the decisions of the popes and bishops are unassailable. At the same time, however, it is also emphasized that in any *ex cathedra* definition the pope is acting not as a private individual, but as the supreme teacher of the universal Church. His charism is the charism of the infallibility of the Church herself, and not one that is separate from this. And it is emphasized further that it is the effective power of the one Spirit of the Church as a whole that ensures that the Church herself can never fail to agree to such decisions. It is further stated in Dei Verbum No. 8 that the deposit of faith to which the teaching office is bound includes all 'that she herself is, all that she believes'. This, then, constitutes a further pointer to the fact that the teaching office is not only actively orientated towards the Church with a content of faith which she initially possesses on her own account, but is at the same time derived from this believing Church herself. In a true sense all this is, in fact, obvious. Only in this particular context, in which we are speaking of the teaching office, it is generally overlooked. In this connection the teaching office appears simply as deriving from God and Christ alone, and as consisting in the possession of the deposit of faith and of a formal ratification enabling it to bear an authoritative witness to the content of this faith. The situation is of course such that in the concrete the bearers of this deposit of faith and the teaching authority that goes with it are necessarily men who as simple believers have already received this faith from the Church and from her life as these exist in the concrete – from the concrete Church, therefore, who in her faith, in the history of her faith, and the development of her dogma, is not simply the passive and obedient object of a teaching authority in the Church. The de facto bearers of the teaching office are, at least in respect of the content of their teaching, dependent upon a Church who is not constituted simply by the one-sided functions of the official authorities in the Church. This faith, this history of faith, this development of dogma on which the teaching office depends in the concrete, are factors to which all the members of the Church contribute, each in his own way, by their lives, the confession of their faith, their prayers, their concrete decisions, the theology which they work out for themselves, and their activities in all this are very far from being confined merely to putting into practice truths and norms deriving from the teaching office itself.[8]

[8] Cf. M. Löhrer, 'Träger der Vermittlung', *Mysterium Salutis* I (Zürich, 1965),

But the doctrinal authority attached to the teaching office has a derivation from the Church as a whole and in herself not merely in respect of the content of what is proclaimed, or in virtue of the fact that those who do proclaim it are always first and foremost themselves believers involved in the single developing history of faith in the Church as a whole. More than this the actual power to teach, the authenticity and effectiveness ('infallibility') of the teaching have a certain derivation from the Church herself as a whole. We do not need to conceive of the reality and effectiveness of this authority, which must in fact be something more than a mere formal right to teach as constituted by a continually renewed intervention on God's part from without taking place in a miraculous manner in the course of the Church's history. For otherwise saving history and revelation history as abiding factors in the Church would not in fact constitute the Church's history itself, but would merely be present at those isolated points within that history as a whole at which God intervened to correct the course of the history of the human spirit and to preserve it from deviations arising from its own interior dynamism. The real effectiveness of the authority vested in the Church's official teachers must consist rather in the fact that through God's grace-given bestowal of himself upon the world, and through the historical manifestation of this in the absolute in Jesus Christ, which renders this self-bestowal victorious and irrevocable, the Church is constituted as the experience in faith of this self-bestowal of God, which can no longer be defeated by error. This entity, then, constituted by the experience of the irreversible victory of God's self-bestowal, is called the Church. As a community and a society she is of her nature institutional, and this means that she has an office, an officially constituted body to be the organ through which she realizes the fulness of her own true nature. Now because of this this office, as a teaching office, participates in this abiding victory of the truth of God in the world which constitutes the innermost entelecheia of the history of the world, and the self-realization of the world in its relationship to God.[9] In Jesus Christ the Church constitutes the achieved self-realization of the eschatological

---

pp. 545–555. Likewise the comprehensive presentation of the relevant dogmatic history by Y. Congar, *Lay People in the Church* (London, 1957). On Newman's thesis to the effect that the real resistance to Arianism in the fourth century was achieved by the 'people' cf. J. Guitton, *Mitbürger der Wahrheit* (Salzburg, 1964).

[9] This idea has been still further developed by K. Rahner, 'Ekklesiologische Grundlegung', *Handbuch der Pastoraltheologie* I (Freiburg, 1964), pp. 117–148; *idem*, 'The Church and the Parousia of Christ', *Theological Investigations* VI (London and Baltimore, 1969), pp. 295–312.

victory of God's self-bestowal upon the world. Moreover, as a community of faith the Church always continues also and necessarily to be a society composed of men with an official constitution. It is because of this that there is also a teaching office. Hence both in what it teaches and in the power and infallibility with which it teaches it this office has a derivation from the Church. This derivation from the *Church* is precisely the concrete form in which the derivation of the teaching office from Christ and God is realized.

Now while all these points are in themselves self-evident truisms, it is nevertheless all too easy, both in theory and still more in the practice of the Church, for them to be covered over by the formal and juridical framework in which the doctrinal power of the teaching office is conceived of, for it tends to be thought of in merely formal and juridical terms as a commission coming from God and Christ. And on this view we cease any longer to enquire what this conceptual model, in itself perfectly correct, is really intended to convey in terms of content. Precisely today, when all merely formal claims to authority are being called in question and disputed, it must be emphasized that the doctrine of the Church's teaching office has a concrete content of its own of a theological kind, and this fact must be clearly recognized and included as a factor in Christian thinking and in the exercise of the Church's official functions in the concrete.

In fact it must be recognized as a basic and universal principle that the situation is not that the formal authority vested in an official body in society and the authority inherent in the realities themselves which that body is designed to represent and uphold really have to be two different entities. The two entities can perfectly well be conceived of as really identical in objective fact. The only proviso is that we must realize and hold firm to the truth that the reality itself and the authority inherent in it as such need to be upheld and given concrete application by an authority of a formal kind existing in society, and further that this authority, which depends upon the authority inherent in the reality itself, can in the concrete individual case make claims of its own and interpret the reality itself, and can thereby claim a 'formal' authority whenever it is not immediately clear to the individual how the individual decisions derive from the 'reality itself' as a whole. But precisely for this reason, and in every individual case in which such formal authority is exercised, it must be able to make it clear again and again that as a whole it derives from the very reality which it is concerned to uphold.[10]

[10] In this connection very different ideas were developed in the past as to the

What this means in the concrete in the case with which we are concerned is this: the teaching office must show itself as it really is according to its own understanding of its nature. It may not cover over and conceal aspects in this from the short-sighted feeling that these aspects tend more to overthrow the authority of the teaching office itself and entail a danger that it will not be recognized. In Lumen Gentium No. 25 the Second Vatican Council explicitly states that the officially appointed teachers of the Church have to apply the appropriate human means in order to arrive at the truth in official decisions on matters of doctrine. Even this, however, is only a very general statement, and almost excessively mild and vague. For in the very nature of the case it obviously implies that those charged to uphold the teaching office are also obliged to study before coming to a decision. They must consult theologians, work themselves and cause others to work in the fields of exegesis and the history of dogma. They must open their minds to discussion. They must maintain contact with the living awareness of the faith which manifests itself in the Church as a whole. For it is from this living awareness that these bearers of the teaching office themselves derive their ideas. Again in any definitorial decisions which these representatives of the teaching office arrive at the Church's own absolute assent of faith as worked out in history, albeit unreflectingly, must already have gone before, so that in a case of this kind the specific charism of the teaching office consists, strictly speaking, in its 'infallible' confirmation of this absolute assent of faith on the part of the Church as a whole, which has already been arrived at.

All these factors are implied in the very nature of the case in the statement of the Second Vatican Council referred to above.

Now it must not be disputed that these and similar 'suitable means' of the teaching office have by and large de facto been applied, although perhaps it should also be emphasized that in particular epochs and at particular stages in the history of the world and of the Church the means and procedures employed in a process of discovering truth of this kind need not necessarily always be the same. Today, for instance, means and procedures may be necessary and obligatory for the representatives of the teaching office which could not possibly have been present in earlier

---

precise connection between authority and 'objective truth'. In addition to the work mentioned in n.7 cf. esp. J. M. Todd (ed.), *Probleme der Autorität* (Düsseldorf, 1967); Y. Congar, *Pour une Église servante et pauvre*, L'église aux cent visages 8 (Paris, 1963), and also *idem* in M. Nédoncelle, R. Aubert *et al.* (edd.), *L'Ecclésiologie au XIXe siècle*, Unam Sanctam 34 (Paris, 1960), pp. 77–114.

ages.[11] But I cannot escape the impression that attempts are still constantly made to conceal these genuinely human factors in the concrete process by which the Church's teaching office arrives at the truth. And this is manifestly because there is a tendency to feel that belief in the divine assistance accorded to the teaching office would be endangered or even disappear if the normal Christian were to realize the sort of concrete personalities who were involved, the sort of institutional factors and procedures which were brought to bear, the sort of struggles, discussions, factional divisions etc. which arose in the process of arriving at the truth in this way. On this question there is a tendency tacitly to proceed from the assumption that there is a kind of 'synergism' at work here, to point to forces that are extrinsic to the human debate, and so to regard God's intervention as commencing only at that point at which human efforts are suspended. In reality, however, God works precisely in and through these human efforts and his activity does not constitute a distinct factor apart from this. Precisely for this reason we should bring these human factors into the open. Instead of concealing them we should throw light upon them and make it possible to assess them at their true worth. For in themselves they constitute something more than merely a supplement to the divine activity, a prior condition for it, or an obscure residue, otherwise unaccounted for, in the exercise of the teaching office. Rather these human factors constitute an intrinsic element in the exercise of the teaching office itself. We are deceiving ourselves if we suppose that the teaching office of the Church meets with more respect and trust on the part of modern man when it withdraws itself into a mysterious remoteness, when it conceals even the material questions with which it has to cope beneath the veil of a *Secretum Sancti Officii*, when it prohibits a realistic and open discussion of the suitability of the theological advisers who are engaged, when it fails to make clear what objective and really relevant criteria have governed the choice of these, and when its decisions are not accompanied by any arguments, or at least any that do justice to the importance of the realities involved.

Of course at a time like the present, in which many more advanced stages of development are to be found side by side, and are being achieved

[11] The author has developed proposals for this in other contexts. cf. K. Rahner, 'Theology and the Church's Teaching Authority,' *Theological Investigations* IX (London and New York, 1972), pp. 83–100; and in addition 'Pluralism in Theology and the Unity of the Creed in the Church' *idem* XI (London, 1970) pp. 3–23; see also G. Baum, 'The Magisterium in a Changing Church', *Concilium* I/3 (1967), pp. 34–42 (Dogma).

almost hourly in the Church, there are still many individuals for whom
any sober and realistic view of the work of the teaching office as it is and
as it actually must be as a matter of theological necessity represents an
attack upon their faith. But for those people who really do provide the
standards by which the present and future of the Church will have to be
shaped the converse is true. Hence today the Church has a vital task to
perform in so educating her members that they are effectively conversant
with the nature of the Church in all her aspects and the forms in which
this must necessarily be manifested today.

Perhaps even here we have already reached a point at which it is possible
to make some explicit statement about that question which is customarily
referred to as the question of 'the teaching office and democracy'.[12] In
formulating this subordinate theme in these terms we are of course aware
of the fact that 'democracy' is not a concept for which any authorization
can be claimed from scripture, or which arises in any traditional ecclesiology. This fact in itself shows that we must be cautious in seeking to
introduce 'democracy' into any ecclesiology as a theological concept. It is
clear from the ultimate nature of the Church that she can never be *allowed*
to be a 'democracy' in the sense in which a secular society can or should
be this. What has to be said about 'democracy' in an ecclesiology could
be expressed without ever using this term at all. We could take as our
starting-point the biblical doctrine of the Body of Christ and the pluralism
of its functions, no one of which can be allowed to exclude the others, and
all of which must work together. Alternatively we might take as our
starting-point the concept of 'brotherhood' etc. Our true reason for
speaking of democracy in connection with the Church at this point,
therefore, is simply that it is precisely this key term that is used today in
treating of this question. In this connection we can point out to those
theologians and believers who all too uncompromisingly reject any such
key term as 'democracy' from the outset in their theology that the traditional ecclesiology works freely with concepts which derive from the
experience of what it is to live in society at the secular level.

First in the very nature of the case it is obvious that that reality which
the term 'democracy' can be used to signify or to stand for has, and
necessarily must have, a quite different relationship to the faith and creed
of the Church and to the truth of divine revelation from that which it

[12] On what follows cf. also K. Rahner, 'Demokratie in der Kirche?', *Gnade als
Freiheit* (Freiburg, 1968), pp. 113–130, and O. Semmelroth, 'Demokratie in der
Kirche?', *Martyria, Leiturgia, Diakonia* (Festschrift für H. Volk), (Mainz, 1968),
pp. 399–415.

bears to those realities consisting in institutional factors, modes of life and practices in the Church, which according to the Church's theological understanding of her own nature, are from the outset regarded as 'juris humani', and as such subject, in a way which is quite different from that which applies to the truth of revelation, to historical change and to free evaluation on the part of the Church's members. Right from the outset the meaning of the term 'democracy' and the place accorded to it in our scale of values differs according to whether it is the first or the second of these two realities that is being treated of. In our present study, therefore, we are treating exclusively of the question of the *teaching office* and democracy, and any answer which we arrive at to *this* question is still not an answer to the further question of in what ways, and to what extent the Church could be 'more deomocratic', for instance in the manner in which its office-bearers are selected, the exemption of ecclesiastical laws from human justice, the degree of autonomy granted to particular Churches within the one Church etc. If the subject of our discussion is to be democracy and the teaching office it is necessary to reject straightway any 'reactionary' prejudice which might lead us to suppose that any democratic system of voting is from the outset incompatible with the nature of the Church's teaching office. From the time of the Council of the Apostles right down to the Second Vatican Council votes have been taken in questions of doctrine, and this system of voting was the manner in which decisions were arrived at which were binding in conscience upon the faith of every member of the Church. Nor let it be said that at least since the First Vatican Council any such system of voting on the part of a *collegium* can no longer have any true significance or any real democratic character on the grounds that it could be blocked or rendered ineffective by the decision of the pope acting as an individual and in isolation. For when any such fully ratified decision of a Council is arrived at by a voting process – and this is what has in fact taken place – then it has the force of an effective decision on the part of the *collegium* as such, and not merely a consultative procedure prior to the decision of the pope. Conversely it is quite impossible for the pope to take an *ex cathedra* decision in opposition to a clear majority of the bishops of the Church, though the term 'impossible', as applied here does not signify any limitation of his formal and juridical authority, but rather constitutes a limitation which is inherent in the reality itself and in the moral norms which have to be observed when the pope arrives at any such decision (seeing that it is through the assistance of the Spirit that he actually does arrive at it).[13]

[13] The doctrine of the Second Vatican Council on this point is clear. Cf. the

THE TEACHING OFFICE OF THE CHURCH

In fact to realize how impossible this is we have only to put to ourselves the following question: Given that the pope proposed to define a doctrine which was contrary to the conviction of the great majority of the Church's members, and that too as expressed by the undoubted representatives of these, and given that, according to the teaching of the Second Vatican Council itself, the pope himself does not receive any fresh revelations, how could he ever know that the doctrine which he proposed to define was in fact contained in divine revelation? If he were to arrive at a decision which was positively opposed to the conviction of the great majority of the universal episcopate, this would be tantamount to asserting that he had received a fresh revelation regardless of whether we did or did not apply the term 'revelation' to this knowledge on the pope's part that *he* was right while the opposite opinion, upheld by the majority of the Church, was wrong. Even if the actual content of the doctrine itself was not held to constitute a fresh revelation which the pope alone had obtained independently of the rest of the Church, still the very statement that this content belonged to revelation would constitute such a fresh revelation in itself. Now according to the doctrine of the Second Vatican Council no such situation is possible. The pope's teaching precisely as formulated in his *ex cathedra* decisions is derived from the faith of the universal Church, and the fact that it is derived in this sense is ensured by the taking of a 'vote', though of course this can take place in the most varied ways, and need not necessarily have the juridical form or the solemnity of a vote taken in a Council. In the nature of the case this 'vote' may be present as the prior condition for an *ex cathedra* decision on the pope's part even outside the context of a Council. If we decide to regard any 'vote' as a democratic element, then we must uncompromisingly assert that the teaching office has something to do with democracy even though in saying this we are still leaving certain more detailed questions not fully answered, the questions, namely, of the theological nature of a voting procedure of this kind, and still more that of which members in the Church are or can be qualified to participate in this voting procedure. With regard to the theological nature of a voting procedure of this kind it must be said that in any such vote the voter does not simply declare what is his own personal free choice (as is the case in votes taken on civic laws in secular

author's commentary on chapter III of the Constitution 'Lumen Gentium': *LTK* Suppl. Vol. I (1966), esp. 221–229. But the pronouncements of the First Vatican Council too on this point must not be ignored. On this cf. H. Fries, 'Ex esse non ex consensu Ecclesiae', *Volk Gottes* (Festschrift für J. Höfer) edited by R. Bäumer and H. Dolch (Freiburg, 1967), pp. 480–517.

society) but bears witness to that faith which he is conscious of possessing and which he finds within himself as a divine gift. In secular society a decision of this kind, even though arrived at democratically, is of its nature binding upon society as a whole. In contrast to this, however, a vote of this kind taken within the free community of the faith which is the Church, and pertaining essentially to the Church, is restricted in its binding force to the individual conscience of the believer.

In a secular society which is democratic in its constitution the outcome of a vote implies a situation in which even those who have voted against the majority are bound to observe the majority decision (otherwise we would have to support a utopian idea and hold that no truly democratic society had yet been evolved at all. We would have to say that it is something that still has to come in the future, and that it is only achieved when the goals which opposed factions have set themselves to achieve can be, and actually are, realized simultaneously). By contrast with this the situation essentially produced by a vote on questions of faith admits of the following two alternatives: first, prior to the decision being taken, the personal faith of those belonging to the minority party may still have remained ultimately open in conscience to the view of the opposing party on the concrete question of faith that was being discussed. In that case *after* the decision has been taken and the convictions in faith of the majority party have been adopted as the convictions of the Church as such, the minority party can re-orientate its ideas in conformity with this. The *second* alternative is that the conscience of the minority party with regard to their faith was such that the decision of the majority is conceived actually to separate its adherents from the Church. In that case the minority party remains free because on the concrete question concerned its own faith taken as a whole is committed firmly to a position which is felt to be diametrically opposed to that of the majority party. From this it follows as a matter of necessity that the majority party must be considered to have separated themselves from the Church, and the true Church must be deemed to be constituted by the minority.

With regard to the question of which members of the Church may be considered as qualified to take an active part in such a vote all that we can briefly say here is the following:

According to the Catholic understanding of the Church the universal episcopate must be considered qualified jure divino to take part in such a vote in union with and under the pope in exercising the Church's doctrinal authority. But 'jure divino' here does not signify in any primary sense that others too cannot be given the right to take part in such a vote in union with the college of bishops in virtue of human laws enacted within the Church. In fact this has actually been the case in all the more recent Councils. There have always been non-episcopal members of the Council who were given the right to vote.[14] The reasons for admitting a non-episcopal member to a consultative vote at a Council or similar occasion do not necessarily have to consist in the fact (though formerly this was, generally speaking the case) that the member concerned, though not a bishop, was nevertheless exercising quasi-episcopal functions (e.g. as the head of a religious order). Another and equally valid reason which was admitted in principle could be the special competence of the individual concerned in a particular field. Roman prelates who had a seat and vote in the Council, on a serious theological view of their functions, rely more upon the competence of specialist theologians of this kind than upon the mere fact of their episcopal consecration, which, after all, constituted them as 'bishops' only in a very formalistic sense. In other words it is at least *possible* for the Church to extend such a right to non-episcopal members even though, when she does so she is acting *jure humano*. In this connection a point to be borne in mind is that in principle it may be *morally demanded* of her in the very nature of the case that she shall extend the right to vote in this way in situations arising at particular epochs, in particular cultural conditions, and in questions arising in specific fields. For it is at any rate not in principle or *a priori* inconceivable that a case of this kind might arise in circumstances such as these. Now if such cases were to arise then the difference between divine and human law in the Church would be only a very relative one, since on the one hand the divine law of the Church's constitution must always and inevitably exhibit a concrete form that is subject to the conditions of particular epochs, while on the other every *jus humanum* entailing a moral duty to act in such and such a way in a specific situation conceals within itself a basic core of necessity that derives from God. From this it follows that the *jus divinum* attributed, in the case which we are considering, to the universal episcopate ultimately signifies merely that the united bishops, and no-one else beside them, represent the abiding assurance and the abiding visible manifestation of the *continuity* of the right of the teaching office in the Church to be heard and obeyed.

The *jus divinum* belonging to the universal episcopate in union with the pope, therefore, does not imply that *it alone* can always and in every

[14] On the practice of earlier Councils in this connection cf. the study by Y. Congar adduced in n. 8, and also *idem, L'Ecclesiologie du Haut Moyen Age* (Paris, 1968), esp. p. 96.

epoch be the sole bearer of the teaching office in the concrete. It is at least perfectly conceivable that a historical situation might arise in which the concrete bearer of the teaching office *need not* necessarily be simply identical with the episcopate alone, and this for moral reasons which in fact do not necessarily have to entail obligations applicable to all ages, but certainly can make claims of this kind at specific epochs and in specific situations (in terms of intellectual, cultural or social development). Now even though one who is a representative of the Church's teaching office does not necessarily have to be fully a member of the episcopate, still in the very nature of the case there will be individuals who are, in spite of this, what we now call bishops (and whom, presumably, we will continue to call by this name in the future), and in virtue of this fact the *jus divinum* of the episcopate itself considered as an official authority to teach is assured, and at the same time we are assured of the fact that the teaching office even as upheld by such individuals can be traced back through the ages in unbroken succession right to apostolic times.

Up to this point we have been following two lines of thought with regard to the possibility and the significance of exercising the teaching authority of the Church in the form of a vote, and with regard to the individuals to whom such voting power could be extended. Now the only way in which we can develop these considerations any further is to attempt to define still more precisely the significance which such a voting procedure would have. We have already said that a vote of this kind is of its nature different from the sort of vote that takes place in the context of secular politics. This latter constitutes a public statement of a voluntary decision taken by the voters themselves. By contrast with this the sort of vote we are speaking of is an attestation of certain beliefs held by the voters which as a matter of their own personal conviction they discover within themselves and recognize as brought about by God.

The next stage in our considerations must be to examine the question of the weight and significance to be attached to a majority vote. How far, and in what sense must this be allowed to prevail over a minority of the voters? The first point that must be made is that (abstracting for the moment from the position of the pope) on a Catholic understanding of the Church the fact that a given position is upheld by the majority of the voters does not represent any absolute guarantee, so far as the conscience of the individual Catholic believer or the individual Catholic bishop is concerned, that the doctrine assented to by the majority does in fact belong intrinsically to the deposit of faith bequeathed by the apostles, and as such binding in faith upon the conscience of the individual believer or bishop. (This does not invalidate what has been said above with regard to the *negative* function which such a majority vote has in contributing to the decision of the pope.) A further point is that on a Catholic understanding of the Church no majority decision arrived at in the present can ever prevail over the absolute assent of faith accorded to a given doctrine by the Church of earlier ages. If such a case should arise, the true Church would unquestionably be constituted by the minority alone. This would remain true even if the pope himself took his stand on the side of the majority in such a case, a situation which, as we know, is not regarded by theological tradition as simply and absolutely impossible from the outset.[15]

It must be recognized *a priori* therefore that we can regard the opinion of a majority as theologically relevant only if in coming to a decision on some open question it continues to affirm the absolute assent of faith upheld up to that point by the Church of earlier ages, and moreover only if in arriving at its decision it has worked in positive collaboration with the pope. And in that case the majority is not merely putting forward its opinion in this sense as constituting what it feels to be the better one, but is rather attesting this opinion as commanding the allegiance of its faith. When a majority has arrived at a decision in this way and under these conditions the minority both can and must agree to it if that minority is not insuperably convinced that the decision of the majority goes against the substance of its own faith as a whole as upheld by it up to that point. In that case this decision would show that even the formal authority of the Church's teaching office was an illegitimate presumption. The Catholic as such is of course convinced as a matter of his faith that any such radical case will never arise in the Church. In other words: when the pope, together with a majority of the bishops (or, supposing that they are in a minority it is a minority purely în the numerical sense, but one which still gives the agreement of the pope the force of moral law) arrives at a decision which is binding in faith on some open question, then this decision is preserved from any real or radical error by the assistance of the Spirit (though this does not mean that any such decision is in every respect successful in the way in which it is formulated, or that it covers all the

---

[15] On this point the ecclesiologies of the Middle Ages were far more open, and despite their universal recognition of the principle, 'Prima sedes a nemine judicatur' they did to a large extent reckon with the possibility that on a very wide variety of grounds, ranging from sickness to heresy, the pope could lose his office. Cf. chiefly H. Zimmermann, *Papstabsetzungen des Mittelalters* (Graz, 1968), and A. Fransen, 'Conciliarism', *Sacramentum Mundi* 1 (New York and London, 1968), pp. 401–403. It is no argument against the kernel of truth in these ideas, which theologically speaking is extremely important, that they could lead to an extreme form of conciliarism.

factors which such a question may involve of its very nature in a full or adequate way, or that it is opportune etc.). But even the Catholic can, and today actually must concede that it is possible for an individual in the concrete to arrive at a judgement in conscience which cannot be overthrown, that a decision of faith of this kind is radically opposed to the ultimate essence of the Christian faith, and in that case the claim which this teaching authority of the Church makes upon his conscience would lose its validity.

In any case these considerations show that some form of democratic collaboration in the decisions taken by the teaching office as such in the Church is not impossible from the outset, quite apart from the fact that in questions of the Church's practice, life in the Church, and discipline, and also in questions of Church law, it is in principle possible from the outset to accord a far wider sphere for such democratic collaboration to be exercised. Here, too however, the interplay between divine and human law which we have touched on above would have to be more clearly borne in mind than is the case in our present considerations. A further point which has already arisen from the very nature of the case in the present discussion is that any such collaboration on the part of the Church as a whole in the progressive articulation of the faith in the course of history is not present primarily or exclusively in those cases in which this collaboration is manifested in forms which are 'democratic' in an explicit or juridical sense. The derivation of the teaching office from the universal Church as supported and sustained by the Holy Spirit even in the progressive development of her faith is far wider and deeper in its ramifications, and does not begin, as many believe, only at that point at which it is given concrete expression in juridical forms.

What we are considering here is a worldwide Church with many millions of believers, all of them in principle called upon to collaborate. But for technical reasons alone any formal or juridical process of democratization represents no absolute guarantee of the fact that the people of God are effectively and actively taking part in the life of the Church in a way which corresponds to the movement of the Spirit of God. Our experience of the contemporary democracies of the masses, whether in the forms in which these may appear in the western or the eastern spheres, serves to show how cautious we have to be in this matter. It may be argued that the people of the Church should collaborate to a greater extent and more 'democratically' even in the functions of the teaching office, and this cannot be rejected from the outset as un-Catholic. At the same time, however, it should first be shown how some scheme can be devised for achieving this in the concrete which is both realistic and practicable. It should be shown which Catholic Christians have achieved a position in secular society such that they are not merely equipped and willing seriously to take part in such collaboration, but also that they are justified in doing so in ecclesiological terms, and it should be shown how Catholic Christians of this type can be distinguished from the rest. The present-day situation of the Church is one in which we are faced with the phenomenon of individuals only *partially* identifying themselves with her, and so too of varying very greatly in the degree in which they do so identify themselves with the Church. Now in this situation there is a very real danger that under cover of the watchword of democracy many individuals will be carried away from the Church into positions which are un-Christian and un-Catholic. Hence the officially constituted authorities of the Church cannot be blamed when they suspect such dangers to be present and attempt to avert them.

In this connection a further factor may be pointed out, one which both reveals the relativity of the majority opinion in any voting procedure of the kind of which we have been speaking, and at the same time also enables us to understand that there is an intrinsic connection between the teaching office and the pastoral office as exercised in the Church. In any such voting procedure we are presupposing from the first that both the majority and the minority accept, with the full assent of their faith, the basic substance of the faith, for the decision actually arrived at in any given case is, or is intended to be, an explicitation of this. It is obvious that we must assume this much, but if we do assume this, then strictly speaking it is no less obvious that the decision of the majority materially speaking implies more a specific definition on the Church's own part[16] on the question involved than a decision which is directed against the opposite opinion on the actual matter itself which is concerned as upheld by the minority. In this respect it is ultimately speaking a secondary question whether the parties themselves have been aware that the controversy between them has this special character, or whether they have supposed that they were radically disunited on the actual matter itself. In any case when we look back on history we can recognize retrospectively that the controversies which have taken place between genuine Christians have only been controversies with regard to the terms in which the truths of the faith should be defined. It is not possible here to corroborate this assertion by means of historical

---

16 A more detailed treatment of this idea is to be found in K. Rahner and K˙ Lehmann, 'Kerygma und Dogma', *Mysterium Salutis* I (Einsiedeln, 1965), pp. 693–696.

examples, nor does the assertion itself imply that it is always easy to distinguish between content and expression in matters of controversy. And again in maintaining this position we are not implying that the controversy with regard to the terms of the definition is in itself a matter of indifference. But it is possible to state that in all decisions in matters of doctrine *one* of the factors included is always that of the terms in which the decision should be defined, because in theological questions it is quite impossible that any given formulation should be the only one and the only correct one. This would only be possible if the truth which it was intended to define contained nothing more than was explicitly stated in the formula. And when it is a theological reality that is being treated of this can never be the case.

However when, if, and to the extent that it is a terminological controversy that is involved in a voting procedure of this kind (whether the parties involved are aware of it as such or not) the taking of such a vote is essentially an exercise of the pastoral office, and it is relatively easy to understand why in this context a majority can be more important than a minority in tipping the scales to one side rather than the other. The majority declares that with regard to the real substance of the faith (which in fact all agree to) it is able to express this better and in a way which is more intelligible to it by means of a particular form of definition, and that therefore, while having to respect the claims of charity towards the others, it has a right to demand that the minority shall fall in with this definition. This is not too much to demand since on the one hand a definition of this kind does not prohibit others from explaining what has been expressed in it in different terms, while on the other any such expression, even among those who respect it, is wide enough and 'analogous' enough to be able to include and implicitly contain within itself the 'special concerns' of the minority.

Now surely this applies especially to the contemporary situation. For today the situation in which we all find ourselves in terms of ideas is such that we are very well able clearly to recognize and to evaluate the historical factors and the analogous nature of any such expression, even, therefore, one that is produced by the official authorities of the Church. The situation of the Church today in terms of theology and speculation is such that we may presume that any authentic, and still more definitorial decisions on doctrine on the part of the Church will in the future consist not so much in fresh explicitations and developments of the ancient teaching of the Church as in the special emphasis which she gives to particular points of doctrine in order to maintain their truth against false interpretations.

Hence in producing authoritative pronouncements of this kind the Church will not be restricting the necessary scope for interpretation which should be allowed for in a situation of pluralism among the various orthodox theologies. Precisely in the future, therefore, decisions on doctrine on the part of the Church will take the form of 'justified and important' definitive formulae in which to express the one creed of the Church, and will be understood as such. Now on this showing any discovery of truth which is arrived at democratically, even though it transcends mere considerations of 'voting' is both more appropriate to the realities involved and also easier to understand and accept than was the case in earlier times.

So far we have been attempting to consider the teaching office of the Church in its relationship to the Church as a whole. We must now consider the question of the teaching office from yet another point of view. In our introductory remarks we have already drawn attention to the fact that in the usual theology of the seminaries, by reason of the formal and juridical categories in which the nature and power of the teaching office are conceived of, the formal authority to be attached to the teaching office is thought of almost independently of the actual *truth content* which it attests. In this seminary theology the content of the faith on the one hand and the formal authority of the teaching office on the other are presented as two separate entities almost without connection. It is true that it is stated clearly that the teaching office is obviously constituted under divine revelation, that it must be subordinate and obedient to it, and that through the power of the Spirit that has been promised to the Church it will also be preserved in this obedience. But this in itself is not enough really to make clear the precise relationship which exists between the formal authority of the teaching office and the *fides quae* which is intended to mediate it to the *fides qua* of the individual believer. We shall enquire into this relationship in respect both of its essential constitution and of the forms which it inevitably assumes today.

With regard to the basic relationship which constantly exists between the formal authority of the teaching office and the content of the faith which that teaching office is designed to present it must first be stated simply and unambiguously that according to the fundamental theology and the interpretation of the faith of the Catholic Church the formal authority of the teaching office is not the first and most fundamental *datum* in the content of the faith such that all other elements in it are based upon this one as their necessary foundation. There is a well-known saying of Augustine[17] (which unfortunately is quoted all too often and in

[17] PL 42, 176.

a sense that is misleading) to the effect that he would not give the allegiance of his faith to the gospels unless the authority of the Church had moved him to do so. Now taken in a strict and absolute sense, and as a universal principle applicable to the faith as such this statement is simply false. Of course it is true as a matter of history that the gospel has come down to me, the individual, historically separated as I am from Christ, through the mediation of the Church. It has come down to me in this sense as that which at once commands and makes possible my belief, as the grace-given power of the Kyrios and as containing the fundamental truths of the Christian faith. But this is still very far from saying that the *formal* authority precisely of the *teaching office* of the Church is in the specifically theological sense the first and most fundamental datum for a Catholic Christian in his faith. Ultimately speaking he believes in the formal authority of the Church's teaching office because prior to this he already believes in God, his grace, in Jesus Christ the crucified and risen Lord, and not *e converso*. In the hierarchy of truths[18] referred to by the Second Vatican Council the fact that there is in truth and in reality a teaching office of the Church is not in fact a first and fundamental datum, but a relatively secondary one, though this is not for one moment to deny that this truth does belong, albeit in its due and proper place, to this hierarchy of truths.

Both in reality and also as recognized in the subjective conscience of the believer, the doctrine of the teaching office is itself based upon certain more radical truths of faith and is not either logically or ontologically speaking the basis upon which all else rests. Precisely in order to be Catholic in our belief we must turn Augustine's axiom 'the other way round' by saying 'I would not believe in the authority of the Church if I were not moved to do so by the gospel'. This is not to deny that in the unity of the whole structured hierarchy of the Catholic faith there is also, in a certain sense, a *mutual* relationship of interdependence between the Church, her institutional structures, and her officialdom on the one hand, and the true substance of the faith on the other as recognized in the conscience of the individual believer. Nor do we deny that Christian faith is always the faith of the Church as well.

[18] A full treatment of the history of this dogma is to be found in U. Valeske, *Hierarchia veritatum* (Munich, 1968). On the subject itself cf. also H. Mühlen, 'Die Bedeutung der Differenz zwischen Zentraldogmen und Randdogmen für den ökumenischen Dialog', *Freiheit in der Begegnung*, edited by J. L. Leuba and H. Stirnimann (Frankfurt, 1969), pp. 191–227, and P. Schoonenberg, 'Geschichtlichkeit und Interpretation des Dogmas', *Die Interpretation des Dogmas* (Düsseldorf, 1969), pp. 58–110, esp. pp. 80–88.

But in this unity and in this wholly *mutual* relationship, in which each of the individual elements in the faith conditions and modifies the others, there is still an overriding order. From this point of view belief in the Church's teaching office is both objectively and subjectively sustained by a reality of the faith which is prior to this teaching office and to faith in it. Hence too in any book on Catholic fundamental theology even of the traditional kind it is taken for granted – indeed we might almost say too much taken for granted – that the section dealing with the existence and authority of the teaching office in the Church as vested in the pope and bishops is included only at a very late stage. A further point is that the truth that in founding his Church Christ gave it an official authority to teach in this sense in virtue of his own authority and promise is obviously no easier to recognize than any other truths of the Christian faith which subjectively and objectively speaking are of a more fundamental character. Since the Second Vatican Council and in the age of a sincere ecumenism a Catholic should not hesitate to conceded that the more fundamental realities of faith common to all Christians, and at the same time more vital to their salvation (whether logically speaking or at least under God's saving providence as it *de facto* exists) are actually *easier* to apprehend in faith than the specifically Catholic truth of the teaching office of the Church. Now these facts, however self-evident, have certain consequences for the teaching office of the Church as applied in practice which, as I feel, are not always recognized and observed.

When the teaching office of the Church arrives at decisions (whether definitorial or merely provisional, albeit authentic ones) if in doing so it relies simply and exclusively on its own formal authority it is in a real sense acting against the obvious truths mentioned above. It is true that within the theoretical system of the Catholic faith this formal authority is itself an obvious factor. But it is not so in the subjective conscience of the individual Catholic believer to which such a decision is addressed. Here this authority is no primary datum, but rather a dependent function, a truth based upon other truths, indeed a truth which is more assailable and more easily imperilled than the fundamental truths of the Christian faith. Hence in taking such a decision the teaching office of the Church has the duty of showing that the content of this decision does not rest merely on its own formal authority. Rather it must show as clearly and convincingly as possible that it is intrinsically connected with the original basis of the Christian faith in general. In doing this it will at the same time have again and again to enable believers to understand afresh that this authority of the teaching office derives from this basic essence of the Christian faith which the subject to whom this particular decision of the teaching office is addressed must already have apprehended prior to any assent on his part to the formal authority of the teaching office.

If, and to the extent that, the Christian faith is ultimately *one* and all elements in it *mutually* condition one another it can uncompromisingly be asserted that there is a mutual interdependence here too. It is just as true to say that the formal authority of the teaching office depends upon the power of the truth of faith as proclaimed to command the allegiance of our faith as to say that the latter depends upon the former. This relationship in which either factor influences the other is distorted, however, if we rely exclusively upon the formal authority of the teaching office. It can be stated absolutely as a matter of principle that in its individual decisions and the preliminary proposals leading up to these the teaching office of the Church acts best and most correctly when it allows the truth which is sustained by grace and inherent in the reality itself which it is treating of and seeking to teach to make its own impact, and allows its own formal authority almost completely to be effaced by giving pride of place to this truth. As we have said this is the right approach to adopt simply because the truth that the teaching office has this formal authority is in any instance supported and kept alive by faith in the fundamental truths of Christianity. Hence in the concrete exercise of its functions the teaching office must again and again re-establish its connections with these truths.

The urgency of the point which we are making here becomes still clearer when we reflect upon the way in which the teaching office of the Church exercises its functions in the situation which prevails *in the present day*. Very many authorities whom we encounter in the world and in the course of human living have a certain power regardless of whether or not the legitimacy of their formal claims to power are recognized by the individual in his own conscience. For the most part these various kinds of authority (that of parents, of groups in secular society, of teachers or experts, or of the state) are reinforced with a certain degree of *power*, whether explicit or implicit, consciously adverted to or unconsciously taken for granted. So far as the conscious awareness of the individual is concerned moral authority and the power accompanying this are far from being clearly distinguishable from one another. When we recognize authority we are very largely, without actually noticing it, submitting ourselves to the power (which itself in turn may take many forms), and when authority is claimed by those in whom it is vested these likewise are aware of and rely upon this *power* which they take for granted without explicitly reflecting upon the fact. This is particularly true in those cases in which the parties involved take it for granted that their authority is accompanied by such power. In such cases authority imposes itself in virtue of the power attached to it and not in virtue of itself. Now right down to these present times in which we live the authority of the Church and of the Churches has had power of this kind which extends to their teaching function as well. They have had this power in virtue of public opinion, many institutional factors, the extremely close connection which they have had with secular society, and all the opportunities they have enjoyed of influencing public awareness in general.

This is not the place to enquire how far such power should be attached to the formal authority of the Church's teaching office as of right, what historical factors and situations have caused this supplementary power to be attached to the teaching office in society and in the awareness of the individual, or what reasons, whether regrettable or providential, have led to a situation in which it has to a large extent lost this power. At any rate the situation which prevails today and which will come to prevail still more in the future is that the power which in earlier times was ascribed to the teaching office in addition to the authority which it was recognized as having in itself has to a large extent disappeared and is in process of disappearing more and more. The teaching office has less and less 'authority' in itself in virtue of this power which was formally attached to it prior to and independent of the assent of faith in which the individual recognized its existence as legitimate. In other words what it lacks now is any effective influence upon the individual prior to his assent of faith precisely to this teaching office. The only real significance which it still has depends almost exclusively, and in increasing measure today, upon the question of whether and how far it succeeds in making its own spiritual authority credible on the basis of the gospel itself. Today less than ever before can it assume *a priori* that its own formal validity as a teaching office has already been acknowledged as *de fide* in the conscience of the individual Catholic Christian, and so rely simply and exclusively upon this as a justification of the specific doctrine which it promulgates. Every time a specific doctrine of this kind is promulgated without its own intrinsic claim to truth being made clear (this does not necessarily have to mean rationally comprehensible in itself, but it surely does mean intrinsically intelligible and following logically from the Christian faith as a single whole) it always entails a threat to the formal authority of the teaching office as a whole such that there is a real danger that it will not be acknowledged. The reason is that, as we have already said, this authority does not of itself command any greater degree of credibility in terms of fundamental theology than other truths of the faith. And since today all kinds of purely formal authority are under attack it follows *a fortiori* that this particular kind of authority cannot constitute the fixed and unquestionable point of departure for considering questions of truth in the subjective conscience of the individual with regard to truth. Hence any appeal merely to the formal authority of the teaching office as a factor which is given and can be assumed as obvious and beyond all dispute will to a large extent be ineffective even though in itself it may, from one specific point of view, be perfectly legitimate as following logically from the faith.

Again in the situation which prevails precisely today every time the teaching office proclaims a specific doctrine of the faith it must justify its own formal authority in doing so, and it must of course do this not merely by speaking in abstract terms about its own formal authority, but by establishing the connection between the content of the individual doctrine which it promulgates and the totality of the Christian faith and the Christian interpretation of existence. It must do this in order that it may, to some extent, lighten the burden which is placed upon its own formal authority, and at the same time state the basis on which it itself rests.[19]

In other words: when an individual doctrine is promulgated by the teaching office the actual content of the truth that is proclaimed should impart credibility to the formal authority of the body which proclaims it. It should do this in virtue of the conviction which it carries of its own nature, and which is immanent within itself, and in virtue of the clear connection which it has with the totality of the faith. Moreover it must do this in a manner which is in conformity with the contemporary situation as well as the actual truth which is involved. This does not render the significance of the formal authority of the teaching office superfluous. On the contrary what we are requiring here is, as we have already said, justified on the grounds that the formal teaching authority is based on a truth which is prior to itself, and on the fact that the individual truth which is being taught can never be a truth of the faith as an isolated doctrine, but must always be so only in virtue of its connection with the totality of the Christian faith in general.

If these two factors are borne in mind then the requirement which we have stated above is in a real sense self-evident; the requirement, namely, that the teaching office itself must so act as to render itself in a certain sense, and speaking approximately, more and more superfluous. This requirement is further strengthened by the fact that it would be quite

[19] It may be doubted whether all the more recent pronouncements of the Church's teaching office have in fact met this requirement.

untrue to say that the progressive development of the Christian faith has ever found its anchor-holds or its turning-points first and last in the teaching office as one particular institution within the totality of the Church. This is of course not to exclude the fact that in the life of the individual believer and of the Church as a whole particular situations have arisen, can arise, and will arise in the concrete in which the assurance that a specific doctrine is a genuine explicitation of the faith as a single whole is provided by the pronouncements of the teaching office.

It is not possible here to develop these considerations any further so as to show, by means of individual examples of the practice of the Church's teaching office, that in the life of the Church in the concrete it has consistently been taken for granted right from the first that these requirements must be fulfilled. Still less should our readers be left with the impression that in what has been said here everything is covered or at least touched upon which it is necessary to demand if in the contemporary crisis of authority the teaching office is to achieve what it is capable of in order to survive this crisis. The present-day situation is such that many further consequences arise from it in addition to those mentioned here which have a bearing on the continuing function of the teaching office. Thus for instance a situation has arisen today in the development of ideas in which it is necessary and inevitable that there should be a pluralism of theologies even within the one Church and in spite of the unity of her creed. This again implies a quite new situation for the exercise of the Church's teaching office, because precisely in its pronouncements and critical judgements it is quite impossible any longer to assume. that there is any one theology common to all with a single uniform language.[20] It would even be possible to raise the further question of whether the future development of dogma in the Catholic Church, and so too the further functioning of the teaching office either can or will lead to further dogmatic explicitations of individual points of doctrine which, as it were, are still waiting to be developed over and above the existing hierarchy of truths, or whether alternatively the future task of the teaching office will consist simply in preserving the basic substance of the Christian message in a far more radical and concentrated way than hitherto.

If we hold the second opinion then it will become still clearer that in the present and future situation of crisis the best and most effective way for the Church's teaching office to defend its own formal authority is for it to present itself as the official body which bears witness with the uncompromising courage and hope that arises from faith itself to that basic

[20] See n. 11.

substance of the faith which is common to all Christians. Perhaps we ought to express this more cautiously by saying that this is what ought to be the case. If the teaching office of the Catholic Church bears witness with unwavering faithfulness to faith in God and Jesus Christ, and again and again gives fresh life to this faith, then even it has its greatest opportunity for achieving advances in the ecumenical field.

2

THE POINT OF DEPARTURE IN THEOLOGY FOR DETERMINING THE NATURE OF THE PRIESTLY OFFICE

THE priestly office in the Catholic Church is an extremely complex entity, and one which is subject to historical changes. As realized in the concrete its form is determined not merely by the dogmatically definable nature of the Church herself, or by its own real theological nature, which belongs to the 'jus divinum' of the Church, but also by the concrete forms which the Church has assumed under historical influences and, arising from this, by the changing positions which the priest has occupied within the Church as a society, as also by the role ascribed to him by secular society. Our present considerations, however, will be confined merely to the point of departure in *theology* for determining the nature of the priestly office in the Church. All other factors will remain outside the scope of our present study even though they do contribute to the contemporary crisis in our understanding of the significance of the priesthood at least as much as the specifically theological problems which it entails. Obviously there is a constant and active interconnection between the theological essence of the priesthood which abides, and the other basic factors and influences in history and society which play their part in determining its form in the concrete. To that extent these questions too (even though they will remain untreated of here) constitute the background for the question with which we are specifically concerned. It is true that even from the point of view of its theological nature the priestly office is an extremely complex entity, so that we must guard against an over-'speculative' approach in which we attempt to deduce the fulness of its reality by a process of logical deduction from one simple and radical characteristic inherent in its nature. But however true this may be, still it is manifest from the contemporary theory and practice of priestly life that we *must raise the question of* where the *initial point of departure* lies for determining the theological nature of the priesthood. Because only in this way can it be made clear what belongs to its abiding nature and what per-

31

tains rather to those changeable factors which are the outcome of historical conditions and the circumstances of particular epochs.[1]

Preliminary Remarks

1. Both from the point of view of the concrete contemporary situation of the priest and also on theological grounds there seem to be disadvantages in taking as our initial starting-point for defining the nature of the priestly office those *sacramental powers* which, according to the teaching of the Councils (chiefly that of Trent) belong to him alone in contrast to the laity and the lower ranks in the hierarchy of order (especially that of deacon). The powers we are speaking of here, therefore, are those of presiding at the celebration of the Eucharistic sacrifice and the sacramental forgiveness of sins (including the administration of the anointing of the sick). There is no need here to enlarge upon the fact that at least in the present age this approach can be adopted only with difficulty, if indeed it is not totally inadequate as a primary and basic starting-point for understanding the true nature of the priesthood.[2] In any case this

---

[1] It is impossible in a brief study such as this to set forth each individual idea in detail. For this reason I may refer to other basic studies in which I have defined my position on the theme in question: K. Rahner, *The Church and the Sacraments*, Quaestiones Disputatae 9 (Freiburg, 1963); *Handbuch der Pastoraltheologie* I (Freiburg, 1964), pp. 149–215 (those charged with ensuring that the Church shall achieve the due fulness of her own nature), esp. 154 ff. (the institutional and charismatic factors), 189 ff. (the priesthood and the individual priest) (New and expanded edition in preparation [2nd ed. 1970]); *Vom Sinn des kirchlichen Amtes* (Freiburg, 1966); *Knechte Christi* (Freiburg, 1967); 'Priestly Existence', *Theological Investigations III* (London and Baltimore, 1967), pp. 239–262; cf. also 'One Mediator and Many Mediations', *Theological Investigations IX* (London and New York, 1972), pp. 169–186; also cf. my address to the Catholic Conference entitled 'Dogmatische Grundlagen des priesterlichen Selbstverständnisses', *Mitten in dieser Welt* edited by the Zentralkomitee der Deutschen Katholiken (Paderborn, 1968), pp. 96–115 and the study entitled 'Theological Reflections on the Image of the Priest of Today and Tomorrow' in this volume pp. 39–60; on the concept of office cf. also my commentary on the third chapter of 'Lumen Gentium', The Constitution on the Church, *LTK* suppl. I (Freiburg, 1966), 210–246 (on No. 28 cf. the commentary by A. Grillmeier, *ibid.*, 247–255).

[2] On this approach the tendency would be to take the hierarchical element and the traditional concept of the priestly ministry too much for granted.

For this reason it is, however, extremely questionable whether any adequate starting-point can be found by envisaging merely the functions of the priest as leader of the community or the merely spiritual element in his ministry. On this cf. also H. U. von Balthasar, 'Das priesterliche Amt', *Civitas* 23 (1968), pp. 794–797;

starting-point would have no directly perceptible basis in scripture.
2. We can also see disadvantages in seeking to define the nature of the priestly office in the first instance *on the basis of the concept of 'mediator'*. This approach too would not find any immediate support from the witness of the bible, for in scripture the concept of mediator is applied only to Jesus Christ. Such an approach would immediately give rise to the difficult questions of how in more precise terms we should conceive of participation in the mediatorship of Christ through the priestly office, what the connection would be between a participation of this kind and the other functions of mediating salvation which are exercised in the Body of Christ even apart from the priestly office, how any such mediatorship should more precisely be conceived of seeing that after all it must always be a mediation between God and the individual man endowed with grace such that the mediator makes them *im*mediately present to one another. Such an approach would also have to come to terms with the dogmatic principle that all sacramental mediation constitutes only one particular manifestation, albeit an effective one, of a grace-given relationship of man to God which extends throughout all dimensions of human life even without any mediation on the part of the official priesthood.

3. It is admitted both from the point of view of biblical study, the history of dogma, and theology, that in order to obtain any understanding of the theological nature of the priestly office (as distinct from the 'episcopal' office, the 'diaconate' and the 'lay state') we must not immediately assume that there is a hierarchical order in the Church divided into three stages, and that this sets its holders apart from the rest of the 'people of God'. On the contrary the approach which should be adopted – though of course this is not possible here – is to take as our starting-point the nature of the Church as a sacrament of God's utterance of himself to the

---

W. Breuning, 'Zum Verständnis des Priesteramtes vom "Dienen" her', *Lebendiges Zeugnis* (1969), pp. 24–40; J. Ratzinger, 'Zur Frage nach den Sinn des priesterlichen Dienstes', *GuL* 41 (1968), pp. 347–376; W. Kasper, 'A New Dogmatic Outlook on the Priestly Ministry', *Concilium* 3/5 (Pastoral), 1969, pp. 12–18.
  In this connection cf. likewise E. Niermann, 'Priest' *Sacramentum Mundi* 5 (New York and London, 1970), pp. 97–101; O. Semmelroth, 'Die Präsenz der drei Ämter Christi im gemeinsamen und besonderen Priestertum der Kirche', *Theologie und Philosophie* 44 (1969), pp. 181–195; H. Vorgrimler, 'Der theologische Ort des Priesters', *Handbuch der Pastoraltheologie* IV (Freiburg, 1969), pp. 432 ff.; K. Lehmann, 'Das dogmatische Problem des theologischen Ansatzes zum Verständnis des Amtspriestertums', *Existenzprobleme des Priesters*, Münchener Akademie-Schriften der Katholischen Akademie in Bayern 50 (Munich, 1969), pp. 121–175.

world as accepted in faith, hope, and love. From this point we should go on to show – always of course with reference to scripture – that the Church as understood in this sense is always in need of that which can be called 'office', the nature of which is determined on the one hand by the nature of the Church herself and on the other (since it signifies a particular function in the Church) must also be negatively circumscribed and distinguished from other ways in which the Church achieves her own due fulness. This factor of office is primarily one as the Church herself is ultimately one. This *single* office can and must be subdivided into particular departments both in respect of its holders and also with regard to the task and functions which it entails of its very nature because in view of the nature of the Church as a socially constituted reality it is quite impossible to conceive of it assuming any other form. But the ways in which this subdivision of the priestly office can be achieved are very varied, and this remains true even if we assume that a development took place during the apostolic age in which the priestly office was divided into three ranks and that this is permanently and irreversibly binding upon the post-apostolic Church and is in this sense *'juris divini'*. For in the New Testament itself this subdivision of a *single* sacrament of order is still extremely fluid. The question of precisely what functions are to be attached to each of the three degrees of order (assuming for our present purposes that there are indeed three degrees) still remains to a large extent an open one both in the New Testament itself and in later ages. From the standpoint of dogmatic theology, even if we recognize this division of the priestly office into three degrees this does not mean that other functions, no less genuine, may not arise within and in addition to the functions attached to these three degrees, albeit as the outcome of the fresh subdivisions of the *single* priestly office which emerge from the ever-changing conditions of history. Indeed the very fact that in the course of history further and quite different official functions and holders of official functions can be discerned in addition to, and also within, the three degrees into which the priestly office is initially divided is in itself enough to demonstrate this point. The same is also true with regard to the process by which such a function is sacramentally imparted to a specific holder of office. The idea that it is only the official process by which the orders of bishop, 'priest' and deacon are imparted that can constitute a sacrament, so far from being part of the Church's official doctrine, is actually in contradiction to the theology at least of the Middle Ages. In the light of these considerations, which we have only been able to touch upon here, it is theologically speaking perfectly conceivable (though naturally the question of whether it would be opportune still remains open) that, while preserving the three degrees of the priestly office in some sense, some different way might be devized of distributing and sacramentally conferring the various functions contained within this *single* priestly office in the Church. Thus for instance the concept of the 'priesthood' might come to cover a very different range of functions in respect of both the official role of the priest in the Church and of the sacramental powers conferred upon him. Again it is possible for there to be other sacramentally conferred 'leadership' functions (e.g. those of 'teacher' or 'community leader') apart from the priesthood itself. We may defer to tradition and the terminology in vogue at the moment by confining our use of the term 'priestly' as applied to such functions only to those which include presiding over the celebration of the Eucharist and the rest of the so-called sacramental powers. But this precisely does not invalidate the point that the Church is free to choose between a wide range of possibilities, or that she can exercise her own free judgement as to how best to divide up this *single* office between various functionaries according to the requirements of the situation at any given time, or how to distribute the functions themselves inherent in this *single* office as determined by the very nature of the Church herself.

4. There is a further point which we must not overlook in our quest for a simple point of departure comprehensible in terms of biblical theology and at the same time capable of 'realization' in the current circumstances, for determining the nature of the priestly office. This point is that in principle the word which has been entrusted to the Church has the force of an event, an exhibitive and effective character. It does not imply merely the communication of some reality which exists in total independence of the actual doctrinal process of communicating it. The Church fulfils her own nature as the sacrament of God's self-utterance to the world in the word, and hence this word has in principle an exhibitive character. That which this word proclaims takes place through it. As with human words in other contexts so too with this word the degree of 'event' character to be attributed to it is essentially variable. And it is in that form which we call the sacrament in the theological and technical sense of the term that this 'event' character achieves its highest point. Nevertheless the fact that this word is essentially variable in the degree of 'event' character to be attributed to it and in respect of its power to take 'effect' does not deprive it of that basic force inherent in all the Church's words of rendering present the single event of salvation both as anamnesis and as prognosis. The proclaiming of the word and the dispensing of the sacrament, therefore, spring

from a single common root and are ultimately one in nature.[3]

The Point of Departure Itself

In the light of these considerations we can arrive at the following definition (although it must be admitted that in doing so we are adopting a
somewhat audacious 'short-cut'): *The priest is the proclaimer of the word
of God, officially commissioned and appointed as such by the Church as a
whole in such a way that this word is entrusted to him in the supreme degree
of sacramental intensity inherent in it. His work as proclaimer of the word in
this sense is essentially directed towards the community* (which is at least
potentially in existence). To express the matter quite simply, he is the one
sent by the Church to proclaim the gospel in her name. He is this in the
supreme mode in which this word can be realized, that namely of the
anamnesis of the Death and Resurrection of Christ which is achieved in
the celebration of the Eucharist. In defining the concept of the priesthood
in these terms we are not seeking to set it apart from the episcopal office.
The very fact that mediaeval theology denied that episcopal consecration
had a distinct sacramental character in itself shows that it is not altogether
easy to separate the two entities one from another even though since the
Second Vatican Council the position of the mediaeval theologians can no
longer be maintained.[4] On the basis of this definition of the concept it
becomes clear that the priest is not simply a 'cult official',[5] and that this
task of bearing witness to the word of God as exhibitive and effective of
salvation is one that lays claims upon his whole existence (viewing this

---

[3] For a more detailed justification of this point cf. 'The Word and the Eucharist',
Theological Investigations IV (London and Baltimore, 1966), pp. 253–286; 'The
Theology of the Symbol', *ibid.*, pp. 221–252; 'The Presence of the Lord in the
Christian Community at Worship', *Theological Investigations* X (London and New
York, 1973), pp. 84–102. We may refer to the points that have been demonstrated in
the articles referred to in order to guard against any misunderstandings of our obser-
vations here.

[4] On this problem cf. chiefly Y. Congar, 'Tatsachen, Problem und Betrachtungen
hinsichtlich der Weihevollmacht und der Beziehungen zwischen dem Presbyterat
und dem Episkopat', *Heilige Kirche* (Stuttgart, 1966), pp. 285–316; also L. Ott, *Das
Weihesakrament, Handbuch der Dogmengeschichte* IV/5 (Freiburg, 1969).

[5] The limitations of this idea even prior to the Tridentine decree are very ably
demonstrated by K. Lehmann, 'Das dogmatische Problem des theologischen Ansatzes
zum Verständnis des Amtspriestertums'. *Existenzprobleme des Prietsers*. Münchener
Akademie-Schriften der Katholischen Akademie in Bayern 50 (Munich, 1969),
pp. 121–175.

from the theological standpoint), regardless of the extent to which it may also determine his calling in secular society or how far it may or may not supply his economic needs. Since the essence of his priesthood consists in proclaiming the word of God this imparts to it from the outset a *missionary* character. It orientates him from the outset towards a community, regardless of whether he can assume this as already in some sense in existence, or whether he has to create it *ab initio;* and regardless too of what the precise sociological constitution of this community may be.

What we have said does not rule out either the possibility or the fact of there being quite different ways in which the 'ministry of the word' may be realized, these too being 'official' ways and capable of being sacramentally imparted to an individual as a commission from the Church.

In this connection the *concrete form* which a priestly commission of this kind may assume in the social structure of the Church and in secular society may *vary very greatly*, and many of the functions which are *de facto* exercised by priests can in practice also be conceived of as special and non-priestly official functions in the Church without the theological essence of the priesthood itself being affected by this. The way in which the word is proclaimed, the concrete form of the community to which the priest is attached, the precise manner in which the various official functions, whether actual or possible, are co-ordinated in the Church, and the status of the priest in secular society – all these are factors which can vary very greatly. But we should not identify all these from the outset with that which constitutes the real theological essence of the priesthood. Not only are all these factors subject to change as a matter of empirical fact, but the Church herself ought actively to take the initiative in imparting ever new forms to them. Up to the present there has been a failure to realize sufficiently the extent to which official functions in the Church in general and the priesthood in particular are capable of being changed in this way both interiorly and exteriorly. Often the indelible character of the priesthood has been appealed to by those opposed to ideas of change of this sort. Contemporary exegesis, the history of dogma and of the Church, the sociology of the Church, and the needs of the Church in the present day all compel us to a radical re-appraisal of the mutable and immutable factors in the Catholic priesthood. If this re-appraisal is carried through boldly enough two points will become clear: first, there is indeed an abiding element in the priestly office such as justifies an individual in the concrete circumstances of his life as a man of today in entering upon it boldly and confidently; second, from the standpoint of dogmatic theology almost unlimited scope is available to the Church in subdividing and giving concrete form to her official institutions in those ways which most effectively correspond to her own mission and the contemporary situation.

3

THEOLOGICAL REFLECTIONS ON THE PRIESTLY IMAGE OF TODAY AND TOMORROW

I

I MUST begin by saying that I am well aware of the fact that the article which follows represents only a very small selection, based on my own subjective preferences, from the totality of the subject-matter which falls under the heading mentioned in the title. The subject of our consideration is connected with so many problems in the fields of biblical theology, dogmatics, the history of religion, psychology, the sociology of religion, social politics, canon law and pastoral theology that in our present treatment our choice of subject-matter will almost of necessity be an arbitrary one, and we can say only very little on the subject as a whole.

With regard to the priestly office and the priest's own personal understanding of his office we find ourselves in a period of transition which is conditioned by both theological and social factors. Without prejudice to the fundamental theological nature of the institution of the Catholic priesthood – something that is inherent in the nature of the Church herself – the concrete form which the priestly ministry assumes in the course of the history of the Church can, may, and indeed should undergo repeated modifications. The very fact that the Church herself both is and should be an historical entity is in itself enough to make this necessary. The actual rate at which changes of this kind take place is not always the same. In the last hundred and fifty years we have lived through an epoch in which the concrete form of the institution of the Catholic priesthood has been relatively fixed and immutable both with regard to the priest's own theological understanding of his own function and with regard to his position in the Church, as also in secular society. Today, however, we are certainly in a situation in which the process of such changes is notably accelerated. The old image still survives. The old image still defends itself. But suddenly the old image is no longer taken for granted, and is

39

threatened. The new image makes itself felt, but has not yet acquired any clear outlines. In such a period of transition and the uncertainty which it inevitably entails, in which experiment is justified and tentative trials are made, in which there is a right and a wrong way of holding firm to the traditional and the accustomed, we priests must maintain an attitude of patience and courage with ourselves, our office, and the Church whom we serve. We must learn to live with those factors in our office which are questionable, and which today we must inevitably feel as burdensome. We must calmly endure those elements in our priestly situation which seem to be troubled, obscure and confused. We cannot simply entrench ourselves in the accustomed ways, in that which has been tried and proved over a long period and enacted a thousand times over, nor can we, simply by a revolutionary act of force, produce in priests *ex nihilo sui et subjecti* that conception of their own role, that mode of priestly life and work, which future generations of priests are perhaps destined to have the happiness of achieving in all its classic and fully refined purity in the near or more distant future.

Such problems in understanding one's own role arise in other callings too in virtue of changes in the social situation, and the individuals concerned cannot forcibly apply that interpretation of their role which is appropriate to the present to the future also, because problems of this kind call for concrete decisions and not merely speculative considerations. No-one is free to choose any situation he likes for his life, and hence it is that we priests of today have had the great task and burden imposed upon us of enduring this period of transition in patience and hope. Yet this is something which God can demand of a priest and a Christian. Sometimes from sheer perplexity and insecurity we find ourselves asking what the role of the priest of the future is to be, and how he is to work. But this has nothing to do with prophesying, the capricious conjuring up of fantasies, or wishful thinking and dreaming. What is involved in such a line of enquiry is simply a realistic confrontation with a future state of affairs, in so far as we are already in a position to foresee this, in order (as far as possible and with all necessary provisos) to deduce consequences from this for the priestly way of life. Our uncertainties with regard to the form which the priesthood will take in the future – uncertainties which oppress us so much today, and in many respects even reduce us to perplexity (something which we can freely admit to ourselves) – are perfectly reconcilable with the firm and unquestioning conviction of faith that the official institution of the priesthood will always exist in the Church.

For at least fifteen hundred years, and since the much criticized Constantine era, the institution and function of the priest in the Church have also come to be regarded as a profession so far as the world is concerned, one which, like any other profession, has been fitted almost without any friction into the structure of secular society adopted by the *corpus christianum*. For this, after all, has been more or less identical with society at the political level. Certainly from the theological point of view the priesthood has always been a profession *sui generis*, with powers and functions which distinguish this particular office from any other worldly calling. Nevertheless within secular society at the social and political level the priest as such has himself had a definite place of his own, carrying a social prestige more or less inherent in the office itself and independent of the personality of its holder, and carrying also a degree of economic support accorded to the priest by secular society, albeit in the most varied forms. In virtue of these the priestly office has been a profession in the normal and modern sense of the term. The priest has had a function in human society which has been recognized and valued by that society itself. It has been taken for granted that the divine calling to the priesthood is at the same time an earthly profession too.

There is nothing in the nature of the priesthood itself which makes this necessary. Nor can we, on the basis of our personal conviction of faith, assert from the outset that this will continue to be the case. The priestly vocation and the office of the priesthood need not necessarily or in all cases also imply a profession taken for granted as such in society. There can be great differences between a vocation and a profession. Indeed there already are in the secular sphere vocations, missions, and forms of human activity extending even into the public life of society which do not *ipso facto* imply any particular profession which is either desired, expected or *ipso facto* recognized as a way of earning one's living by society itself. In fact the very nature of missions of this sort can be imperilled to the utmost in those cases in which they are also institutionalized and accepted as ways of earning one's living in society. This is the case, for instance, with poets, philosophers, artists, or the prophets of a new ideology. Even in the secular sphere there can be a great difference between vocation and profession. The tension between the two may be so great that it can actually be a criterion of the genuineness of a vocation of this kind that it is impossible to institutionalize this vocation in any calling such as society can recognize. Now if this is already true in the secular sphere then the priestly vocation can certainly not *ipso facto* and as a matter of course be conceived of, without any further distinction, according to the conceptual model of a profession in society, even though a habitual outlook extending over a millenium and a half represents a constant temptation to us to conceive of the priestly vocation in these terms. Today we are actually in a position to say with Paul in a completely realistic and objective manner that he who ministers at the altar should also live by the altar. Nevertheless in this period of transition we will have to ask ourselves again and again whether from the very heart and centre of our existence we are succeeding in really understanding and constantly renewing our acceptance of our own priesthood without tacitly attaching to this understanding the prior condition that the priesthood itself must be capable of being lived in such a way that it also constitutes our worldly profession.

II

After these preliminary remarks let us attempt to develop a few thoelogical considerations with regard to the nature of the priesthood. This is something which has become obscure to many priests of today, not merely because the social status which it carries no longer appears to them to be taken for granted and secure, but also for theological reasons. A fresh problem has arisen with regard to the very relationship between that which is religious in the sacramental sense on the one hand and the secular on the other quite in general. This is because modern man has the impression that if he is to find God at all he must seek him in the sphere of his secular and everyday life, that that which is cultic and religious in the specific sense is *ipso facto* and of itself suspect, that it is 'religion' rather than Christian 'faith'. In the light of the New Testament a question arises ever anew of whether the presbyter of the primitive Church should be interpreted at all in terms of the religious category of the priest, that is to say the 'mediator' between the holy God and an unholy people empowered by a higher authority for cultic activities. In the light of the true and biblical doctrine of the royal priesthood of the holy covenant people of God the question presents itself of what place there can still be on such a view for the official priest within this holy covenant people, seeing that its relationship to God is immediate. How can any such official priesthood still constitute a special calling, and that too both in the society of the Church as such and at the same time in secular society. These are a few specific reasons for the sense of insecurity that a priest feels in his understanding of his own role. They relate to the official priesthood as such. But to these and similar specific reasons other and more general ones must be added, reasons which, though they are less specific, are nevertheless far-reaching in their effects. The authentically religious element as it exists today – even when it is a real and living force, and indeed most of all here – manifests itself as that about which we maintain a tactful silence, that which must not be spoken of, that which does not fall within the sphere of social and institutional policy making.

Here we have only been able to indicate these reasons for the insecurity which the priest feels in interpreting his own role. But in response to these reasons it cannot be our task at this point to present a biblical theology defining the precise nature of the apostle, the disciple, the presbyter, the deacon, the bishop, the prophet, the teacher in the Church. As found in the New Testament all these concepts are still fluid both in themselves and in their mutual relationship to one another. It is by no means the case that in the New Testament they always have the same meaning, and it is a difficult question, and one which has certainly not yet fully been solved, to decide precisely what elements in all that is referred to by such terms as so many functions in the life of the Church have entered into the hierarchically ordered offices of bishop, priest and deacon as we have them today, and what elements in these primitive functions are still really present apart from these offices in the contemporary Church, although, it may be, in quite anonymous forms or existing under different designations. Here we must confine ourselves to a few theological considerations which on the one hand can be deduced from a wholly traditional theology of the sacrament of order, and which on the other hand still serve to show how even today the essence of the Catholic priesthood can still be conceived of as a unity, although one that is still at the same time vital and capable of change.

If we wish to achieve a genuine theological understanding of the nature of the ministerial functions in the Church which we designate as her official priesthood then we must take as our starting-point the Church as one and whole. An alternative would be to interpret the priesthood of the Church whether explicitly or unconsciously in terms of a general conception of the priest as the mediator endowed with higher faculties between a sacral dimension belonging to God as holy on the one hand, and a secular and unholy world on the other. This concept of the priesthood would be worked out in terms of this history and phenomenology of religion in general. But if we adopted this approach we would constantly be in danger of misconceiving the true nature of that function in the Church which we nowadays designate as the priesthood, departing in this to some extent from the linguistic usage of scripture. We can legitimately designate this function as the priesthood, provided only that we overcome the dangers of misundertanding which such a concept entails. We should take as our starting-point a concept of the Church as one and whole and achieve an understanding of what is special in the function which the presbyters in the Church take upon themselves in the light of the nature of the Church herself.

God loves the *world*. His grace is at work everywhere and in every age. Considered as God's self-bestowal offered to man it summons man in all dimensions, including the 'secular one', to a decision: the decision namely of whether or not he accepts this self-offering of God in the living of his everyday life, although his acceptance of it may perhaps be at a quite unexplicit level. If the 'sacral' is ultimately constituted by the grace of God, in which God becomes the sustaining basis, the ultimate depths, and the absolute future of man, then in this ultimate sense there is no sacral sphere such as could be marked off as the holy temple and set apart from a profane and Godless world, as though it were only there, and not here, that the holy God of eternal life was waiting for us and was to be found. There is only one ultimate line of division between the secular and the sacral, *that* namely defined by the mortal guilt of man's refusal of God, God who wills his salvation to be everywhere and in all dimensions of man. In relation to this sanctification of the secular world even the Church as a whole is simply the basic sacramental sign of the fact that God has, in this sense, loved the world itself. When the will of God towards the world as forgiving it and permeating it with his own divinity is explicitly proclaimed in this Church in the word of preaching, in the creed, in the sacral sign, then, while this proclamation is certainly effective, what it proclaims is not a saving event which takes place only in the explicitly sacral sphere of the proclamation itself. What this proclamation constitutes rather is an explicit revelation of a saving will on God's part which is addressed in the form of judgement and grace to the whole world in all its dimensions and epochs, and which can still achieve victory even in those spheres in which it is never accepted at all at the level of conscious and explicit decision. For the acceptance can take a purely anonymous form and consist simply in maintaining integrity and honesty throughout the vicissitudes of life.

From this point of view alone, then, the Church as a whole is not simply identical with the salvation of the world. Rather she constitutes the historical and symbolic manifestation of this salvation, the basic sacrament of salvation for the world. Now if this is true, then still more caution must be brought to bear if we are rightly to define the nature of one specific function within this Church. The officially ordained priest is not the sacral representative of God who is equipped with celestial powers and set apart from an unholy people by God. Rather he is the bearer of one specific and necessary function within a people that has already been sanctified by God. The universal priesthood is not an entity deduced from the official priesthood by a process of metaphorical refinement. Rather it constitutes the sustaining basis for this official priesthood. It is because there is a holy covenant people, because the Church as one and whole constitutes the historical and social manifestation of God's will to bring universal salvation to the world as eschatologically victorious, because the Church is she who makes manifest this victory of God's universal will to save – it is because of this that there can be within her such a specific function as the official priesthood. There must be an official institution of this kind in the Church because the Church is an entity which, of its very nature, must necessarily have directive functions at the social and historical levels too, through which she becomes apprehensible and effective for the individuals within her and about her. But for this very reason the nature of these directive functions at the social level is in its turn determined by the nature of the Church herself. This does not exclude, but rather includes the fact that as applied to the individual holder of such functions it both can and must be said that he receives his commission to exercise such functions from God and Christ, and is not commissioned to exercise them as it were from below by the multitude of individual members within the Church inasmuch as this multitude can be thought of as prior to the Church herself as constituted as a society, in other words as structurally organized by her official institutions. Certainly the Church only becomes concrete and effective to the extent that one factor, albeit not the only one, by which she is constituted is the factor of officialdom within her considered as one particular function. But for this very reason this element of officialdom derives its nature, its eschatological character, its special features, and its limits from the Church considered as a whole and as one. In the light of this we can understand, for instance, that it is only a baptized individual who can be a priest, that the Eucharist which he celebrates is from the outset the Eucharist of the holy people of God, that he can only teach inasmuch as he himself hears in a spirit of belief, and inasmuch as it is the faith of the universal Church that he preaches, for the Church as hearing and as encompassed by the victorious grace of God is she who is indefectible. We can understand also that all sacramental power that is conferred empowers the individual to achieve a fulfilment of the Church's own nature, and to do so in such a way that the recipient of the sacrament does not merely remain passive, but himself makes a positive contribution towards this self-fulfilment of the Church in which she makes actual her own nature as the basic sacrament of salvation for the world. In fact this is the almost universal teaching of the theologians, at least with regard to the sacrament of penance.

We should conceive of the priestly office, then, from the standpoint of the Church. We should think of it not as a power which in the first instance sets its holder over against the Church as the people of God, but as the empowering of an individual in one specific area to achieve the fulfilment of that which the Church is as a whole, and moreover, that fulfilment which she must achieve in this way in virtue of her official ministry. And once we recognize this then we can understand how very cautious we must be in enquiring into the specific characteristics proper to the ministerial priesthood in relation to the rest of the members of the Church.

In the case of many priests today we find a degree of insecurity with regard to their understanding of their own priesthood which strikes us as almost neurotic. The question is raised of what a priest really is and why there still are priests today, seeing that on the one hand almost everything which he himself has the power to do and does could also be done by others, and on the other that the little which, according to the teaching of the Catholic faith, can be done only by ordained priests can hardly constitute the content and the function of a 'principal calling'. Certainly the following proposition is true: according to Catholic teaching and practice there is little in that which constitutes the normal activity of a priest engaged in the pastoral ministry which could not also be done by a 'layman'. At least provided that authority is granted on the part of the hierarchical Church (something which it is perfectly well able to do) teaching and directing, indeed baptizing itself, are not acts for which priestly ordination is absolutely required, although in concrete living practice all these constitute the principle part of the priests' vocational work. Of course there is a whole range of further and more subtle problems which might be treated of in this connection. But abstracting from these we can certainly raise a further question with regard to those functions of presiding over the celebration of the Eucharist, the administration of the sacrament of penance and the anointing of the sick which, according to Catholic teaching, can be exercised only by an ordained priest. Even if a special 'class' has to be constituted within the hierarchical structure of the Church in order to cater for these functions we are of course entitled to ask whether in themselves they are capable of constituting a 'calling' in the sense in which this is understood in secular society, one namely which, even from the secular point of view, constitutes the main occupation of an individual in the same way that an official post in secular society does.

Yet if we present the question in this way and divide the function of the ministerial priesthood into its individual components in this way then, even though in doing so we are following the pattern of the established theology of the seminaries itself, we are still putting the question falsely. In this connection it may be pointed out that the problem which we are treating of here is still not precisely the problem of whether the priestly office in the Catholic Church should necessarily also have the status of a profession in the secular sense. This problem of the professionalization of the priesthood, as it is called by the contemporary sociologists of religion, is one with which we shall have to concern ourselves at a later stage. But in order to recognize how false it is to present the question in the manner envisaged here, and in order to achieve an understanding of how the question should rightly be presented, we may begin by pointing to an analogous example, namely the recent revival of the diaconate in the Latin Church.

In the discussion which has taken place in recent years both before and after the Council, the objection has often been raised even by such personages as Cardinal Ottaviani that the diaconate comprises no tasks or functions whatever which, provided the Church authorises it, could not be exercised by laymen also. From this point of view the problem with which we are here concerned arises still more acutely than in the case of the official priesthood. For in this case there are at least some powers and functions which, according to Catholic teaching, can only be attributed to the ordained priest. Nevertheless in response to this attitude of scepticism with regard to the diaconate and its renewal it has rightly been pointed out that to present the question precisely in *this* way is false. It has been emphasized that what is in question here is not whether in ordaining an individual as deacon we are transferring functions to him which he would not otherwise possess and hence has not previously exercised. The question is rather concerned with a whole unified complex of functions and tasks, reasonable in themselves, which the individual holds and exercises in the name of the Church. Does there exist in the society of the Church an explicitly sacramental form and sacramental seal which can be applied to this unified complex of functions and tasks in such a way as to give the individual concerned an assurance of grace in the exercise of his tasks? The question of the legitimacy and reasonableness of a sacramental order, therefore, is not, in the last analysis to be answered by pointing out that one or other of the tasks involved in the Church is only possible provided the individual has actually been ordained for it in this way. This question is to be answered rather by applying the principle that it is reasonable and in accordance with the nature of the Church to confer a sacramental seal and sacramental power upon the official and institution-alized functions exercised in the Church as a society, and moreover this remains true even in those cases in which such functions and tasks are 'in themselves' possible and indeed *de facto* exercised in the Church even when no such ordination has been conferred. The nature of sacramental ordination and the purpose for which it is designed are such that it does not depend upon whether it relates to something and achieves some form of consecration which would otherwise not exist at all.

In the light of this it becomes clear that priestly ordination is in principle and from the outset also related to such priestly functions as are possible and actually practised in themselves even without ordination, such functions, therefore, as teaching, directing, preaching the gospel in the name of the Church and in the word of authority that claims the obedience of faith. In other contexts too sacraments are in fact – especially so far as their recipients are concerned – not symbolic events such that without them the actual reality signified, the *res sacramenti*, would not be possible. Rather they are the historical, social and effective manifestation of those events of grace which are also possible even apart from them, and the effects of which extend beyond that sphere within which these events require to be made manifest at the sacramental level also. Grace, justifica-tion, and even unity with the Body of Christ in his Spirit (the *res sacra-menti* in the Eucharist) are in fact possible and become a reality even apart from baptism, the sacrament of penance and the Eucharist. And yet this does not mean that we have either to deny or to obscure our obligation to receive these sacraments or the '*necessitas medii*' attached to them. In an analogous way, therefore, priestly ordination can perfectly well be applied to the totality of the priestly office as this is exercised in the concrete in the Church. The basic question with regard to the essence of the priestly office, therefore, is not 'What is it which the priest alone can do?' but rather this: Let us say that what the priest assumes and brings to its fulness in his office is a complex of tasks and functions deriving its meaning from the nature of the Church herself, so that it is this that gives the priestly office its justification. On this showing, then, are we to understand this complex as a unity that is conferred on a specific individual so as sacra-mentally to empower him to exercise these tasks and functions, and so constituting a special status in the Church with a distinctive content of its own?

Certainly with regard to the manifold elements in this complex we can impose a structure upon this complex. Certainly we can take as our starting-point in imposing this structure the fact that the individual is empowered to proclaim that effective and exhibitive word which the priest utters in the name of the Church in the celebration of the Eucharist. We can further freely and unreservedly take into account the fact that the complex of such priestly tasks and functions in the concrete is itself subject to a certain process of change in the course of history – the more so since according to the witness of history itself no absolute lines of demarcation can be deduced by which this complex can be separated off from the complex of functions and tasks belonging to the bishop. But the imposing of a structure of this kind on the complex of priestly tasks and functions, and even the factor of change in the concrete realization of this complex, do not exclude the fact that priestly ordination bears upon the complex of these functions taken as a single whole, that priestly ordination consecrates the individual for this complex and confers it upon him as a single whole, and that it is not confined merely to those functions of the priest which are reserved to the ordained individual exclusively. To put the matter bluntly: the priest is not merely ordained to say Mass, but equally to preach the gospel in the name of the Church, and this statement is not invalidated by the fact that it can be said that preaching the gospel can also be done without ordination. The point in question here, therefore, is simply whether the complex of priestly tasks as it exists *de facto* in the present constitutes, when viewed as a whole, a meaningful complex of tasks and functions which must be present in the Church. Now this is a question which can unreservedly and unambiguously be answered in the affirmative, and that too even if we leave the question of whether any particular element in this complex will also continue to be included in it in the future.

In order to understand this more clearly we must first go back somewhat further in history. We should not in the first instance take as our starting-point that threefold division of the Church's office into bishop, priest and deacon which is traditional, and also functioned as legitimate in the Second Vatican Council. The official institution of the Church is ultimately one, and that too not merely in the sense of an *a posteriori* unity among the holders of office in the Church, but in itself. The Church has an office and, moreover, in virtue of the fact that she, without prejudice to the deeper unity in the Holy Spirit of faith, hope and love, of her very essence is also endowed with an historical dimension. At this level too, then, the Church is she who is one and she who must necessarily actualize her own nature as a single social entity, amongst other factors through that one precisely which we call her official institutions, although this does not imply that the Church as such and as one could only achieve the fulness of her own nature in actual terms through her official institutions. It is not easy, and above all not possible in any adequate sense here, to express the basic essence of this single office in a definition that is brief and yet at the same time expresses all that it contains in terms of the nature of the Church herself. To do this we should have to consider this nature in itself, and that too at a most radical level of theological thought, a level to which the dogmatic constitution on the Church of the Second Vatican Council has brought us essentially nearer, but which it has still not succeeded. in achieving in any definitive sense. We should have to consider the unity which exists between that which in ecclesiology is called the 'potestas ordinis' and that which in the same discipline is referred to as the 'potestas jurisdictionis'. And in doing this we should have to ask whether these two concepts, even considered in their ultimate and original unity, provide a basis for the whole essence of the factor of office in the Church, or whether in them functions such as, for instance, the prophetic function, which also belong in some sense to the factor of office in the Church, are not perhaps too inadequately represented. We should have to ask ourselves whether the Church as understood simply in these terms does not after all appear too much as a mere static establishment.

We have no intention of denying the questionable factors in this, or of rejecting as false or misconceived other possibilities of arriving at a radical definition of the nature of the Church at this level, and, arising from this, of the factor of office in her. But even allowing for this, we may perhaps commit ourselves to the following statement: For our present purposes we are viewing the Church not as the society of the saved, though obviously she is also and even primarily this, but rather as the medium of salvation – in other words as the offering of salvation to mankind and not as the acceptance of salvation. On this showing, then, we must describe her as the abiding actualization of that word of promise on God's part which was uttered and made manifest in Jesus Christ in history, and which is eschatologically victorious. This word certainly achieves its supreme point in that proclamation of the Death and Resurrection of Jesus in the Eucharist which renders these events present. But obviously too it is not restricted to this. For this basic word must not merely be doctrinally formulated, developed and expressed in ever new forms corresponding to the concrete situation of the world itself, so that in this sense the word itself has a history of its own, but more than this it must be uttered in a form in which it can penetrate into the concrete situation of the individual man and into all the dimensions of individual human life both private and social so as to become actual for the present and future alike. In this sense, then, this basic word in its unity bears within it a character that is at once doctrinal, juridical in the social sense, sacramental, and prophetic.

The nature of the Church as medium of salvation, therefore, consists in the presence of this word as understood here being actualised ever afresh. Moreover the Church in this sense necessarily has a social character also, and therefore an institutional character and an official establishment, Now it follows from this that with regard to the nature of the priesthood, presupposing all that has already been said with regard to its complexity, this can be specified by the fact that as conferred on an individual it empowers him to proclaim this word as the word of the Church. In defining the nature of the priesthood in this sense we can set aside those elements in it which distinguish it from the episcopate, for these are relatively secondary and, moreover, have varied in the course of history, and for our present considerations they are of minor importance. The priest is he who has been empowered for the ministry of the word in the Church, and we can recognize in this 'definition' all the functions attributed to him provided that we have clearly before our eyes the manifold dimensions intrinsic in this word, the variations in the degree of its actuality, and its exhibitive character, its nature as not merely doctrinal but prophetic too in its orientation, and its character as promise. All these are factors in it which we have already indicated above.

It is unimportant whether the bearers of the word which is, in this sense, 'official' can also be – at least in certain degrees of its actualization and certain specific directions – men who have not been essentially commissioned for proclaiming this word by having that special power conferred upon them which we call priestly ordination. In those cases in which a commission of this kind is given with sufficient breadth (although it may be rather vague with regard to the more peripheral activities which it includes) it should also be ratified, made explicit and reinforced with the sacramental grace necessary for it in the public and social life of the Church. According to the Catholic interpretation of faith this word is present in a particularly intense degree in the word of the Eucharistic anamnesis, in the word of pardon uttered in the sacrament of penance, and in the concretion of this in the anointing of the sick, so that in all normal cases in the life of the Church this sacramental ratification constitutes an indispensable prior condition for the word to be uttered in these contexts, so that everything may take place 'in order' in the Church. The Church is intended to be something more than merely the amalgam of the individual religious enthusiasts, the 'zealots'. For though the Church has a certain freedom, bequeathed to her by Christ himself, as to the precise manner in which she defines the powers attached to the individual offices within her, and as to the way in which she divides her offices into several degrees or orders, still this factor of institutionalized office is something that she must have, and its function is to empower its holders to render present through their official witness this word that is always identified with the Church herself. Now if all this is true then there is in the Church a priesthood of a kind which cannot be reduced solely to the cult of the Church in the narrower sense.

An office of this kind is of its very nature so multi-dimensional, necessarily extending its claims over all departments of the life of its holders, and it depends upon so many prior human factors, that the function it confers upon its holder in the Church is far from being merely a partial one. On the contrary it gives him, amongst other things, a clearly defined status in the social life of the Church as such, and in virtue of this fact implies a vocation and a calling in the ecclesiological sense even though this does not necessarily, or at all epochs in the Church's history, carry with it a professional status in secular society as something that is accorded by that society and is effective in its life. This remains true however much it may be the case that this is likely to be brought about as a result of the interplay between the ecclesiastical and the secular spheres, an interplay which it is quite impossible wholly to avoid.

So long, therefore, as we believe in the nature of the Church and her character as abiding we have no reason to call in question the necessity of the official priesthood as an abiding factor in her. However much the image of this may be charged in secular society its nature will endure. Now the nature of the official priesthood is such as to lay claims upon the whole man in such a way that it certainly implies a vocation and, following from this, a profession too, taking the term profession here to signify a comprehensive and permanent task which an individual exercises on behalf of others, which to a very large extent demands that his whole life shall be committed to it, and which is prior to any process of institutionalization in terms of secular society. If a priest were unable to understand his priesthood in this sense as a vocation and thereby as a profession too, he would have failed to understand the very nature of this priesthood itself. If today he is experiencing the fact that secularized society refuses to recognize his 'profession', then he is simply suffering from the contradiction of the Church as such by the 'world' (something which the Christian layman also has to endure in his own way), and he should ask himself how he can be surprised at this since in fact, after all, Christian faith always implies folly and scandal so far as the 'world' is concerned. Certainly as a result of this contradiction special features will often be evoked in the activities and life of the priest as it *de facto* exists which have nothing to do with the nature of the priesthood itself, and through these we and the Church in the concrete often cause scandal to the world in a way that is unnecessary and regrettable. But for the most part what is implied in this contradiction is, after all, something which constitutes the very nature of the Church and the priesthood, for the word of God both as judging and as liberating is destined to be contradicted and this is precisely something that belongs to its very nature.

III

While recognizing, then, that the priestly office as it exists today, and also as it will exist in the future, constitutes a special status in the Church and, in this theological sense, a profession, this is still clearly not enough to decide the question of the priesthood considered as a profession in the secular sense also. Certainly we might refer to the biblical statement that he who ministers at the altar can also live by the altar, and in fact we have already invoked this principle. We could further point to the fact that in secular society as it exists today, with its extremely wide variation of callings and divisions of labour, there is a whole range of callings and professions in a secular sense within that society which do not play any part in the social productivity of that society in the material sense. Those engaged in the representational arts, authors and musicians for instance, belong to this category. The fact that they live by their activities in these fields is something which society accepts without question. It could further be emphasized that on a right theological understanding of the function of the priest in the Church, which is so very far from being confined merely to the cult, it actually includes today, and will include in the future, so many prior activities and tasks that it can only be fulfilled if it is accepted as a 'principal calling'. All these aspects certainly have a certain significance even with regard to the future, and they will also be capable of taking effect in the future at least provided that society does not become so anti-Christian and hostile that it prevents them with physical force. But this is still not enough to provide any effective answer to the question of the 'professionalization' or professional status of the priesthood. From two points of view a question still remains: on the one hand from the point of view of the reform which the Church and the individual local and worshipping community will assume in the future, and on the other from the point of view of the function which the priest himself will have to fulfil for communities of this kind.

It is not merely that which still lies totally in the future which is affected by these questions. For in some sense this future has already begun even here and now, and hence the questions which we have raised already affect the present-day life of the priest and his understanding of his own function, the more so since, after all, it is the priests of the present day (not alone, it is true, but still amongst others) who will have to conduct the Church into the future that awaits her. For this reason we cannot simply set these questions aside if we want to consider the priesthood as it exists today. We cannot do this even though at the same time we must neither forget nor neglect the point that we emphasized at the beginning of these considerations, namely that calmness and patience which are so needful in a period of transition.

The moment we turn to consider the future form of the Church herself this 'professional status' to be attributed to the priesthood becomes a question. For over the space of one and a half millenia the Church has existed as a national Church, so that her status in the midst of secular society has, on the whole, been taken for granted and never called in question, and on this showing the professional status of the priesthood too has been something accepted without question. Nor do we need, from our contemporary point of view, to condemn this status of being a national Church which the Church has enjoyed since the 'Constantine epoch' as in principle a sinful derogation on the Church's part. This status of being a 'national Church' has been, and still is – to some extent this is still true even today – a historical phenomenon which was probably quite incapable of being otherwise, and which, moreover, has certainly had a positive significance for the true and enduring function of the Church herself. Nevertheless all this seems to tell in favour of the point of view that the Church is changing from being a 'national Church' into a Church of those who believe as an act of their own personal and free decision. Whereas earlier, and right down to our own days the Church has been, despite all her struggles with the state, a social entity in her social constitution and in the status accorded to her by secular society, one which, through her power as a society, her institutions, the value accorded to her in public opinion etc., was prior to the free decision of faith on the part of the individuals, and rather supported this than was supported by it, nowadays this situation is changing at an ever-increasing rate.

More and more the Church, with her offices, the authority attached to these, her value in the eyes of the public etc., is becoming an entity such that her real effectiveness in society is dependent upon the free faith of those who confess their allegiance to her, and incidentally to recognize this is in no sense to deny the fact that she has been founded by God in Jesus Christ. It is true that in a Church which is only gradually becoming a Church of personal believers in this sense, there still always are certain elements (justifiably so not merely with regard to the Church's due mode of existence but also with regard to her real effectiveness) which are prior to the free decision of faith on the part of the individual to believe in the Church. These factors are present first because even a believing community continues to be in specific areas a real entity in secular society which also plays its part in shaping the situation in which non-believers live. A further reason why such elements still remain in the Church is that Christian parents have a right and duty to bring up their children as Christians and to bring them to a positive decision of faith. On the other hand, however, this still does not in the least alter the fact that there is a difference between the national Church of the past and the Church of free personal faith which is gradually developing and which must so develop even though at the same time we hope and work to ensure that this future Church will not be all too small a flock in terms of the numbers of her members.

In a Church of this kind constituted by personal faith it is after all inevitable that the professional status of the priesthood in its secular aspects will in some respects be called in question. Certainly the Church of the future must be open in a missionary and apostolic sense to the whole of society, and this means to non-believers as well. She must not seek to turn herself into a ghetto, a small sect with the sort of cosiness and lack of interest in the 'wide world' outside which is characteristic of this. But the number of her priests, their mode of life, the possibility of their human existence, will be primarily conditioned by the number of adherents, the economic resources which they will have and their mentality in a Church of the kind we are thinking of. For instance it is after all hardly conceivable that throughout all future ages this Church will to a large extent have her economic necessities provided for by those who have no personal relationship to the Church whatever in terms of faith, are hardly Christians at all even in the most superficial sense through baptism, and declare themselves Christians only for the purposes of their official status in secular society (this is in fact the situation which prevails today in central Europe with regard to the administration of taxes on behalf of the Church).

Conversely we can foresee that the resources which a living community of believers of this kind will be able to contribute towards those who are called to be priests will be on a totally different basis, and will be conditioned by quite different factors in terms of education and way of life than is the case today with the great majority of such communities.

Certainly it is desirable that in the future too as many priests as possible will be humanly and theologically highly educated men who can also assume a significant place in secular society. At the same time, however, it is certainly not a matter of necessity in the very nature of the Church that the priests will have simply the same type of academic formation as educated functionaries in the state. Already today in view of the fact that the lack of priests is becoming ever greater we should work to abolish prejudices of this kind, and seek to devize institutional means of enabling men to become priests which need not be identical with those which are nowadays required for so-called late vocations to the priesthood. We shall straightway be going on to develop certain aspects of this point in somewhat greater detail.

A preliminary point that still has to be recognized is that even from the point of view of the function of the priest himself his professional status will be called in question to a notable extent in the future. On any honest and realistic view of our work we priests of today must admit that our work and the success which it achieves, which is still considerable even today, depends upon the conditions provided by the national Church and by a traditional Christianity. People still come to the Church even when we preach badly. The Church taxes are still paid, even though the relationship between these and the Christian faith and the Church is an extremely problematical one. Even today, without having to exert ourselves particularly, we still receive almost all the children of parents who have been baptized Catholics in baptism and religious instruction in the state schools. Even today it is still almost universally regarded as important to be buried with the Christian rites. Our sermons and morning prayers are transmitted over the radio even when they are bad. In the long run, however, we cannot simply count upon this always remaining the case. But any alterations which take place in this situation, whether they are gradual or, as it may be, in the form of spectacular upheavals, we priests will be brought face to face in a far plainer and harsher light with the fact that the success of our work depends upon the vitality of our own personal religious lives, and will survive precisely so long as this survives. Just as an artist (i.e. one who thinks of himself as such) goes hungry and fails if the personal factor in his art is not real and strong, so too the priest of the future will depend, in his concrete living, upon the question of whether he is really a man who lives from the heart and centre of his own personal existence as one who bears witness to the faith and arouses faith in others. To put the matter crudely the priest of the future will 'earn' as much as he himself provides in terms of genuine religion. But this does not imply that we are in any sense calling in question that professional status which is still obviously present among us today, and that too even though we neither wish nor expect the priest of the future not to 'live by the altar'.

Let us attempt, albeit only in the form of questions which are genuinely conceived of as open and unreserved, to express in somewhat more concrete form, the point which we have just sketched out in barest outline. It is perfectly conceivable that a situation might arise in which some future community of believers found itself unable to discover any more priests through the administrative channels customary hitherto. Why, then, should such a community not discover and select from among its own more vital members some senior man who (the due conditions of theological formation and human maturity being fulfilled, and ordination having been conferred by the bishop) would become the 'presbyter' of this community, its priest? Certainly we will always need priests and bishops in the Church who also exercise the priesthood as their 'chief office' and 'main calling' in the secular and civic sense, and also in the manner in which these were to be found in the first centuries of the Church in circumstances of persecution. But does this prevent us from boldly envisaging the possibility that there may also be 'part-time' priests in the civic sense, and that it may be that this will be something that is not merely forced upon us by the ever greater lack of priests, but also something that has positive opportunities and advantages of its own to offer? The term 'part-time' as applied here would in fact only serve to characterize a priesthood of this sort from the standpoint of secular society. But it would not imply that such a priesthood would be, in the concrete existence of the individual, or in a theological sense, a hobby which such priests would practise in their spare time.

Today the 'diaspora' situation of the Church is increasing and extending, and because of this any organization of the cure of souls in the Church on a basis which is in principle territorial will also perhaps become ever more difficult and problematical. Now in view of this would it not be possible to work out the concrete form of the priesthood as vested in a specific individual in terms of a personal group of a specific kind, and not by invoking the territorial principle of the parish, which, after all, still consistently serves as the basic model for priestly activity. After all there may already be today many men, both young and old, who are suitable for the priesthood in the truly theological sense already indicated, and who feel themselves called to it even though they may not on this account *ipso facto* regard themselves as suited or feel themselves inclined to take upon themselves all the various functions exercised by a parish priest as normally envisaged today. Could we not, without prejudice to the theological essence of the priesthood, be bold enough to allow it to become specialized? Could we not from the outset juridically work out institutional forms for it in such a way that when this priesthood was conferred upon the individual through sacramental ordination the range of functions attached to it and the group of believers which that individual was intended to serve would be such as he himself felt himself formed enough to cope with.

We have in fact already come to recognize a similar situation with regard to the deacons who are newly ordained or about to be so. The social worker who has been ordained deacon or the teacher of religion who has been ordained deacon, despite having been ordained, and indeed concomitantly with it, precisely continues in his own calling. He is not obliged to perform all those functions which in principle and in themselves are included and consecrated through this sacramental ordination. Why should not something similar also be conceived of and introduced in the future in the case of the priesthood as well? After all it would for instance be perfectly possible to ordain one of a group of masters attached to a secondary school as priest, without thereby obliging him even in principle to any kind of priestly activity outside the milieu in which he had formerly lived and worked. The established offices in the Church are essentially one, and they are capable of far more variations and subdivisions so as to suit those who hold them than we have been accustomed to recognize hitherto. For generally speaking even when we consider this problem at the theoretical level we overlook the fact of how many concrete variations of form priestly activity has already manifested in former times, as it still does to this day.

We may notice merely in passing that among these possibilities for the future the questions of priestly celibacy would also have to be thought out afresh. I myself have been most resolute in supporting the view that celibacy should be retained even for secular priests. I am convinced that any further secularization of the clergy would not be conducive to the salvation of the Church and the priesthood, and moreover that in accordance with the recommendation of scripture the priest is called to live by, and to bear witness to his faith in that eternal life which is not of this world, amongst other things by his renunciation of marriage, however great this blessing may be. These considerations of themselves are enough to justify my support of priestly celibacy. At the same time, however, the question may very well be raised whether this sacred burden should be imposed upon all those groups of priests who may perhaps be formed in the future within the single priesthood.

The priestly office will endure in the Catholic Church because the Church endures. In the outward forms it assumes in secular society it may undergo great changes. We do not need to introduce such changes violently or in a hysterical and revolutionary spirit. Nevertheless we should not shrink from them either, as though through them the essence of the priesthood itself were to be imperilled. We only safeguard the abiding essence of the priesthood when we maintain an attitude of freedom and openness towards a change in its external forms as and when this is demanded by the situation of the Church today and in the future. And so in accordance with that attitude of mind which prevails today at least in this respect in the hierarchy of the Church we must guard still more against any tendency to a conservative rigidity than against being over-bold in devizing fresh forms of the priesthood. But in an age in which an ecclesiastical defeatism and a general insecurity prevail, an age in which the Christian faith is under attack in the most radical manner, the point of first and last importance with regard to the priesthood is that unconditional hope which springs from faith in its existence and its function in the Church of today and tomorrow.

As Christians we do not have to calculate what the future of the priesthood will be in a futurologist sense. We do not have to estimate its chances and adapt ourselves accordingly. We have to believe in this future unconditionally, and by this act of faith to shape this future precisely when it seems to be improbable. Here too we need to be not those who suffer the future, but rather those who create it. In a spirit of faith, prayer, and self-lessness we have to overcome any tendency to a bourgeois 'establishment' attitude towards our priesthood as though it were a means of earning our living. We have to be the sort of priests who in the boldness of faith seize upon the folly of the Cross. We have to be not hirelings but shepherds who hope against all hope. We have to give our allegiance to the scandal of the Cross of Christ, to have the patience to endure historical situations which are impenetrable to our gaze. We have in a real sense to see ourselves as servants of Christ, that Christ who, through the fathomless darkness of his death, has redeemed the world. We have to be ready to bear unemotionally and in all the realism of our colourless everyday lives the stigmata of Christ. And if we do all this then we are priests indeed, then it is the grace of God alone which is creating through us, and also through our priesthood, that future which the one and unique Lord of history and of the Church has devized for this priesthood and which will come to pass.

4

ON THE DIACONATE

SUCH far-reaching and rapid developments have taken place in the theology and the practice of the permanent diaconate[1] that even twenty years ago it would have been quite impossible to guess at them. Certain theological movements in the last few years before the Council, the Council itself, and certain impulses arising from it, have all undoubtedly contributed to this. In our present consideration however we have no intention of re-opening in any direct sense the discussion of this conciliar theology of the diaconate and the practical effects deriving from this. We must begin by taking all this as already recognized and valid.[2] Since the Council, however, and without any direct dependence upon it, the development of the diaconate has received a quite fresh impetus, and it is this that we shall be concerned with here. For in the light of this fresh impetus which we are on the point of describing the question of the content, the significance, the usefulness, or even the necessity of the permanant diaconate will be presented from an aspect which is quite different from those which have formerly been discussed, and different even from those which were considered in the Council.

The new stimulus to develop a theology, and concomitant with this new practical applications too, of the diaconate stems from the new theology of the priestly office. This is something which in its current developments was still not envisaged at all in the Council, or at any rate,

---

1 This study is the text of a lecture which the author gave on the 7th of December 1968 in Freiburg, on the occasion of a conference on the diaconate. For purposes of publication a few notes have been added to it.

2 On the state of the discussion at the Council itself cf. the commentary on Article 29 of the Decree 'Lumen Gentium' by H. Vorgrimler, *LTK* Suppl. I (Freiburg, 1966), 256–259; cf. also *idem*, 'Erneuerung des Diakonats nach dem Konzil', *Der Seelsorger* 35 (1965), 102–115; K. Rahner, 'The Teaching of the Second Vatican Council on the Diaconate', *Theological Investigations* X (London and New York, 1973), pp. 222–234; also H. Vorgrimler, 'Zur Theologie des Diakonats. Thesen', *Der Diakon heute*, edited by the Cathedral School, Akademie für Erwachsenenbildung der Diözese Würzburg [Würzburg, 1969), pp. 39–43; *idem*, 'Der theologische Ort des Diakonats', *Handbuch der Pastoraltheologie* IV (Freiburg, 1969), pp. 417 ff

if it was so, the statements in which it was referred to did not attract any attention. This new development of the theology of the priestly office, which is of the utmost importance for the diaconate, generates its own forward impulse, and this from two different directions: from the standpoint of the biblical theology of 'office' in the Church, and from the situation both within the Church herself and in secular society in which the priestly office is placed today. Although we must begin by speaking of the fresh problems raised by the theology of the priestly office, our treatment of this must necessarily be extremely brief, and we shall only discuss these problems in so far as they throw some light upon the theology of the diaconate itself.

The first point to be clearly recognized in the New Testament theology[3] of 'office' in the Church concerns the division of this into the office of priest and bishop. In so far as we can discern this division at all in the New Testament it certainly does not consist in any clear line of demarcation drawn between the office of priest and bishop. Moreover it is clear that that which constitutes the essence of this office does not consist in any immediately apprehensible sense in sacramental powers of a specifically sacerdotal kind, or, more precisely still, in any special powers exercised in the community's celebration of the Eucharist. In so far as we can discern any special office in the Christian community as portrayed in the New Testament, with its universal priesthood, it is characterized primarily by a special mission to preach the word and by the function of leading and directing a Christian community, and in this connection the question of the relationship and at the same time the distinction between these two functions represents a further special problem in its own right. Of course we can say, and objectively speaking we are certainly justified in saying, that any official preaching of the word or leadership of the community achieve their supreme point in that proclamation of the Death of the Lord which takes place in the liturgy of the community. And it is in this liturgy that the community itself achieves the fulness of its own nature in a form that is sacramentally most intense. In this sense we can certainly establish a rational connection between the traditional and sacerdotal concept of the priestly office which is also that sanctioned by the Council of Trent, and the conception of office which we find in the New Testament, which is not

---

[3] On this cf. H. Schürmann, 'Neutestamentliche Marginalien zur Frage der Entsakralisierung', I/II, *Der Seelsorger* 38 (1968), pp. 38–40, 89–104; J. Blank, 'Der Priester im Lichte der Bibel', *ibid.*, 155–164. But see also H. Schlier, 'Grundelemente des priesterlichen Amtes im Neuen Testament', *Theologie und Philosophie* 44 (1969), pp. 161–180.

in any direct sense defined in specifically priestly, i.e. cultic and sacerdotal, terms. But even if we recognize this still the question of the nature of the priestly office is presented in a fresh form by the New Testament, and needs to be answered afresh by working out a fresh way of organizing the manifold elements belonging to the priestly office based upon the bible itself.

To this a second point must be added which also derives from the present-day biblical theology of 'office' in the Church. In the light of the New Testament it is surely possible to conceive of official functions within the society of the Church which are quite different from those which spontaneously occur to our minds today when we speak of 'office' in the Church and go on straightway to divide this into the offices of bishop, priest and deacon in the conviction that these three hierarchical degrees can be easily and unambiguously distinguished from one another, and that these alone, when taken together, represent the single totality of 'office' in the Church. It is true that the three terms do occur already in the New Testament: bishop, presbyter, diakon. But even if it appears in the Pastoral Epistles that by the end of the apostolic age the bishop as an individual already possesses a well-defined function of leadership in the local community reserved to him alone, still this in itself is not enough to supply any unambiguous distinction between the three concepts or to assign any unambiguous content to each of the three. In other words in terms of the New Testament there is indeed an 'office' in the Church, and this is ultimately one. But it can be subdivided into various functions according to the concrete needs of any given community. These functions as distributed in this sense between various office-holders will certainly also have to be thought of as hierarchically arranged. But the element of 'office' in the Church is certainly still fluid. Various sociological patterns can be employed in determining the concrete forms which it assumes and the variations which it undergoes, and moreover no very clear lines of demarcation are to be found in the New Testament marking it off from other charisms contributing to the wellbeing of the community, which cannot be regarded as official or institutional in any proper sense. In passing a further point must also be emphasized: the fact that in the New Testament the Church's 'office' is still fluid in this sense, and that variation is still possible in the way in which its different functions are distributed between different office-holders according to the concrete circumstances and requirements in any given case does not gainsay the sacramentality of the three hierarchical degrees of order recognized in our own times. In other words these factors in the New Testament cannot be contested on the ground of the dogmatic teaching of the sacramentality of order as it exists in the present day. There is a further question of what the reasons are, in more precise terms, for ascribing a sacramental force to the juridical act of conferring 'office' in the Church. But this question need not concern us for our immediate purposes. In any case the teaching of dogmatic theology demonstrates the fact that the single sacrament of *ordo*, even though it really is single (otherwise there would be more than seven sacraments) can be subdivided into different degrees, and this teaching also demonstrates the fact that at least as late as the high Middle Ages the theologians uncompromisingly taught that the truly sacramental element in order was further subdivided into very minor and insignificant official posts in the Church. And they also taught uncompromisingly that the conferring of a share in the single 'office' of the Church allowed for a far greater variation and modification of content among the official posts which the Church recognized than we are nowadays accustomed to accept as either possible or actual. What all this implies for the diaconate can be explained only at a later stage.

We must first consider the fresh impetus which the theology and practical application of the priestly office implies for the diaconate from yet another aspect. The problems entailed in the situation of the present-day priest both within the society of the Church and within secular society must briefly be touched upon.[4]

Formerly in virtue of his priestly office, it was taken for granted that the priest has a specific and well-defined position in secular society. In virtue of his priestly office he had also a calling in the worldly sense, a 'firm position' even at the secular level, a plain and recognized 'role' in the body politic. Today this is no longer so obvious. The question is raised, for instance, whether a priest should not follow a secular calling as well in order to achieve an indisputable position in the world, and one which provides him with economic support, so that he may bear an effective witness to the gospel precisely from this well-recognized position. In fact there are here and there in the secular institutes priests who side by

[4] There is a constantly increasing body of literature on this subject, which it is quite impossible to present here. For this reason reference will only be made to the address which the author delivered on the 4th September 1968 at the Conference of German Catholics in Essen: 'Dogmatische Grundlagen des priesterlichen Selbstverständnisses', *Mitten in dieser Welt*, edited by the Central Committee of German Catholics (Paderborn, 1968), pp. 96–115. Reference may also be made to the following articles: 'The Point of Departure in Theology for Determining the Nature of the Priestly Office' in this volume, pp. 31–38; 'Theological Reflections upon the Priestly Image of Today and Tomorrow', in this volume, pp. 39–60.

side with their priestly tasks follow a worldly calling. This, together with the phenomenon of the worker priests, demonstrates the fact that we have already reached a stage which is beyond that of purely academic speculation.

There is a further question, namely whether in view of the dangerous lack of priests today there should not be individuals who, in addition to their priestly office, also follow a worldly calling as a 'full-time job'. These would exercise their priestly functions on Sunday or in the evening as a 'part-time job'. This question points in the same direction. An additional factor is that even regarded from within the Church those who hold the priestly office in the Church at least to some extent have gathered to themselves and exercised functions in the Church which are both very intensive and very numerous, even though precisely if we take the traditional conception of the priesthood as our starting-point we cannot really see why such functions should be exercised precisely by priests. The phenomenon of the lay religious instructor, the so-called lay theologian, and many others besides show that even this question which is interior to the society of the Church is no mere theoretical problem.

These are findings which both at the theological and the practical levels have properly speaking only been realized in their full relevance since the Council, and it is in the light of these that the question of the diaconate too must be viewed today. Although the factor of 'office' in the Church is ultimately one, in respect of its functions and its distribution between various of its holders,[5] it is far more elastic, flexible and fluid, if we may so express it, than has been realized in the last few centuries. We have no intention here of drawing from this the conclusion that we should *ipso facto* call in question or seek to revise the threefold division of the single office of the Church into bishop, priest and deacon, which had already become classic and canonical at the beginning of the post-apostolic age. At the same time it should not be forgotten that the great theologians of the Middle Ages still counted the so-called minor orders as well – in other words those belonging to quite unimportant office-holders in the Church

[5] On this cf. the author's article, 'Die Aufgliederung des einen Amtes der Kirche" *Handbuch der Pastoraltheologie* I (Freiburg, 1964, 2nd ed. 1970), pp. 160–167, together with the chapters which follow. On the concept of office in general reference may be made to the author's commentary on the third chapter of 'Lumen Gentium', *LTK* Suppl. I (Freiburg, 1966), 210–246. On the question of whether it is possible for a way of subdividing the institution of order to be developed *juris divini* within Christian history cf. also the author's article, 'Reflection on the Concept of "Ius Divinum" in Catholic Thought', *Theological Investigations* V (London and Baltimore, 1966), pp. 219–243.

– as to be included also among those degrees of office which are sacramentally conferred. Moreover, even to this day the Church has not produced any official doctrinal decision which rules out such a theory.

But even when we simply take for granted the three degrees in the hierarchical division of ecclesiastical office, still it must at least be concluded from the evidence which we have mentioned both in terms of biblical theology and of the state of contemporary society, that it is possible freely to reconsider in more precise terms both the content of the three offices in the Church and the lines of demarcation between them. Moreover this reappraisal needs to be something more than merely an affair of the reason engaging in theological speculation so as to establish what is the case. Also, and more than this, it must at least to some extent be capable of leading to an alteration in the content of these offices, and to the establishing of new and real lines of demarcation between them (that this is not impossible from the outset is indeed also demonstrated by the fact that, for instance, it cannot be asserted in any very precise terms whether the power of conferring the sacrament of confirmation belongs to the episcopal or the priestly office. This is something that on any showing needs, from this aspect to be determined once and for all as a matter of positive law by the Church).

On this basis it would be theologically justified to say that the function and tasks of the renewed and permanent diaconate enumerated by the Council do not restrict our scope for working out a more profound and also a fresh and creative theology of the diaconate. These functions adduced in the Council vary very greatly in their significance. Taken in isolation any one of them can also be conferred upon one who is not a deacon, although on any right understanding of the single complex 'office' in the Church this does not tell against the significance and the sacramentality of the diaconate itself. These functions enumerated by the Council are not co-ordinated among themselves by it so as to constitute the diaconate as a unified whole in which all these functions and tasks are manifestly interconnected. And finally it is by no means certain that in the diaconate in its contemporary form, in contrast, and also as an alternative to these historical functions of the diaconate, quite other functions may be present which will characterize the diaconate of the future far more decisively than these former ones.

In this theological situation, in which the question of what a deacon is and what he should be in the future is still, to a very great extent an open one, in this situation in which it is possible to work out a new definition of what the diaconate shall mean not merely at the speculative but at the practical level as well, it seems to me that properly speaking only the following fixed points can be regarded as established: the deacon receives his office together with the powers and duties appropriate to it. The conferring of this office on the part of the episcopate has a sacramental character and because of this must take place in the manner required for a sacramental act performed in public, something which is perfectly reconcilable with a considerable breadth of choice in the form which this conferring of the office of deacon is to assume. It is not normal (i.e. legitimate in the ordinary circumstances prevailing in a Christian community) for the deacon to have the power of presiding at the Eucharistic liturgy. For while it is true that this does not simply constitute in itself alone the content of the priestly office or the basic theological starting-point for defining its nature, still this power is, after all, proper to the priestly office, and will surely remain so in the future, although it still does not carry with it any absolute, fixed, or unalterable connection with the official preaching of the word of God and the direction of the community (taking these in turn as constituting a unity). It seems to me, however, that these three specifications of the diaconate constitute at the same time the sole three invariable factors which can be attributed with certainty to the diaconate.

All that has been said up to this point has been intended to convey in barest outline the insight that we cannot properly speaking define the meaning and content of the diaconate of the future on the basis of the New Testament, the ancient practice of the western Church, or of course on the basis of the eastern Church's conception of the diaconate either,[6] although at the same time the three invariable factors mentioned above have to be respected. Today, therefore, what is properly in question is not a restoration of the diaconate in its ancient form, but a creative conception of the diaconate of the future. Ancient models of the diaconate can provide stimuli for this new specification of it. Nevertheless in this new and creative specification what is involved is not merely a restructuring of the traditional functions of the ancient diaconate at the level of speculative theology.

But how is this new specification of the nature, i.e. the specific function, of the diaconate of the future to be arrived at? This is the difficult question

---

[6] This also becomes clear in view of the very different motives adduced at the Council as arguments in favour of restoring the diaconate. In the Decree on the Church the motive adduced is the importance of specific functions (No. 29). In the Decree for the Eastern Churches the motive is the ancient discipline of the sacrament of order (No. 17), and in the Decree on the Missions the fact that the diaconal ministry is already being exercised in practice (No. 16).

with which the Church has to cope today the moment she has resolved
upon a renewal of the diaconate of this kind. Two points should be self-
evident from the outset in this quest for a new conception of the diaconate:

1. Any such creatively new conception cannot be worked out exclusively at the conference table of rational theological speculation, because
in principle and in all cases no concrete decisions can be arrived at solely
and exclusively by a process of theological reasoning. Practical and
concrete experimentation is required. All kinds of attempts have to be
made, even though they do not lead immediately or in all cases to results
that are serviceable or permanent, and even though conversely such
attempts have to be undertaken only with theological speculation as their
concomitant, and with an attitude of realism and prudence.

2. It can readily be accepted from the outset that the diaconate of the
future as it is realized in the concrete will admit of a quite considerable
number of variations of form. This is surely something that we should
expect both with regard to the concrete functions attached to an office of
this kind and with regard to the various holders of this office. For even an
office which, as a matter of theological principle, is conceived of very
much as a unity certainly demands very considerable variations in the
forms it assumes in the situation which exists today both in the Church
and also in secular society with all its extreme complexities and variations.
In fact it can be the case that it will only be from a fairly wide variety of
concrete forms assumed by the diaconate (forms which have been
prompted by the situation of the Church and her concrete practice, and
have almost been forced upon her) that we shall gradually come to recognize the single theological essence common to all these various forms and
underlying them, and constituting the ministry of the diaconate as an
office of the Church.

Now if I am to attempt to say anything with regard to this content and
nature of the diaconate of the future I would like to begin by drawing
attention to the fact that probably the best treatment that has been accorded
to this theme up to the present is that of H. Vorgrimler in the *Handbuch
der Pastoral-theologie*, Vol. IV.[7] In what follows I shall be relying very
much on this study, but I would like to present what I have to say in my
own words and on my own responsibility.

In order to find an answer to our question concerning the nature and
function (which is the same thing) of the future diaconate certain preliminary methodological remarks must first be made, and then certain

[7] On this cf. n. 2.

negative boundary lines must be drawn, and finally an attempt must be made to state in positive terms what the future diaconate will be.

First a few preliminary methodological remarks. In the days of the Council the line of argument which I customarily followed in support of the restoration and renewal of the permanent diaconate was as follows: the diaconate already exists *de facto* in an anonymous form in the Church of today. In these circumstances it is right that those who are already vested with this anonymous diaconate should also have the sacramental commission conferred upon them, because in principle it is possible for there to be a sacramental diaconate in the Church, and such a sacramental commission is reasonable and productive of grace.[8]

This line of argument was, and still is in principle, not unjustified. Today, however, it is no longer adequate, for first in asserting that *de facto* the function of the diaconate was already being exercised in the Church, albeit in anonymous form and without any sacramental commission, we allowed ourselves to be influenced too much by the model of the earlier form of the diaconate,[9] although this in itself did not simply make our assertion false. It was not possible on these grounds to define more precisely what form the diaconate is to assume in the future in terms of its functions and activities. With regard to the functions already *de facto* existing in the Church it could not easily be explained which ones would be conferred by means of a sacramental commissioning and which would not. In the 'institutional Church' in the future, even though it is certain that in the future too there will be functions of this kind pertaining to the administrative practice of the Church such as not merely can be, but actually should be exercised by laymen, even so it will remain to some extent a question of practical judgement to decide where to draw the borderline in the concrete between this type of function and the other type. There is a further point to be noticed, pertaining to methodology. The diaconate of the future will remain an integral part of the official ministry of the Church as hierarchically organized. On the one hand, therefore, it must certainly manifestly be seen to be a subdivision of this official ministry and its functions, deriving from the very nature of the official ministry itself. On the other hand, however, this subdivision can and must be conditioned by the concrete situation in which the Church fulfils her

---

[8] On this cf. my article, 'The Theology of the Restoration of the Diaconate', *Theological Investigations* V (London and Baltimore, 1966), pp. 268–314.

[9] Up to the present the best general presentation is still to be found in K. Rahner, H. Vorgrimler ed., *Diakonia in Christo*, Quaestiones Disputatae 15/16 (Freiburg, 1962).

task through her official ministry. It follows that whatever authentic basis we find for instituting the diaconate of the future in its distinctive form it must be such that it does not in any sense depend upon the postulate that this concrete form of the diaconate as conceived of in the present must have been in existence all along and of necessity, and must continue to exist for all time. This means that the concrete situation of the Church is an essential element in this line of argument. This does not invalidate the 'jus divinum' of the diaconate (and, as the concomitant of this, its sacramentality too) for this jus divinum simply implies that the Church's official institutions belong essentially to the Church herself, that they are communicated sacramentally as such, and that this special quality inherent in them also extends to the concrete subdivisions of these institutions whenever the process of subdividing the single institution of order is demanded by the concrete situation of the Church, or is at any rate reasonable in view of it.

There is one final point which has to be taken into account from the outset with regard to this basic flexibility and adaptability of the single institution of order in the Church and the forms into which it is subdivided. It is that any specific subdivision of this order is itself in turn capable of appearing in various concrete forms as demanded by the concrete circumstances and tasks of the Church, and that in such subordinate manifestations of it various aspects may be particularly emphasized at various times. In seeking a theological basis for the future diaconate, therefore, we do not need to make it our aim to evolve any absolutely univocal and uniform type of deacon. The priesthood itself is subject to a wide range of variations, even though it is conceived of as consisting essentially in the authoritative preaching of the gospel in the name of the Church, and in guiding and directing the community (both functions being thought of as a unity), and this in itself is enough to make it apparent that the diaconate does not necessarily have to be univocal and uniform in the sense indicated. Admittedly it is necessary that a single basic essence of the diaconate, deriving from the very nature of order itself and from the concrete situation of the Church (for it is this that demands that the single institution of order shall be subdivided in this way) shall be common to all these variations of type which the diaconate may assume in the concrete, and shall be recognizable as such in them all. But all that we can demand is that it shall continue to be sufficiently intelligible why this particular subdivision of order is called the diaconate, and how it is adequately to be distinguished in terms of theology from those other 'official' functions which are present in the Church as institutions, and which are both distinct from the priestly office and at the same time not to be conceived of as pertaining to the diaconate. In this respect it is inevitable that in the process of drawing the lines of division certain points will remain unclarified. The reason is first that in view of the variations in the way in which the single institution of order in the Church is subdivided it is quite impossible wholly to avoid such points of obscurity; we have simply to accept them and make due allowance for them. Second, it is perfectly possible that the future situation of the Church will make it necessary, and will actually bring it about that new and hitherto unfamiliar ways of subdividing the institution of order will be introduced, and that concerning these it will not always be easy to say *a priori* whether they constitute a variant form of the diaconate or a subdivision of order which cannot be subsumed under this concept of the diaconate.

Now let us turn to certain negative demarcations of the diaconate. In order to be in a position to define these the following preliminary points have to be made: the Church as a whole, and therefore all her members – including, therefore the so-called laity – have been entrusted with a ministry towards man to work for his salvation. This universal ministry has an individual and a social dimension affecting both those entrusted with it and those to whom it is directed. This universal Christian *diakonia*, binding in the same way upon clergy and layfolk alike, is a Christian duty which no one individual can transfer to the rest. In this universal *diakonia* each has a responsibility towards all, and each Christian has a responsibility not only towards his fellow Christians but essentially towards every man as well. But not withstanding this the concrete form in which this universal *diakonia* or ministry is realized in the individual Christian life, and in which each individual discharges his personal responsibility varies according to the concrete circumstances of those involved, both those vested with this ministry and those to whom it is directed.

Now without prejudice to this universal *diakonia* there is a special *diakonia* proper to those who are officially ordained. The reason for this is twofold: first, ordination considered as an official institution too can be understood only as conferring the authorization, the duty, and the equipment to minister to other Christians and individuals. Second, in the community of Christians called the Church, which is of necessity constituted as a society with institutions, there is need for a special office with special functions and the powers entailed in these attached to it, with a particular part to play (we shall not be describing or justifying this in any more precise detail here) within this universal *diakonia*. On the basis of these prior considerations we can now lay down the following negative lines of demarcation with regard to the diaconate in the special and restricted sense as part of the official institution of order in the Church, with special functions of its own. Its specific nature cannot, in any proper sense, be regarded as consisting in the function of leadership as such. For this is proper to the episcopal and priestly office. In some cases, as in the missions or communities deprived of priests, the deacon is entrusted with leadership functions of this kind, and this is perfectly possible chiefly in virtue of the fact that he belongs to the ranks of those who are officially ordained. But all such cases are secondary, and do not imply that this leadership function belongs specifically to his particular office. Nor does the office of deacon imply that the laity are deprived of their mission and duty to exercise the universal diaconate or that these can transfer their mission to the officially ordained deacon. Again the officially ordained deacon is not, properly speaking, a mediator between clergy and layfolk in the Church, for at least in principle there is no need for any such mediation even though it may be conceded that in specific sociological situations in the Church the deacon does perform a useful secondary function of this kind. In principle, however, this function does not constitute the very nature of his office, and the very fact that he himself belongs to the ranks of those who have been officially ordained – in other words to the clergy – is in itself enough to show that this is not the case. Again the true nature of the diaconate cannot be defined in terms of specific cultic powers, even though *de facto* he may exercise powers of this kind, such as baptizing, conferring Christian burial, giving communion, performing the sacramentals etc. at least provided the official Church gives a certain authorization for them such specifically sacral functions can also be assumed by any baptized layman, and even though this fact does not in itself alone in principle exclude the possibility of empowering the individual sacramentally to exercise a whole complex of such sacral functions, still at least today, in the present situation of the Church and the concrete possibilities thereby entailed such functions should be left to laymen, and should be regarded as functions which are not so important in themselves that they need to constitute a specific office in the Church of today. Nor does the office of deacon in the proper sense imply that bishops and priests should be able to transfer the specifically diaconal functions entailed in the institution of order in the Church in general to the deacon in the strict sense in such a way that they themselves would have nothing more to do with such diaconal functions. The institution of order is ultimately one, and any subdivisions introduced into it do not in fact imply that the various ways in which this single office is shared are simply set alongside one another as so many separate compartments. The significance of the episcopal office at least is such that the institution of order in general in the Church must be present in it in its fulness, and in view of this those who hold it cannot transfer the specifically diaconal functions contained in it (which we shall have to define more precisely at a later stage) in such a way that they no longer remain the responsibility of the bishop himself. And the same applies analogously to the priestly office to the extent that this too involves leading a community constituted by a particular locality or class, analogous in structure to the Church presided over by the bishop. The fact that an office is subdivided does not in fact imply that that single official institution is *a priori* split up into totally different functions. Rather it signifies a graded participation which is made necessary *a posteriori* by the concrete situation, because the technical work, material conditions etc. involved are such that in practice no one individual office-holder can perform by himself everything that is absolutely speaking required of his office.

After applying these negative lines of demarcation to the office of deacon we must now attempt to define its nature in positive terms. Once more we have to emphasize that this process of defining the nature of the office of deacon cannot be deduced solely from any one abstract concept of the nature of officially constituted order in the Church. Rather we have to take into account the concrete situation prevailing today in which this official institution has to fulfil its function.[10]

The office of order in the Church has the function of building up the Church herself, forming the community. Now this function of forming the community implies not merely a function of the kind which might be contrasted with the function of mediating personal salvation to the individual as such. On the contrary this function of forming the community also and precisely implies that in human and Christian terms a place is assigned to the individual as such in the community such that in it he finds a position in the ecclesiastical and social life of the Church from which he can live out his own individual human and Christian life so as to achieve his slavation. This function of forming the community, which also and essentially involves certain prior conditions simply at the human level, and which also implies an integration of the individual into the community (something which is itself different from any totalitarian subjugation

[10] So far as the present author is concerned cf. on this requirement the considerations put forward at the scientific and speculative level in *Handbuch der Pastoraltheologie* II/1 (Freiburg, 1966), pp. 181–188, and further 'Practical Theology within the Totality of Theological Disciplines', *Theological Investigations* IX (London and New York, 1972), pp. 101–115.

of the individual on the part of an ecclesiastical society) is confronted today, in the conditions of secular human life, with special difficulties entailed in the contemporary state of society. Hence those officially vested with the task of forming the community in this sense are required to become specialists in their own right, to learn special kinds of knowledge and skill such as cannot be either presupposed as already present or capable of being acquired by every ordained individual.

In earlier times secular society itself was so constituted as to ensure that men were integrated to a greater or lesser degree, but in any case in sufficient measure, into secular society. Right from the first they had in it that role which best fitted them, and sufficient stability and security at the human level. The ecclesiastical community could from the outset presuppose a society at the secular level which was sufficiently integrated to provide due scope for the life of the individual, and did not need to make any special provision for this social integration of the individual into secular society.

Today all this has changed. The individual man lives in a society which is in a state of great disintegration, and therefore in a state of insecurity as to his proper role, and this also implies a lack of the natural human substrate for a Christian life on the individuals' part, and for his incorporation into the Christian community as such. Of course secular society itself has the task of striving ever anew to achieve this integration of society. But precisely in virtue of the institutional factors which it creates for this purpose, it in turn introduces new forms of disintegration. Now what we have to bear in mind in the case of these individuals who are socially disintegrated in this sense is not merely those who, from the economical aspect, are very poor and oppressed, not merely the conflicts between the social classes in the usual sense of the term. There are other such forms of disintegration also. There are the lonely, those who are in various ways cast aside by secular society, deprived of any secure place or any role in society to give them stability and free them from burdens of care. There are also those who while they are still young and immature have to be integrated into society.

This task of integration is primarily a human one, one from which the Church even as such cannot withdraw herself if she is to serve humanity as such. It is a task for the Church even though in this respect she cannot claim any monopoly in discharging this task in human society. Furthermore this task is a specifically ecclesiastical one to the extent that the integration of the individual at the human level into the human community and society is the necessary prior condition for the forming of an ecclesiastical community, while conversely any such process of forming an ecclesiastical community or of providing a permanent place for the individual in the community of the Church always also has repercussions upon the formation of the human community and the humanization of secular society.

This task, then, of integrating the individual both into a humanized secular society and at the same time in particular into the community of the Church is, from these various points of view, a function of the Church. And it is a function of such a kind that it presupposes specialist equipment and human qualities which can neither be possessed nor acquired by every one of the Church's official functionaries. But if this task, which we may surely describe with justice as a diaconal task in a specific sense, is a task for the *official* Church as such, and if today it cannot adequately be discharged by every one of the Church's officials for want of specialist equipment at the material and human level, then it follows that the Church today must institute a special subdivision within the single institution of order[11] which can be called the diaconate in the specific sense and in the sense which we have defined. And it is precisely this that constitutes the diaconate as it must be today, regardless of whether the earlier diaconate did or did not have this specific content. This is not to dispute the fact that this diaconate of the future as understood in this sense does still continue to have a sufficient connection with the earlier diaconate to make it legitimate for us to apply the old name 'diaconate' to it.[12]

The position is, then, that on the one hand one of the tasks of the Church's official ministers is to build up the Christian community by integrating man into the civic and ecclesiastical community when he exists today in a state that is to a large extent disintegrated from a religious and social point of view, while on the other this task cannot be fulfilled unless those charged with it have specialized formation of the most varied kind at their command, such as bishops and priests cannot possess. It is this position, therefore, that makes it necessary to have the diaconate as a special official institution.

We have now explained the starting-point for determining the nature of the future diaconate on the basis of the nature of the institution of order itself and of the contemporary situation of the Church in the concrete. But even though we have done this many questions still remain open with regard to the forms in which it is to be developed in the concrete. It is in

---

[11] On this cf. also the section in the *Pastoralhandbuch* adduced in n. 5.

[12] On this cf. also the author's 'Practical Theology and Social Work in the Church', *Theological Investigations* X (London and New York, 1972), pp. 349–370.

a true sense evident in the light of our basic position that even in respect of the sphere allotted to him from the very nature of the diaconate itself the future deacon cannot be an 'all-round' deacon, but must rather be himself in turn a specialist even within this sphere. The question of which specialized tasks pertaining to this diaconal ministry have to be discharged in a particular branch of the Church or local community by such a specialist holder of the office depends of course on the concrete circumstances of the particular branch of the Church or local community concerned. With regard to these specialist deacons we should not seek to deduce too much *a priori*. For uniformity within the individual groupings within the Church is far from being an aim to be striven for. At this level the particular and special forms of the diaconate which are developed should be arrived at on the basis of the concrete needs and requirements of the Church's life. A deacon may be working in a factory or trade, he may be running a community home, he may be a welfare worker, an assistant in pastoral work, a specialist in marriage counselling, engaged in preventing suicides, or in similar tasks. All these are perfectly possible concrete forms of the diaconate which may be developed, although it is clear that those engaged in them should have a minimum of specifically religious powers and duties, and by actively engaging in the celebration of the Eucharist on Sundays should give expression to the fact that the diaconate, as the spirit of fraternity put into practice, finds its starting-point and its supreme sacramental realization in the sacrament of unity. It seems to me that with regard to these concrete forms of the diaconate that are developed the question of the teacher of religion in primary and secondary schools represents a special problem. Perhaps it is not necessary to conclude without further ado that the function of the 'teacher' who is not a priest in the Church, the function of the 'lay theologian' in the Church, should be subsumed under the diaconate as understood here. The 'teacher' (*didaskalos*) in the Church already figures prominently in the New Testament, and it must be remembered first that he does not necessarily have to be identified with the priestly leader of the community, and second that it cannot simply be taken for granted that the only possible role for such a teacher in the Church of the future will be as a teacher of religious doctrine to immature schoolchildren. These facts in themselves are enough to show that the role of 'teacher' in the Church does not necessarily have to be subsumed under the diaconate as understood here. But at least certain concrete roles which will be developed for the 'teachers' in the Church, i.e. those in which the teaching given to adults is designed to introduce these to the Christian life, and so into the Christian community, can perfectly well be understood as a specialized form of the diaconate. The theological nature of the diaconate has nothing in it that decides the question beforehand of whether a deacon should work as a 'full-time' deacon, i.e. engage himself in this ministry as his chief calling in the secular sense, or whether he should exercise his office on what is, from the point of view of the state, a 'part-time basis'. The theological nature of the diaconate does not predetermine from the outset the question of whether a combination of ecclesiastical office and secular calling of this kind constitutes simply the *de facto* combination of two roles which do not have much to do with one another, or whether, as in the case of the worker priests properly so-called, these two tasks compenetrate one another. The theological essence of the diaconate does not predetermine from the outset whether deacons should be drawn from the ranks of younger men, or from the class of those who have been prematurely relegated to retirement by contemporary society because their physical powers have been somewhat reduced even though they have reached the full maturity of their experience of life. All these possibilities are given, and which of them are to be realized in practice is a question which must be decided in the light of the concrete circumstances involved. The same applies to the question of whether a deacon should work as an individual in isolation, or in a team made up of several deacons, whether he should work directly under the bishop in the fulfilment of his task or should be assigned to one particular parish priest.

In any doctrinal review of the nature of the diaconate one thing further must also be said concerning the sacramental grace which is imparted through this sacrament. A sacramental grace which is ritually communicated by the conferring of a given office in the Church has, in virtue of that fact in itself, a quite peculiar character. The reason that it is imparted by means of a ritual conferment of office is because this office can only be exercised in accordance with its true nature if it is fulfilled in faith, hope, and love. The reason is that while the absence of any personal or 'existential' engagement on the part of the individual (i.e., in the case supposed, an engagement that is sustained by grace) certainly does not simply 'invalidate' the ways in which this office is fulfilled, still it is contrary to the nature of the office itself, and hence something that is indeed conceivable in individual holders of office, but not in the Church as a whole. For in her the dimension of her social and historical reality can never totally and definitively be separated from her endowment with the Spirit. Any conferment of office by the Church and in her, therefore, always also constitutes the offering and the promise of that grace which alone really makes the fulfilment of this office an ecclesiastical fulfilment in the full sense. Any such 'grace of office', therefore, is given precisely in order that the individual holder of the office may fulfil his ministry for the other members of the Church in accordance with its true nature. It 'sanctifies' the holder of the office precisely inasmuch as it equips him not to seek his own sanctification in an 'egoistical' manner, but rather, by directing his gaze away from himself and forgetting himself, to serve his neighbour in the Church.

It is in this that the very essence of every charisma of office, every 'grace of office' consists. It 'sanctifies' the individual on whom it is conferred precisely in virtue of the fact that he forgets himself in the service of his neighbour. Hence it is that on any true understanding of the nature of the Church as a society and as pneumatic at the same time the grace of office is not, properly speaking, something that is supplementary, that fills out the basic equipment that is given when an office is conferred within her, but rather actually constitutes this basic equipment of office in itself. This in itself *ipso facto* implies the further point that this grace of office is not something which takes place solely at that particular point in time when the office is sacramentally conferred and actually constitutes that point, but rather implies the promise of God to support with his grace the whole conduct of office on the part of the ordained individual in his life, a promise which, therefore, is constantly achieving fresh actualization in the life of the deacon. Once we recognize that to be appointed to the diaconal function in the Church is something abiding and ultimately irrevocable, and recognize too that the promise entailed in this of the assistance of the Spirit of the Church for the fulfilment of this task as something that is likewise abiding, we have *ipso facto* also achieved an understanding of that which in tradition and in the teaching of the Council of Trent is called sacramental character, something which is present in every 'degree' of the single sacrament of order in the manner appropriate to each degree. It is really superfluous to embark on any lofty speculations over and above what has already been said concerning this 'character indelebilis' inherent in the sacrament of order. Such speculations would merely give rise to ideas which are inessential or else would state in other terms something which is, in the very nature of the case, entailed in the enduring nature precisely of this specific ministerial task and the abiding nature of the offer of grace inherent in it.

Now if we are to give any adequate account of the sacramental grace of the diaconate, we must now consider this event of grace from yet a further aspect. For this purpose we must undertake a consideration which touches upon the relationship which exists between grace and sacrament in general.

Any short-sightedness in theology, or any excessively naïve piety constantly entails the danger of unconsciously falling into the position of regarding the sacraments exclusively as *the* events of grace alone (even though this is in contradiction to other firmly held theological positions). Such a position, however, is false. He who seeks God in a spirit of faith, love and hope is *ipso facto* justified, a child of God, and a temple of the Spirit even before he has received the baptism of water, though of course even in any such 'subjective' attitude the will to receive baptism is implicitly and unconsciously included. At least in normal cases he who comes to the sacrament of penance as a repentant sinner comes as one who has already been justified, and whose sins have already been forgiven. The prayer of the 'confiteor' before Mass, if it is uttered with a sincere heart, is not merely the desire addressed to God for the forgiveness of some sin, a desire emanating solely from the individual himself. Rather it is an event of grace which God himself brings about in the individual and through his act. The question of why, without prejudice to these obvious points, the sacraments are, nevertheless, meaningful and, under certain circumstances necessary is one which cannot explicitly be discussed here. The reasonableness of and necessity for the sacraments arises ultimately from the nature of man as a physical person, and from the 'incarnatorial' dynamism of grace itself. For as the grace precisely of *Christ* this seeks to project itself beyond the source and centre of human living as endowed with grace, and to achieve a dimension of historical concretion in space and time. For it is in this alone that even grace achieves its full effectiveness and power over all dimensions of human existence.

Let us therefore apply these points which we recognize as evidence to the diaconate. First it is clear that there can be powers in the social dimension of the Church which, in order to exist at all and to be validly applied, presuppose in the society concerned a specific conferment of office achieved in a manner that is juridically defined. Speaking quite in general it is also perfectly conceivable that such official functions in a society can be conferred in various ways. Now it has already been said that the particular functions inherent in the diaconate, however they are to be thought of in more precise terms in their particular details, and whatever possible new forms are to be conceived of for them, are 'in themselves' also within the power of a 'layman' and can be exercised by him even though this fact does not call in question the reasonableness of such a complex of tasks and powers as are involved in the diaconate, and therefore of the diaconate itself as an office in the Church. If we consider this point in conjunction with what has been said above with regard to extra-sacramental and pre-sacramental grace, then we can freely arrive at the following conclusion: that amalgam of functions which is or can be unified and sacramentally conferred in the diaconate already exists independently of any such sacramental conferring of office, and this complex amalgam of functions is exercised in its 'lay' practitioners (provided the necessary conditions are present for grace to become effective) with a grace which is, in its effects, the same grace directed towards the service of neighbour which is manifested and conferred '*ex opere operato*' in a sacramental mode in the sacramental order of the diaconate. We say this for the 'consolation' of those who, in virtue of the functions which they do *de facto* exercise in the Church are striving to attain to the diaconate as a sacrament, but have not yet had it conferred upon them through the imposition of hands. In a Church that is permeated by the Holy Spirit even such a ministry as this cannot be 'devoid of the Spirit'. Conversely, however, it follows from the same radical connection between sacrament (sacramental sign) and grace that the fact that the lay 'deacon' is endowed with the Spirit does not invalidate the reasonableness and relative necessity of the sacramental diaconate. Precisely this extra- and pre-sacramental grace enjoyed by the lay 'deacon' demands, in virtue of its incarnatorial dynamism, to achieve its due sacramental manifestation in the Church in which this grace in itself finds the full realization of its essence. So true is this, indeed, that conversely this 'incarnation' of it becomes the sign that effects the grace itself. This is true just as it is also the case that when diaconal functions are exercised in the Church, and when these are entrusted in a more or less informal way to individuals there is a tendency for them to become recognized and entrusted to those individuals in that more formal manner in which the recognition and the conferring of them can be called a sacrament in the proper sense, appointing the individuals concerned to the office of deacon.

5

OBSERVATIONS ON THE FACTOR OF
THE CHARISMATIC IN THE CHURCH

I

THE Catholic ecclesiology of former times from the period of the
Reformation onwards was concerned almost exclusively with the
institutional factors in the Church. It viewed the Church as a
'*societas perfecta*', unified, organized, and directed by the official hierarchy,
which is in its turn summed up in a supreme and effective manner in the
pope. It is true that in this period also it was recognized that the Church
is holy, and that this holiness is one of her essential characteristics and
notes (characteristics which make a given entity recognizable and distinguishable for what it is), but this holiness was looked for almost exclusively in the sacraments and other objective means of holiness present in the
Church, in other words, once more in the institutional factors. Meanwhile
the interior subjective holiness achieved by justifying grace was regarded
as consisting almost exclusively in grace at the individual level and as
present in the individual for himself. Whenever the holiness of the saints
(either canonized or worthy of canonization) was spoken of, this was, it is
true, valued as a proof of the 'outstanding holiness and inexhaustible fruit-
fulness in all good' of the Church, something in virtue of which the
Church as '*signum levatum in nationes*' manifests herself as instituted by
Christ to 'outsiders' as well.[1] But this objective holiness was not regarded
as an element intrinsic to the life of the Church herself, standing in a quite
specific dialectical relationship to the institutional factor in the Church
such that each influenced the other, instead of this holiness merely being
the product of the institutional activity of the official functionaries in the
Church.

Now in the most recent times, prior to the Second Vatican Council, in
it and after it, a more explicit theology of the charismatic factor in the

[1] DS 3013/33014.

Church has been developed[2]. First a clearer emphasis has been laid upon the fact that the Church is not simply a society at the merely external level, and constituted as such by institutional factors, not merely a means of salvation but also the fruit of salvation in herself. It has come to be emphasized that the opposite of ecclesiological Nestorianism is that the Spirit and grace are constitutive for the Church as an eschatological reality[3]. Now on this showing the gifts of the Spirit, the 'charismata' can be conceived of not merely as present in the Church but actually as constitutive for her and for the life that is proper to her. These charismata belong to the very nature and life of the Church just as much as the institutional factors. It is further emphasized that in a Catholic ecclesiology we find neither in practice nor in the linguistic usage of the New Testa-

[2] Admittedly no comprehensive work on this subject has yet been written. The basic principles are to be found in Y. Congar, 'Le peuple fidèle et la fonction prophétique de l'Eglise', *Irenikon* 24 (1951), pp. 289–312, 440–466; K. Rahner, 'Das Charismatische in der Kirche', *LKT* II (2nd ed. 1958), 1027–1030; *idem*, *Das Dynamische in der Kirche*, Quaestiones Disputatae 5 (Freiburg, 1958), pp. 38–53; Cardinal Suenens, 'Die charismatische Dimension der Kirche', *Konzilsreden*, edited by H. Küng and D. O'Hanlon (Einsiedeln, 1964), pp. 24–28; H. U. von Balthasar, 'Charis und Charisma', *Sponsa Verbi* (Einsiedeln, 1964), pp. 319–331; H. Küng, 'The Charismatic Structure of the Church', *Concilium* 1/4 (1965 (Ecumenism)), pp. 23–33; *idem*, *The Church* (London, 1969); B. v. Leeuwen, 'Die allgemeine Teilnahme am Prophetenamt Christi', *De Ecclesia* I, edited by G. Baraúna (Freiburg, 1966), pp. 393–419, esp. 409 ff.; E. Bettencourt, 'Charisms', *Sacramentum Mundi* I (New York and London, 1968), pp. 283–284; G. Hasenhüttl, 'Die Charismen in Leben der Kirche', *Der Seelsorger* 39 (1969), pp. 167–174; *idem*, *Charisma, Ordnungsprinzip der Kirche* (Freiburg, 1969).

[3] On this view of the Church cf. K. Rahner, *The Church and the Sacraments*, Quaestiones Disputatae 9 (Freiburg, 1963); *idem* 'Ekklesiologische Grundlegung', *Handbuch der Pastoraltheologie* I (Freiburg, 1964), pp. 117 ff.; *idem*, 'The Church and the Parousia of Christ', *Theological Investigations* VI (London and Baltimore, 1969), pp. 295–312.

In this connection ecclesiology has come, from the nineteenth century onwards, increasingly to be conceived of in terms of christology. This appears in the work of theologians such as J. A. Möhler, J. Perrone, F. Pilgrim, J. Görres, C. Schrader, M. J. Scheeben, H. Newman, K. Arnold, O. Semmelroth, Y. Congar, F. Malmberg and many others right down to the documents of the Second Vatican Council. Cf. most recently H. Mühlen, 'Das Verhältnis zwischen Inkarnation und Kirche in den Aussagen des Vatikanum II', *Theologie und Glauben* 55 (1965), pp. 171–190; J. Alfaro, 'Das Geheimnis Christi im Geheimnis der Kirche nach dem Zweiten Vatikanischen Konzil', *Volk Gottes* (Festschrift für J. Höfer) edited by R. Bäumer and H. Dolch (Freiburg, 1967), pp. 518–535; in the light of this tradition it is of course astonishing that a merely juridical conception could have continued to be maintained so long in the official ecclesiology.

ment any opposition or hostility between the official institutions of the Church on the one hand, and the charismatic elements on the other.[4] The Church is not only the 'holy Church' the 'communio sanctorum' in the objective sense, a community of *the* holy one, the dispenser of the goods of salvation, in virtue of her truth, her foundation by Christ, her sacraments and the salvation present in her. As an eschatological community, sustained in being by the victory of God's grace, she is also holy as a totality in virtue of the actual faith that exists and that is brought about by this victory of grace, and in virtue of the love of God and neighbour practised by her members. As such she manifests herself as she who demands faith and provides the basis for it, and she must bear witness to her own nature in this sense.[5] Now this is possible only through the working of charismata, the more so since in fact the sacraments can become effective for sanctification only through the extra-sacramental grace of God predisposing the subject for them.[6] Moreover under certain circumstances even one who has been sacramentally justified stands in need of a special and exceptional measure of extra-sacramental grace..[7]

There is no need at this stage to enter into a distinction which, while it may be possible, is not very decisive, between actual and effective grace for supernatural Christian activity on the one hand, and charismatic gifts of grace in the narrower sense on the other. Of course it is possible to draw a distinction of this kind if we take the charismata to signify that which, empirically speaking, is in some sense out of the ordinary, but bestowed upon an individual by God to benefit others. It must be remembered, however, that each particular instance of sanctifying grace enjoyed by a given individual is always at the same time designed to benefit the Body of Christ as a whole. In other words there is no such thing as a mere

---

[4] A more detailed treatment of the relationship between these two basic elements in the Church as she really exists is to be found in J. Brosch, 'Amt und Charisma', *LTK* I (2nd ed., 1957), 455–457; K. Rahner, 'Amt und freies Charisma', *Handbuch der Pastoraltheologie* I (Freiburg, 1964), pp. 154–160; *idem*, 'Grenzen der Amtskirche', *Schriften zur Theologie* VI (Einsiedeln, 2nd ed., 1968), pp. 399–520; *idem*, 'Dialogue in the Church', *Theological Investigations* X (London and New York, 1972), pp. 103–123; *idem*, 'The Teaching Office of the Church in the Present-Day Crisis of Authority', in this volume, pp. 3–30; *idem*, *Vom Sinn des kirchlichen Amtes* (Freiburg, 1966); cf. in addition O. Semmelroth, 'Die Kirche als Hierarchie und Pneuma', *Die Zelle in Kirche und Welt* edited by A. Spitalen (Graz, 1960), pp. 129–150; *idem*, 'Institution und Charisma', *Geist und Leben* 36 (1963), pp. 443–454; *idem*, *Das geistliche Amt* (Frankfurt, 2nd ed., 1965); *idem*, 'Office and Charism', *Sacramentum Mundi* 2 (New York and London, 1968), pp. 171–173.

[5] DS 3013.   [6] DS 1526; 1559.   [7] DS 241.

individual sanctifying grace benefiting one particular member in isolation from the rest. It must further be remembered that any power, whether it be an official authority that is conferred or an endowment with gifts of a non-institutional kind, can be applied by the holder in a way that is morally right only when the exercise of such endowments proceeding from sanctifying grace also sanctifies their holder (this is in fact clear in the case of sacramental powers and their use). A final point which must not be overlooked is that the borderlines between that which is normal and that which is extraordinary in Christian living are wholly fluid.[8] Now when all these points are considered the distinction between actual or effective grace on the one hand, and charismata on the other is a very secondary one, which to a large extent we can confidently leave unexplored for our present purposes. What we have to bear in mind above all, therefore, is the ecclesiastical and social function of every effective actual grace, and we must not overlook the fact that as effective (distinguishing this from sufficient grace) this grace falls under the sovereign disposition of God, which can neither be coerced nor taken for granted as always present. These are factors, then, which impart a 'charismatic character' to effective grace, and in the light of these considerations we can conclude that the charismatic element belongs no less necessarily and abidingly to the nature of the Church than her official institutions and the sacraments. The charismatic element was not merely bestowed in order to facilitate the initial stages of the Church's life, though in the alarm which followed upon the Montanist crisis this view was often maintained, since then any spontaneous manifestations of the charismatic were all too easily suspected of being 'enthusiasm', and there was an exaggerated tendency to recognize the charismatic as manifested in certain specific historic forms which in fact are out of date. Against this view it is in fact the case that the very nature of the charismatic as an essential trait inherent in the Church demands precisely that in contrast to the official institutions and the continuity apparent in these the charismatic manifests itself in ever fresh and unexpected forms, and hence too needs to be discovered ever anew.

The truth that the charismatic element belongs to the very nature of the Church is also an explicit doctrine of the Church herself. It was already put forward as such in the encyclical 'Mystici Corporis' of Pius XII.[9] The Second Vatican Council too speaks relatively at lengths of the charismata

---

[8] In 'Lumen Gentium' No. 12 the Council too takes into account the factor of gifts of grace which are disseminated universally.

[9] DS 3807.

of the laity.[10] They are imparted by the Holy Spirit in the Church according to his good pleasure.[11] They contribute to the renewal and further development of the Church, and they can be extraordinary, exceptional, or equally well be merely simple and broadly disseminated. In principle it pertains to the Church's official functionaries to judge of them, and it is their task to examine these charismata. At the same time, however, they must not suppress them when they are genuine. A similar emphasis on the existence of charismatic, as distinct from merely hierarchical, gifts, in the Church is to be found in the Decree on the Missions.[12] The terms 'charisma' and 'charismatic' occur in fourteen passages in the documents of the Second Vatican Council. Admittedly it must also be stated that apart from the insistence on the point that the officials of the Church have on the one hand to respect the charismata, and on the other hand to examine their genuineness, not very much is said in the Second Vatican Council with regard to the relationship between the charismatic and the institutional elements and their mutual interplay. Certainly in contrast to the ecclesiology of post-Reformation times the charismatic element in the Church is explicitly referred to. But, as 'Lumen Gentium' shows, the Church of officialdom still continues constantly to occupy the centre of the ecclesiological stage despite the fact that the second chapter, concerning the people of God has been placed before the third, concerning the Church's official functionaries. Perhaps, even at the risk of seeming over-subtle, we might be permitted to characterize the position of the ecclesiology here in the following terms: In the ecclesiology of former times the official institutions were concentrated upon almost to the exclusion of all else, and were at most regarded as also being the channels through which the charismata were mediated. Today, on the other hand, the charismatic factor is felt in some sense to supply the institutional one with the motive force necessary for it. The question still remains whether in any future ecclesiology we shall not have to regard the official institutions as the necessary regulators of the charismatic element, so that it will be this that constitutes the true pith and essence of the Church. When we consider that the distinctive characteristic of the Church as compared with the Old Testament synagogue, consists precisely in the fact that she constitutes the presence of grace as irreversibly victorious, and that the difference between these two is not to be found in their institutional aspects as such, then it should in

[10] Cf. the decree on the Apostolate of the Laity, 'Apostolicam Actuositatem' Nos. 3 and 30, and on the Ministry and Life of Priests in 'Presbyterorum Ordinis', No. 9.
[11] Cf. the Dogmatic Constitution on the Church, 'Lumen Gentium', Nos. 4, 7, 12.
[12] Cf. the Decree on the Church's Missionary Activity, 'Ad Gentes', Nos 4 and 23.

reality be perfectly possible to regard the Church primarily as the historical concretization of the charismatic as brought about by the Spirit of Christ, and to regard the specifically institutional element in her simply as one of the regulating factors (albeit a necessary one) for this charismatic element. Now precisely from this consideration the converse actually follows, namely that the official element in the Church has a charismatic character. For it is evident that ultimately speaking the gifts of the Spirit can only be regulated by a gift of the Spirit. In other words any attempt to regard the official and the charismatic elements as simply opposed to one another would be totally at variance with the real situation. It is perfectly reasonable to suppose that some of the charismata as such are destined for the official functionaries of the Church such that without them these functionaries could not rightly perform their duties. This would imply a promise which in itself and from God's point of view cannot fail that the necessary charismata will be bestowed for the performance of these offices in virtue of the eschatologically definitive possession of the Spirit on the part of the Church as socially constituted, and in virtue of this eschatological character of the Church this promise would actually constantly be being made good in the Church as a whole, even though we cannot say with any certainty that it is actually being made good in any given individual case, and even though we cannot adopt the Donatist view that the individual act of the official Church is *ipso facto* invalid whenever it is not supported in a visible manner by the charismata.

In this connection, and in order to understand what has just been said, reference must be made to the so-called sacramental grace in the sacraments constitutive of particular callings within the Church, and it must be emphasized that such 'graces of calling' (order and matrimony) are capable, under certain circumstances, of achieving heroic dimensions, and therefore as a moral miracle of being charismatic in a narrower sense as well. This means that the transition between the graces of calling (as actual and effective) on the one hand, and the charismata of office in the narrower sense and extending beyond the scope of official authority as such on the other, is extremely fluid. It is certain that indefectibility and life promised to the Church, and in virtue of this to her officials also, is *de facto* made good in the concrete in part through the charismata bestowed again and again precisely upon her officials. But over and above these official charismata there must also be non-institutional charismata. For the Church as holy and as bearing witness in the world to the eschatological victory of God's grace through the manifestation of her own true nature is in fact not a Church which is constituted solely by her official functionaries. Rather she is the holy people of God. The charismata which can be present in all Christians, and which therefore actually are present at least in germ in every justified individual who, as a member of the Body of Christ has a quite specific function to perform in that Body, are different from the Christian virtues and the actual and effective graces necessary for the exercise of these only in that in these virtues they make manifest that which is *ipso facto* present (albeit with varying degrees of effectiveness) in order for any Christian virtue to be practised in the Church, namely the outward sign of her nature as a society, of revelation, of the creed, of witness and of mission on the Church's behalf. Of course these charismata necessarily have a significance for the world as well, corresponding to the whole meaning of the Church as 'the sacrament of the world'. It is through them that the Church fulfills her mission towards the world in serving it. It follows from the connection between virtue, effective grace and charism as described above that in addition to the major bestowals of charisms and 'enthusiastic' movements which have arisen and must arise again and again in the Church, the acts of heroic faithfulness in coping with everyday life, in standing firm in situations which are unfavourable to religious life and similar virtues can perfectly well be charismatic also, and that too in a relatively strict sense in that by their endurance and indefatigable force in the totality of an individual life or the life of the Church these virtues clearly make manifest the power of the Spirit of God.

If charismata belong to the very nature of the Church it follows that the official functionaries of the Church must not merely tolerate them but actually examine them and cultivate them too (1 Thess. 5:19 f.), a point which is emphasized by the Second Vatican Council. The official functionaries must recognize, and in practice act upon, the truth that the impulses of the Spirit on the Church's behalf do not always or necessarily have to manifest themselves in and through the official institutions. On the contrary some of them can also proceed from the holy people to the extent that in that people the Spirit makes effective his gifts of grace. The Church's officials must not suppose that any movement from below *ipso facto* proves that it is not sustained by the Spirit and not charismatic merely on the grounds that the officials themselves succeed in suppressing such a movement. The officials of the Church can 'quench the Spirit' just as much as individuals when they do this through their own fault. Certainly it is a truth entailed in faith in the Church and in the promise of God to her that there is no question of any radical or definitive opposition to the workings of the Spirit taken as a whole in the Church's institutions taken as a whole. But this does not exclude the possibility that in many cases, even important ones, the officials may erroneously or culpably suppress charismatic movements of the Spirit or condemn them in an attitude of mistrust. Nor should we euphemistically term such acts on the part of the Church's officials as simply a necessary and prudent process of testing the charismata. The officials must have the courage to allow fresh and hitherto unknown forms of the charismatic factor in the Church to appear[13]. The officials must also require, make legitimate, and give a place in the life of the Church as a whole to the further processes by which these charismatic factors are given that institutional embodiment in some form to which they have a right, and which they must achieve at a very early stage in order to be effective and to endure.

II

In the previous section we have stated, in somewhat brief summary, the basic essentials with regard to the charismatic factor in the Church, though admittedly without entering into the biblical theology[14] or the history of the charismatic element in the Church.[15] We have now to approach the question of this charismatic element from yet a different aspect, and one which has rather to do with the sociology of the Church. The following proposition is put forward for further discussion: The charismatic element in the Church designates that point in the Church at which God as Lord of the Church presides over the Church as an open system.

In order to make this statement intelligible we must first explain what we mean when we call the Church an open system. There is a certain approach adopted both by the exponents of apologetics within the Church and also by those who oppose them, in which both either explicitly or implicitly take as their starting-point the axiom that the Church is a closed system. What we mean by a closed system here is that this system, i.e. a

---

[13] On this requirement, which has also been taken up by the Council, cf. K Rahner, 'Do not stifle the Spirit!', *Theological Investigations* VIIA (London and Baltimore, 1972), pp. 72–87.

[14] For a more detailed treatment see E. Käsemann, 'Geist und Gesitesgaben im NT', *RGG* II (3rd ed., 1958), 1272–1279, and H. Schürmann, 'Die geistlichen Gnadengaben', *De Ecclesia* I, edited by G. Baraúna (Freiburg, 1966), pp. 494–519.

[15] Admittedly to a large extent this history also proceeds outside the Church. On this cf. the comprehensive studies by R. A. Knox, H. G. Steck, H. Grundmann and E. Benz.

complex of realities of various kinds which, despite their variations, are related to one another and contribute towards a common task, is defined and directed from a point within the system itself. At least so far as the life of the Church as a society in the true sense is concerned (as distinct from any purely private sphere in the life of the individual or from the merely secular dimension), friends and foes alike of the Church conceive of this system more or less explicitly in such a way that all initiatives, in so far as the only real validity they have is within the Church as such, are thought of as proceeding wholly from her official functionaries and among these ultimately from the pope as the supreme pastor of the Church. The Church is conceived of as an absolute monarchy or totalitarian system in which in principle the only measures having any force in the dimension of the social are those decreed, ordained, or at least approved in a positive manner by him who stands at the supreme point within this system. Of course in such a conception it is held that in order that the Church may abide, this supreme figure endowed with totalitarian dominion is preserved from making any erroneous decision in any essential or decisive matters by the assistance of the Holy Spirit, and hence that as constituting a society in the formal sense this totalitarian and closed system, which is adequately directed from a point immanent within the system itself, is nevertheless, in virtue of this assistance of the Spirit, precisely not a totalitarian system of the kind which must radically be rejected by reason of its total subjection to one who is omnipotent and at the same time liable to error. But however much this idea of a closed system of this kind may be furthered by a certain kind of papalism, by reason of its authoritarian outlook, the Church is not a closed, but rather an open system, i.e. a system such that the definitive condition in which it actually stands and should stand neither can nor should be defined in any adequate sense in terms of any one point immanent within the system itself. On the contrary its definitive state can only be defined in terms of a point outside the system, i.e. in terms of the dominion of God, so that to do justice to the state in which the system exists at any given stage we must say that its operations are charismatic rather than institutional in character.[16]

This last statement calls for a little further explanation. Of course within the dimension of the Church's official institutions and juridical system there is a supreme position within her which, so far as this dimension in itself is concerned, is not in its turn determined by any further point of

---

[16] In this connection cf. also the various works which the author has written on the subject of 'Freedom in the Church', as well as the study entitled 'The Question of the Future' in this volume, pp. 131–201.

reference existing in the same dimension. To that extent there is a supreme universal authority in the Church which is not itself in turn dependent upon any other legal authority as such. In the Catholic Church the pope and the united episcopate are the bearers of this supreme authority as constituting a special kind of unity which is quite incapable of being adequately defined in terms of any further formal or juridical factors. In other words taken together they constitute a supreme authority which is both monarchic and collegiate (however contradictory this way of putting the matter may sound).[17]

At this point we may set aside this question of how, on a Catholic view, the supreme holders of the highest universal juridical authority in the Church are to be conceived of in more precise terms, because this point does not affect the question of whether the Church is a closed or an open system. But it must be urgently insisted upon that this whole juridical dimension, taken strictly as such, is only one of the elements in the social reality of the Church herself, and that too not one such that it can dominate over the total reality and the total functioning of the other elements even at the merely social level. In this statement it is of course presupposed that there are elements in the Church, at least in the social dimension, which must not be thought of simply as subordinate elements, subdivisions etc., of the dimension of the juridical, in other words that the social dimension and the organization of a society by law are not identical at least so far as the Church is concerned.

In the deliberations leading up to the doctrine of the papacy embodied in 'Lumen Gentium' at the Second Vatican Council a statement proposed by the Pope himself was rejected and deleted with a certain force, the statement namely that the Pope is only answerable (devinctus) to the one Lord (Jesus Christ).[18] The very fact that a statement of this kind could be proposed at all illustrates the tendency touched upon above to understand the Church as a closed and totalitarian system. Of course this statement can be taken as an expression of the fact that the highest, and in fact

[17] Treated of in greater detail in my studies, *Episkopat und Primat*, Quaestiones Dispuatae 11 (Freiburg, 1961), pp. 13–36; 'On the Theology of the Council', *Theological Investigations* V (London and Baltimore, 1966), pp. 244–267; 'The Episcopal Office', *ibid.* VI (London and Baltimore, 1969), pp. 313–360; 'On the Relationship between the Pope and the College of Bishops, *ibid.* X (London and New York, 1972), pp. 50–70.

[18] On this text proposed by the Pope, but referred back by the Theological Commission cf. my commentary on chapter 22 of 'Lumen Gentium', *LTK* Suppl. I (1966), 227/228, and in addition to this the observation of J. Ratzinger on the 'Nota explicativa praevia', *ibid.* 355/356.

personal supremacy within the officials of the Church is not in its turn subject to any other authority at the juridical level within the Church, that the supreme position (*suprema sedes*) is not judged by anyone else, as it is stated in the CIC, and clearly in this sense the statement which was rejected would be correct. But it almost inevitably conjures up the misunderstanding that in all that concerns his own functions the Pope acts merely on his own volition, merely as autonomous, and not as accepting the ideas of others; that his position is not merely an essential element of an indispensable kind in a greater whole, incorporating the contribution proper to himself into this greater whole without being able to recognize or define in any adequate sense what develops from this contribution of his within this whole, and what the whole itself becomes through this contribution of his. The statement that was rejected conjures up the mistaken impression that at the social level of the Church the Pope is the sole sovereign and active determining factor, so that everything that takes place in the Church, even though it is carried out by many subordinates, is properly speaking his work. It suggests that Peter is the Church, and that the Church is adequately contained, reformed, and determined in its activities in Peter.[19] It is to rule out this position that we say that the system of the Church is open, and in this sense charismatic. What we *de facto* observe in the Church throughout her entire history is a genuine pluralism within which the papacy has a position of its own without thereby being able to determine or to initiate the whole of that activity. And this fact is not one which must be misinterpreted in terms of a mistaken ideology in favour of a totalitarian papalism by saying, for instance, that such realities are, after all, positively integrated into an absolute system of this kind by being approved of and explicitly or tacitly consented to. The first Councils, almost the whole history of dogma, the origins of the religious orders, the greater part of the history of spirituality, the life of the Churches of the Far East including their juridical systems, the history of theology, and much more besides, have developed, as a matter of history, without any influence – at any rate any notable influence – on the part of the Pope. This is, as has been said, a fact which must not be interpreted away. In dogmatic ecclesiology it is explicitly taught that even the office of the bishops, despite their necessary union with the apostolic see, is *juris divini*. In other words the bishops rule their flocks not in the name of the Pope but in the name of Christ, and hence are not mere officials of the Pope. And in this doctrine, even at the juridical level

19 S. H. Meyer, *Das Wort Pius XI: 'Die Tradition bin ich'*, Theologische Existenz heute 122 (Munich, 1965).

of the Church, a certain inalienable pluralism is recognized, so that even at this juridical level the authority accorded to the Pope is not a totalitarian one.[20]

Now at the juridical level it is not merely the relationship between Pope and bishops briefly delineated above and culminating in the doctrine of the united episcopate as the body vested with supreme powers in the Church that could be further developed and applied in the concrete. There are other phenomena too in this sphere precisely of law which demonstrate the openness of the system. For instance there is a doctrine in canon law, and that not merely the canon law of the Middle Ages, to the effect that any new law needs to be accepted by the people of the Church. And this phenomenon actually exists in practice too down to the present day, albeit only in a few striking instances.[21]

All these observations might equally well be extended − albeit prudently − to the sphere of the discovery of truth within the Church. Here too, without prejudice to its real authority, the official teaching institutions constitute one particular element in an open system, and do not constitute that point from which, taking it simply as a point within the Church herself, the Church's awareness of her own faith can alone or adequately be defined. The official teaching institutions are not merely bound by scripture and tradition as two factors to which they are subordinate. It is also true that they can only carry out their own work in preserving, and especially in developing, the deposit of faith with the help of theology and of religious awareness in general, neither of which are simply dependent upon those official institutions.[22] So far as theology is concerned it is admittedly the case that the official teaching institutions are rightly empowered to censure or reject opinions in matters of theological doctrine, but they cannot simply dictate the direction in which theology proceeds in positive terms, if only because they cannot direct anyone *in concreto* to work actively at theology. A further point that is demonstrated again and again is that the history of the ideas that are applied in the official pro-

[20] On this cf. also n. 17 and the commentary on the Constitution on the Church referred to in n. 18.

[21] An example of this from the disciplinary sphere, and belonging to recent times would be the 'Constitutio Apostolica' of John XXIII, 'Veterum Sapientia'. The, prescription contained in it to use Latin as the language for lectures in the Catholic faculties has not been carried out, and hence manifestly no longer has any validity. See *AAS* 54 (1962), 129–135, esp. 133 f., and also the definitive interpretations *ibid.* 339–368.

[22] On this cf. also my study 'The Teaching Office of the Church in the Present-Day Crisis of Authority', in this volume, pp. 3–30.

nouncements of the Church's teaching authorities are quite incapable of being directed in any complete or adequate sense, although of course the teaching of the official Church too has some influence on the history of such concepts. Thus a position can arise in which the official teaching authority itself is compelled by a developing history of ideas of this kind, independent of the teaching office, to express the content of the faith in fresh concepts which run counter to its earlier opinions in order to avoid the danger of doctrines previously expressed in terms which have become petrified no longer being understood, or being rejected as impossible to apply.[23] In the dimension of her awareness of truth too the Church is an open system within which even a Pope cannot know beforehand what course the further history of faith and dogma will follow.

All the elements which either condition or constitute the concrete life of the Church in all her dimensions, revelation, the history of the world, the history of ideas, science, political influences that are brought to bear etc., have a mutual interplay, mutually modify one another, and all this goes to make up a history which even in terms of this present world tends towards a future that is unknown and which cannot in any adequate sense be prognosticated. Even the Pope is not merely the pilot who guides the history of the Church, but he who is himself guided as well in a history the true pilot of which does not himself belong to this history. It could be said that this is something which is not peculiar to the Church, but rather constitutes a characteristic present in absolutely all forms of human history which everywhere and in all cases is open and can never consciously or totally be guided by any futurology towards a preconceived future. It may be that the openness of any social system, constituted as it is by the openness and unpredictability of the future, and present in it perhaps against its own will, is, at least in a certain sense, a mere remnant of obscurity, untouched by man's own will to plan the future rationally, and something which he is precisely forced to put up with in shaping the world and manipulating the course of human life. But even if this is true, in the Church this openness is not a mere remnant to be put up with in a system which has failed to achieve a totalitarian constitution governed from one single point, and thereby to achieve complete control of itself. This openness, rather, is precisely that which positively asserts itself as an essential element in the system. The Church must positively will to remain open because only in this way can she be true to her own nature as the exodus, the people on pilgrimage towards the inconceivable mystery of God, as

---

[23] See K. Rahner, 'Demythologization and the Sermon', *Concilium* 3/4 (Pastoral), (1968), pp. 12–20.

she who is endowed with that radical promise and hope which cannot be defined in 'this worldly' terms otherwise than as the will to the absolute future which precisely in this form is mediated through the willing acceptance of the openness to an unknown future within the present world.[24]

It is from the nature of the Church in this sense, as constituting an open system in a radical and abiding sense, that the charismatic element in the Church derives its ultimate and truest essence. This charismatic element is not merely, not even primarily, something like one particular individual factor introduced into the Church by God from without as something belonging to a particular category, and almost as an element of disturbance. On the contrary, when we use the term charismatic we are using a key word to stand for that ultimate incalculability which belongs to all the other elements in the Church in their mutual interplay. This means that the charismatic is, if we may so express it, transcendental in character, not one element in the system of the Church but a special characteristic of the system as a whole. At the same time, however, that in the charismatic element in the Church which is concrete and belongs to a particular category could perhaps, without doing violence to the nature of this charismatic element, be conceived of as constituted by the openness of history within this present world considered as creative freedom. This element of the free in history, of that in secular history which cannot adequately be controlled from any point within the world, and which is in fact also an element and a condition of the history of the Church, would on this showing become that which is charismatic in the true sense in the Church in virtue of the fact that precisely this openness of the future in the present world becomes, through the grace of the Spirit, a medium for the Church's own members to reach out to the absolute future.[25]

III

A third consideration should now be introduced: the question of the interplay between official institution and free charisma as it exists in the concrete. In accordance with what has been said in the first section let us leave

[24] On this see the study already referred to entitled 'The Question of the Future' in this volume pp. 131–201.
[25] Cf. K. Rahner, 'Marxist Utopia and the Christian Future of Man', *Theological Investigations* VI (London and Baltimore, 1969), pp. 59–68; *idem*, 'A Fragmentary Aspect of a Theological Evaluation of the Concept of the Future', *Theological Investigations* X (London and New York, 1972), pp. 235–241.

on one side the interplay between the teaching office of the Church and the charismatic development of faith or theology. In other words let us concentrate upon the connections between the Church's official institutions and the charismatic element in her at the level of the Christian life and the Church's life in the concrete, and recognize at this level that in this interplay within an open system of the Church the very nature of the system is such that it is quite impossible to avoid cases of conflict. In the light of this we can then formulate our third question quite simply as an enquiry into the nature of ecclesiastical obedience. The question with which we are here concerned has also arisen again and again in the course of the Church's history, and particularly in those cases in which charismatic prophets, filled with a consciousness of their own mission, have come into conflict with the official Church and her leaders.[26]

When we speak of obedience in connection with the charismatic element it is evident that we are presupposing that obedience to the Church on the part of a Christian, a priest, or a member of a religious order is indeed one virtue, but not the only one, in which all else is subsumed, and further that within the scope of a Christian life, even though his obedience plays its part in determining its course, autonomous personal initiatives, conscious judgements, and a personal and inalienable responsibility for his own actions must be present; in other words that in an open system obedience, no less than official juridical authority, makes it necessary for there to be mutual influence and interdependence between those vested with authority and those who are 'subordinate' to them. Within the Church, therefore, obedience is to be conceived of otherwise than would be the case if it consisted in the legitimate response of a 'subordinate' to an authority conceived of in totalitarian and authoritarian terms. In a closed system such authority decides everything and is itself influenced by no-one. The obedience we have to consider, then, is such as is to be found in an open system in which each party influences the other; in other words an obedience which allows for personal initiative, and in which we have absolutely to allow for the possibility, even in the Church, that in certain circumstances the individual may feel called upon by the dictates of his own conscience to refuse to carry out some directive. Now on this view of obedience, and on the basis of the concept of the open system, it is clear that in all these cases of conflict there can be no formal principles on the basis of which, and purely at the level of theoretical consideration, it is

[26] Cf. A. Müller, *Das Problem von Befehl und Gehorsam im Leben der Kirche* (Einsiedeln, 1964).

possible to arrive at a single univocal solution applicable to all such cases.[27]

The very process of striking the right balance in the concrete between personal initiative and obedient fulfilment of the directives from above can no longer be clearly and unequivocally arrived at on the basis of general principles. The same applies to innumerable further questions in which charismatic movements and tendencies on the one hand, and the official institutions on the other, may come into conflict. The national peculiarities of a particular local Church, and the way in which it is incorporated into the single universal Church, centralism and decentralization, freedom in theological research and certainty in matters of doctrine, devotion to the sacraments and personal devotion in the life of the individual in the concrete, interior attitudes and cult on the one hand, and Christian responsibility towards a secular world on the other, withdrawal from the world and assent to the world etc. – all these contrasting attitudes are such that each of the separate tensions involved may be maintained, preserved or evoked either by the official institutions or by the charismatic element, and hence conflicts can arise with regard to the way in which these tensions are to be smoothed out and reconciled in the concrete. For the reconciliation that is arrived at in the concrete is not in any sense itself a firm and unchangeable factor laid down once and for all. Rather it is something that must constantly be rediscovered afresh as a matter of concrete decision, and in this process it cannot be arrived at in the concrete solely on the basis of abstract principles. It might be suggested that we should content ourselves with a statement that in cases of conflict between the official institutions and the charismatic elements it is the official institutions that have the last word (although not the penultimate one), so that our obedience is due to them. The validity of this can indeed be admitted as a certain practical rule of thumb. But the problem is not solved thereby. For the only 'last word' in the true sense is concerned with that which has already taken place or is brought into being by this word. So far as the future is concerned there is no 'last word' in the proper sense. For even one who actually obeys a directive can still always take into account the fact that at a later stage such a directive will be withdrawn, that the situation will change radically and will thus render the controversial directive superfluous, that as generation suceeds to generation in the Church, as theology progresses etc. many

---

[27] On the whole range of problems entailed cf. K. Rahner, 'Marginalien über den Gehorsam', *Sendung und Gnade* (Innsbruck, 4th ed., 1966), pp. 487–509; *idem*, 'Christus als Beispiel des priesterlichen Gehorsams', *Knechte Christi* (Freiburg, 1967), pp. 142–145.

directives are rendered out of date, and thus a whole new scope for the charismata is created in the Church.

It must be remembered that obedience itself in its turn had its due place in the open system of the Church, and that the obedient man cannot possibly be obedient and nothing more, but must rather work out ever afresh, and on his own responsibility, a synthesis between the responsible taking of personal initiatives on the one hand and obedience on the other, even having to exercise his own critical judgement on the law and the directives of the Church. In other words it must be remembered that in the practice of obedience there is no such thing as any 'once and for all' universal and formal law laying down precisely what *form* this exercise of obedience must assume in the individual case. Now in view of all this one of the factors entering into obedience in relation even to the institutional element in the Church is actually a charismatic element, a movement of the Spirit which cannot be foreseen or controlled either by the representative of the institutional or by those who respond to their directives.

To put the matter quite simply: obedience in itself and as such must call upon the free initiative of the individual seeking to obey in the Church, and upon the decisions he takes of his own personal responsibility. And on these grounds alone, while the institutional factor in the Church is a legitimate entity, it nevertheless remains encompassed by the charismatic movement of the Spirit in the Church, the Spirit who again and again ushers the Church as an open system into a future which he himself, and no-one else, has arranged, and in a manner which can never adequately be planned for beforehand by any man or any institution. The charismatic element does exist in the Church, and it does not merely stand in a dialectical relationship to the institutional factor as its opposite pole, existing on the same plane. Rather it is the first and the most ultimate among the formal characteristics inherent in the very nature of the Church as such.

6

SCHISM IN THE CATHOLIC CHURCH?

EVERYWHERE in the post-conciliar Church we are afraid of new schisms, and believe that we can recognize signs that the danger of schismatic division is no mere nightmare on the part of reactionary Catholics, but a reality which has to be taken seriously into account. A short time ago the Pope[1] himself spoke of such dangers of new schisms arising in the Church. Everywhere groups of priests are formed who feel themselves to be in some sense opposed to the bishops as the leaders of the Church. Such groups may sometimes, perhaps, give the impression of being pressure groups because in certain circumstances they actually seek to make the hierarchy agree to their demands by means of threats. Here and there, for instance in Holland, Eucharistic confraternities have been set up which, on any normal Catholic understanding of what the Church is, seem to be schismatic in character so far as the Catholic Church is concerned. In Amsterdam Catholic priests have threatened the lawfully constituted bishop that they will set up a non-episcopal Catholic community unless he allows married priests to remain fully in their official positions. Even in the pre-conciliar age we were forced to face the question of whether something similar to a schismatic separation from Rome had arisen in China under the pressure of the communist régime. As the ecumenical movement has become stronger the lines of demarcation between the individual Churches have seemed less clear and less significant. Such a trend can actually lead to individual groups of Catholics forming premature amalgamations at the ecclesiastical level with other Christian groups to the point at which in reality, albeit not of set purpose, something like a schismatic separation from the Catholic Church is brought about. This means that the theme, 'Schism in the Catholic Church?' is not lacking in a certain interest and immediate relevance. We have no intention here of describing or even analysing any further the facts and symptoms indicated

[1] In his address in the Lateran Basilica on the 3rd April 1969. It is interesting that shortly before in 'La Croix' Cardinal Suenens had declared that he did not believe that there was any danger of schism in the Church today.

above which are indicative of a danger of schism in the Church. Instead we shall be putting forward certain basic theological considerations bearing upon this theme of 'Schism in the Church of Today'.

Heresy and Schism

First the difficulty of drawing a theological distinction between heresy and schism must be pointed out. The difference between heresy and schism has been recognized from ancient times. Moreover in the history of the early Church certain particular cases can be found in which this distinction seems, at least at first sight, to be actually illustrated in the concrete. At least in those cases in which the point of dispute was merely the legality of a given individual holding a leading office in the Church, whether subordinate or supreme and nothing more than this, we seem to encounter an instance in which schism is present without any heretical split having taken place. Again the present-day *Codex Juris Canonici* (c. 1325 § 2) draws the relevant distinction between heresy and schism, and seems to presuppose (without providing any clear definition on this point) that schism does not necessarily imply heresy and vice versa. And indeed at first sight this seems readily comprehensible. Schism arises in those cases in which someone explicitly and directly, or by implication through his actions, refuses obedience to the Pope as the supreme leader of the universal Church and the representative of unity in her, and (or) unequivocally separates himself from the Church as a living community. This can be the act of an individual or a group, and in fact it makes no difference whether the individuals who do separate themselves from the community of the Church do or do not attach themselves to some other Church or churchlike group. Now such a separation does not seem necessarily to imply the denial of any Christian doctrine explicitly taught as such by the Catholic Church.

In reality, however, the distinction between heresy and schism is not so simple. It has long been noticed that ever since the primacy of the Pope has come to be numbered among the explicitly defined doctrines of the Catholic Church, on any Roman Catholic understanding of the Church's nature the distinction between schism and heresy is no longer so simple. For to withdraw obedience from the Pope seems, after all, if it is radically carried through, to imply a denial of the dogma of the primacy of the Pope, in other words to be heresy as well. The Second Vatican Council does not state this with regard to the Orthodox Churches because it consistently avoids the concepts of 'haeresis' and 'schisma'. But this does not eliminate the problem. We could of course say that the problem of whether or not it is possible to arrive at any real distinction between heresy and schism is unimportant, since we have in fact accustomed ourselves to regarding heretics and schismatics alike as in good faith, or to presume that they are so. In other words we have grown accustomed to regarding the separation from the Church which these involve as existing merely at a specifically external level, albeit an important one, either that is to say at the level of a specific conscious and abstract formulation of a reality of the faith or at the level of the Church's organization as a society. If this is the way in which we regard heresy and schism in the case of one who is, in all good faith, following the dictates of his conscience, in other words one who is merely materially speaking a heretic or schismatic, then the distinction between the two realities is from the outset not very important. Nevertheless this question, which we have no more than indicated above, has a certain importance for our considerations as we shall straightaway have to show.

A first point that strikes us is that today we speak almost more of the dangers of a schism arising in the Church than of the dangers of fresh heresies arising. The reason for this is surely not that there is no danger of fresh heresies arising in the Church.[2] Surely the explanation of this state of affairs is to be sought elsewhere in the fact that the lack of interest in theoretical questions of faith in the case of many young men is far too great to give rise to any directly theoretical dissent from the official Church at the level of conscious will and opinion. On this showing we can understand that resistance to the Church today is enkindled first and foremost at the level of concrete living, and is directed against her juridical dispensations and her 'establishment', and because of this when any such revolt becomes manifest and socially relevant in the Church it is easier to subsume it under the ancient name of schism or of the danger of schism than under the concept of heresy as formulated at the theoretical level. In the light of this we can, however, go on to ask whether in fact the phenomena which are referred to as schisms or entailing the danger of schism can appropriately be subsumed under this ancient concept at all. For this does, after all, presuppose that the theoretical reason has a certain primacy over the practical because it precedes it in time. Properly speaking, therefore, it would from the outset relegate schism to the level of a secondary phenomenon by comparison with heresy, something which properly speaking could only constitute a reaction against very secondary factors at the

[2] Cf. K. Rahner, 'Heresies in the Church Today?' in this volume, pp. 116–141.

social level, as for instance the question of whether this or that individual is the legitimately elected Pope, whether this or that bishop is or is not exercising his authority legitimately, etc.

It is true that in the times in which we live the practical reason has, at least *de facto*, attained a certain primacy because on the one hand, in the active control of the life of man and his environment by technical means, it has come to have quite new functions, and because on the other in these functions it is no longer thought of as merely the carrying out of the speculative reason. Now on this showing the dissent manifested by the Church's members comes to be quite different in kind and to have a quite different significance from what has been called schism hitherto. Basically speaking this new kind of dissent carries with it the dissent of the speculative reason because the practical reason is regarded as the more comprehensive. And because of this it is properly speaking heresy too, even though this term too can only be applied in that modified sense which has just been indicated with regard to the use of the term schism.

Schism as a Contemporary Phenomenon

From all that has been said, inadequate though it is, it surely follows inevitably that what we of today are confronted with is not simply the new danger of a schism which has remained unaltered in its essential character as such, but rather a phenomenon the true theological and social nature of which is still far from being clearly recognized. It cannot be our task here to embark upon a theological and sociological examination in order *ex professo* to describe this new and different phenomenon. This would be too great and too difficult a task. A point which we shall be treating of more fully at a later stage is that not everything new that is desired and striven for in the Church today in the way of doctrine and living practice is also *ipso facto* schism or entails the danger of schism. On this basis, however, certain insights will be provided, albeit indirectly and without being explicitly stated, into that phenomenon of modern times to which the ancient term 'schism' can be applied only hesitatingly and with reservations. For these 'schisms' are the distorted forms of those pluralist factors in the Church which are justified in the present times and only possible in the present times. And it is of these that we shall have to speak. And it is because it is only in these present times that these pluralist factors are possible that it is only now that a phenomenon arises which can only very inadequately be designated by the ancient term 'schism'.

Abstracting, however, at this preliminary stage from the problems of terminology and the material questions implicit in them, we must begin by pointing out that schisms still can arise even today in which individuals or even more specific groups in the Church can separate themselves from the Roman Catholic Church by refusing to give their allegiance to the universal Church or to a legitimately established division of it to the extent that is necessary, and by refusing to obey the officials legitimately vested with authority in the Church. Just as this sort of thing was possible and actually happened in earlier times, so too it can also be possible today. The occurrences mentioned at the outset in the contemporary Church provide concrete illustrations of the fact that there is a danger of such schisms arising. Admittedly it must be pointed out at the same time that even when this general statement has been made very many individual problems of a more concrete kind still remain wholly unsolved. Presumably when men separate themselves to a certain extent from the concrete unity of life within the Church, or refuse to obey the authorised officials in the Church today this is not the outcome of a quite general *a priori* attitude in which this concrete unity of life with the Church and obedience to legitimately constituted authorities in the Church are rejected in general and in principle. Rather it represents a reaction against specific modes of living in the Church which are historically conditioned and are regarded as no longer in keeping with the times. These modes of life in the Church can then also be maintained and defended in the concrete by specific laws and prescriptions on the part of the Church's authorities (the Pope or a bishop).

In any cases in which an attitude was adopted of radical rejection of the concrete unity of the Church and her legitimately constituted authorities, and in which a schism arose as a result of this attitude, a heresy would be present from the outset and unequivocally, and it would be this alone that would be the source of the schism. Such a case, therefore, would imply not so much the problem of schism but that of heresy. But let us envisage the second case, i.e. one in which a reaction arises which (at least) appears to be schismatic against a particular way of life in the Church which is no longer in keeping with the times or reasonable to impose, and the ecclesiastical laws and prescriptions upholding that way of life. In such a case the question arises whether in the concrete case the ecclesiastical law or official ordinance has or has not any objective authority binding in conscience. The case of an unjust command, an unreasonable ordinance, or one in which an ecclesiastical authority exceeds its own competence is in principle possible in the Church, and it cannot be regarded as schismatic to react against this by refusing to obey it even when the form this takes in a specific instance is not merely a failure to fulfil the ordinance or law in question, but a radical rejection of such a specific and particular law or ordinance. Something of this kind is at least conceivable when the law that is being questioned or the dubious directive not merely prescribes that which is less good, but actually does violence to a genuine human right, or commands something which, when all the circumstances have been taken into consideration, must be judged to be immoral. As we have said, the possibility of such ordinances being issued in the Church cannot be excluded *a priori*, however true it may be that the individual Christian in the individual case must exercise great caution before he presumes such a situation to have arisen. It is true that within the official hierarchy of the Church there is in principle such a thing as an authority over authority, at least in the prime instance of the Church's teaching office as vested in the Pope or in a Council. This means that when an officially defined doctrine in the strict sense is issued by the Pope or Council then it is also clear so far as the Catholic understanding of the Church is concerned that in this case the Church's teaching office is not exceeding its authority.

But this absolute authority over authority is primarily present only in official definitions of doctrine, and not in other authentic statements of doctrine. And in the case of laws and prescriptions on the part of the Church's official pastors it is only in the most exceptional cases that it becomes possible to deduce a law or prescription of the Church as a rule of action at the concrete level unambiguously and compellingly from the teaching authority of the Church in an absolute sense, and so to demonstrate that any rejection of such a law or prescription amounts to heresy by a usurpation of the authority that governs authority. This means that any resistance to a concrete law, the real binding force of which is in fact precisely disputed, cannot so easily and simply be proved to be unequivocally schismatic provided we do not fall into the false assumption that a directive issued by an ecclesiastical authority in all sincerity can never be immoral. In those cases, therefore, in which it is not any definitorial decision of doctrine that is in question, and in which a specific directive cannot be proved unequivocally to follow from a doctrine of this kind, it is in principle conceivable that a conflict between an ecclesiastical authority and one who refused to obey its directive might be a case of open conflict, one which cannot univocally be decided from either side. In such a case the question of whether the refusal to obey does or does not constitute a schism remains open, so that such a conflict can be decided not in terms of theory or formal law, but only in terms of the facts themselves.

Now given that a conflict of this kind remains insoluble at the level of theory and formal law, so that the question remains open whether it does or does not constitute a schism, we cannot solve it by saying that in such a case the officially constituted authorities of the Church can eliminate a case of conflict by threatening or actually imposing an excommunication. For this would merely be to transpose the problem and turn it into the question of whether an excommunication of this sort is just and effective.

From these indications it will be recognized that the question of whether it is a schism or merely a legitimate resistance to possible excesses on the part of the Church's official authorities in a given concrete instance will in many cases be difficult to answer, and that in many such cases it will often be quite impossible for the situation to be controlled by decisions at the level of theory and formal law. Such control will only be achieved, on the contrary, by the practical reason which in this case consists in patience and a Christian attitude of readiness to renounce and to serve. Despite all this it still remains valid as a principle that even today schisms can arise in the Church which really are such. Nor do we need to enlarge any further upon the point that very often if not always today, to the extent that a genuine and not merely a presumptive schism has arisen it proceeds from a heretical attitude of mind even though this may not become wholly apparent in every case. For even when individual groups attempt to assert their rights, whether supposed or genuine in a way that involves force and is devoid of charity against that concrete unity in the Church of which the official authorities are the respresentatives, a heresy at least of the practical reason can be present by the very failure to accord due valueto the importance of this concrete unity, and also to the formal authority of the official functionaries of the Church. While, therefore, it may be perfectly true that there are real dangers of schism arising in the Church of today, still very many tendencies or actual situations occurring in the Church today should not *ipso facto* be condemned as constituting a danger of, or a tendency towards a schism. Alternatively we may say that the dangers involved here are such as are also inevitably involved in every good in our present world and age, and such as do not *ipso facto* make us suspect the genuineness of such goods. Let us identify a few such tendencies and real situations which must not be confused from the outset with schism or the danger of schisms.

The Degree of Autonomy of the Subsidiary Churches

The first factor we may point to is the tendency of the subordinate Churches to achieve a specifically greater degree of autonomy. The right of the subordinate Churches to a certain degree of autonomy and the importance of this both in itself and for the universal Church were in principle recognized at the Second Vatican Council. But the inferences envisaged in this recognition were nevertheless chiefly the subordinate Churches of the east. Obviously an autonomy of this kind could readily and unhesitatingly be conceded to these. We were already accustomed to them, and a recognition of this kind was still far from affecting *that* Church in which the majority of those who expressed this recognition live, namely the Church of the west, the western hemisphere, her daughter Churches in America, and the missions All of these are governed by one and the same *Codex Juris Canonici,* which manifestly affords little scope for the distinctive way of life proper to the subordinate Churches. The tendency to insist more strongly on their own distinctive ways of life and to achieve a more manifest degree of autonomy on the part of the subordinate Churches, therefore, is something which, though it has been recognized by the Second Vatican Council, has still been recognized primarily at the theoretical level, so that numerous grounds for conflict are concealed within this recognition, even to the point of threatening to turn into schism. But in itself this tendency is legitimate, and must not from the outset be suspected of being schismatic. Obviously this tendency meets with resistance on the part of the Church of the west, which is *de facto* to a large extent reduced to uniformity. If we take as our starting-point the assumption that whatever the forms in which the particular degree of autonomy enjoyed by a subordinate Church is expressed they must fall within the uniform pattern which has hitherto prevailed, then this tendency would from the outset be deprived of any real force and reduced to a mere theoretical ideal. As a matter of right and in practical terms the tendency to achieve a more emphatic degree of autonomy on the part of the particular subordinate Churches demands a wider scope than has hitherto been accorded to them by the general law of the Church and the practice of the Roman curia. On the other hand the unity of the subordinate Churches within the one Church is certainly not constituted or assured by the unity of the *creed.* On the contrary, it also demands, and that too precisely today, in an age in which an ever greater degree of unification is being achieved within a single world civilization, a certain measure of universal law and universal patterns of life within the Church, over and above the *jus divinum*.

How to strike the balance in the concrete between these two principles of the autonomy and the unity of the subordinate Churches still remains a very obscure question, the more so since in many respects today the Church is actually confronted with fresh tasks and fresh decisions which require a greater degree of unity than was formerly the case. Obviously the concrete point at which to strike the balance in the contemporary scene between these two principles, and that too in terms of the particular concrete questions being treated of in any given case, is something that has to be discussed afresh again and again. But this is a point which cannot be discussed any further here. The question which remains in this connection is how such a balance can be *discovered* afresh in the concrete. Now the actual situation prevailing in the Church, and that too even at the human level and in all areas of the Church's life, is that generally speaking a right and a measure of power in the concrete is only granted under the force of a certain compulsion and not on the basis of a dialogue and the arguments put forward in this. It cannot be said that a degree of compulsion in some form, brought about by newly created situations, by a certain resistance etc. is from the outset or in every case an illegitimate way of altering a given state of affairs in the Church. In human life and in human society it is in fact not the case, and can never be so, that the process of arriving at decisions takes place *solely* through discussions of the *facts* involved (however important it may be to strive for such discussions), in other words that the authority of an official institution is demonstrably nothing else than the representation of the material arguments on which a given decision is (or should be) based. Now if this is the case on any Catholic and realistic view of the matter from the point of view of the 'authorities', then we cannot fall into the utopian idealism either of demanding that the desire for some change on the part of those 'subject to authority' shall only be arrived at *exclusively* on the basis of a reasoned discussion of the realities involved (however true it may be that these must be the most important factor) which comes to be accepted by the officially constituted authorities as correct. In any decision one of the factors which is constantly at work is a certain 'compulsion' from above *and* from below, and we do not make the process of arriving at a given decision more human by suppressing this. Only if we recognize this obscure element in the process of arriving at any decision can we restrain and control it, be self-critical in our application of it, and concede that the other party too has a right to it, recognizing that it is all too easy to condemn it as immoral even while we are all too ready to overlook it as a factor in our own activities. If all this were not the case, then the very idea of *consuetudo contra legem* could not have any legitimacy, not even in specific instances.

On the other hand it can never be legitimate to use a schism or the threat of a schism as a means to impose by force a new balance between the unity of the Church on the one hand and the autonomy of the subordinate Churches on the other. This statement is intended to apply to those cases in which there is question of a real schism, and not to that radical situation mentioned above in which it is only a presumptive schism that is involved in the process of resisting a directive of the ecclesiastical authorities prescribing something which is not merely the lesser good, but something that is actually immoral, or against an excommunication which is objectively speaking unjust, and at the same time definitive. The reason, therefore, that it is illegitimate to use a real schism or the threat of one as a means of achieving a new balance between the two principles mentioned above is that any real schism breaches the unity of the Church, which for a Catholic, and in the light of the Churches doctrine, is an entity which he can dispense with only by dispensing with the Church herself as necessary for salvation, and also that the will to enter into schism in this way runs counter to the eschatological hope of the Christian, who holds firm to the truth that, in spite of all, the good that God wills always finds its due place in the long run through the exercise of humility, patience and courage, without any revolutionary irruption into the continuity of the history of the one Church. For once and for all the Church is not a broken-down synagogue, but the Church of the final age such that the only stage which is to come after it is the eternal kingdom of God.

This eschatological hope does not imply any canonized immutability on the part of an established Church, but simply holds firm to the fact that this change within the Church and through her can take place and does take place repeatedly within her hierarchical constitution without us having to separate ourselves from the unity of the Church as it exists in the concrete, and not merely as an ideological postulate. He who attempts to oppose the due and justified differences of constitution of the subordinate Churches within the one Church by schismatic force overlooks the fact that thereby, and precisely in this present age of a growing socialization of man, he is turning himself into a religious individualist. And the ideologies on which this state is based have no real future. We can reform the Church only from *within* the Church, and while maintaining an eschatological hope which humanly speaking can never be proved in any adequate sense. Now it belongs precisely to the very nature of this hope that even in conditions which seem to be unfavourable or hopeless it takes up the cudgels against any establishment within the Church. But when all this has been said, the fact still remains that the tendency on the part of the subordinate Churches to achieve a greater autonomy is legitimate and must not be suspected *a priori* as a schismatic tendency, because without a certain gentle force this aim is impossible of achievement.

Pluralism in Theology

A second phenomenon in the contemporary Church must likewise not be suspected *a priori* of being a schismatic or even heretical tendency. This is a growing pluralism in theology.[3] We cannot at this point set forth the reasons for this increasing pluralism in terms of the history of ideas or the history of the Church. But the time when one and the same scholastic philosophy and theology prevailed throughout the Church has passed. It is clear that several different theologies have emerged within the one Church and within her one binding creed, and that these differ from one another according to their respective intellectual backgrounds, the linguistic and philosophical presuppositions on which they are based, the concrete situation in terms of ideas to which any given theology of this kind is addressed and to which it must respond. Of course to say that there is a pluralism of theologies of this kind is not to assert that they have not all in common emerged in order to contribute to the understanding, the interpretation and the proclaiming of the one Christian creed. Nor is it to assert that these theologies should cut themselves off from this one and abiding Christian creed as it is proclaimed by the Church's authorities, the bishops and the Pope.

But surely this does mean that the theologies which have been developed today on the basis of various intellectual presuppositions and aims cannot simply be reduced to one and the same theology in any one higher synthesis worked out as a complete and positive system at the level of abstract speculation, however much we may have to strive for this as an ever asymptotic goal. Each of these theologies has its own special aspects, presentations of subject-matter, terminology, historical stiuations etc., on which they lay special emphasis at particular points, and this means that in certain respects they are irreducibly alien and unassimilable one to another.

[3] Cf. K. Rahner, 'Pluralism in Theology and the Unity of the Creed in the Church', *Theological Investigations*, XI (London, 1973), pp. 3–23.

Indeed it may perfectly well be the case that in specific questions the underlying agreement between these different theologies in the one area designated by the creed can never be defined at all in any positive or adequate
terms by any process of speculation on the part of the particular theologies,
or by recourse to an overall authorty. Instead it may well be the case that
we have to be satisfied with trusting to the fact that each of the individual
theologies unequivocally gives its allegiance to the one creed for all the
variations of theological language between them, and that each of them
adheres in a spirit of obedience to this one creed. For it is obvious that
these theologies still have a duty to adhere to the creed even when the creed
itself is in its turn partly determined in its very formulation by the language
of one specific and historically conditioned theology. A pluralism among
the theologies of this kind, even though it does not exclude, but rather constantly demands, a dialogue between them is something that we have to
take into account today, and learn freely to live with as an unavoidable
fact. This means that any one of these various theologies must refrain
from over-hastily concluding that it can discern heretical or schismatic
tendencies in the others. Of course this is not to say that a theologian no
longer has the right of appealing to the teaching office of the Church to
which the true and ultimate judgement belongs in expressing his opinion
that a specific theological proposition put forward by some other theologian is no longer reconcilable with the creed of the Church, even though
in principle this other theologian continues to submit to the teaching office.
But in view of the pluralism among the theologies of today, which can no
longer be avoided, any theologian has to be extremely prudent and cautious before expressing such an opinion.

Again, so far as the teaching office of the Church herself is concerned,
with its task of watching over the unity of the creed and the purity of the
faith, it finds itself, as a result of this insuperable pluralism among the
theologies, confronted with fresh tasks in the way of working out procedures which will do equal justice alike to the task of the teaching office
itself and to the contemporary situation of an abiding pluralism in theology. Concerning these fresh tasks with which the teaching office is faced
we cannot enlarge any further at this point. On any showing, however, it
remains a fact that a pluralism in theology has of itself nothing to do with
schismatic and heretical tendencies, provided that the theologies concerned constantly and consciously submit themselves to the one creed of
the Church, and are willing to make ever-renewed efforts to listen to one
another's message.

The formation of Groups within the Church

One of the points that is spoken of today is the necessity of achieving a process of democratization in the Church. Here we are abstracting from the question of whether any such concept as 'democracy', belonging as it does to the realm of secular society, is suitable to any extent to be incorporated into the terminology of the Church and her ecclesiology and the discussion of her interior problems. Nòr can we treat of the problem of democracy in the Church at this point as a problem in itself. The question we are raising is simply what this problem has to do with that with which we are properly concerned. Moreover, however the nature of a democracy and the methods, limitations and needs of democratic life and the procedures of a democratic society should be defined, it is clear on any showing that in the broader social groups, and so too in the Church, democracy is inconceivable without the formation of informal and even formal groups too within the Church which emerge from below and are not formed as executive organs of the official leaders within the Church. Again these groups do not find their justification only at that point at which, and in virtue of the fact that they enjoy explicit approval from above. They do not have to be the upholders of a policy which is either intended (with the necessary provisos and in legitimate ways) to become general throughout the Church and to establish itself even in her institutions, or alternatively is at least intended as a struggle to achieve some recognized, albeit particular, place in the Church's life.

In order that there may be democratic procedures within the Church (to the extent that it is possible and reasonable for there to be such even in her, and that certain forms of democracy are allowed for) such groups are indispensable. Moreover such groups have always existed in the Church even though the key term 'democracy' has not been applied to them. In earlier times groups of this kind were generally informal and tended rather to bear the character of charismatic movements, at least at the beginning, inasmuch as they were not represented by religious orders or even by secular institutes. To this extent the difference between earlier times and the present day is to be found rather in the fact that on the one hand such groups are appearing more clearly than was the case as formal groups, and on the other that they regard their efforts as falling under the heading of a process of democratization or of collegiality within the Church.

It is self-evident that with a programme which they seek to carry out in one or other of the ways that have been mentioned such groups all too easily incur the suspicion of being schismatic in tendency. They are in fact groups which clearly stand apart from the *corpus ecclesiae* considered as a totality and from the official institutions in the Church, and uphold a specific attitude and specific aims which do not *ipso facto* and from the outset enjoy the positive approval of the official authorities in the Church. If such groups sought to give their aims a concrete social embodiment in the sphere of religion without any regard to the Church as one and whole, and without any attempt to adapt themselves to her order, or in persistent and unequivocal defiance of the Church's official authority and the unity of this as represented in the Pope they would be *de facto* schismatic, though this is not to contest the fact that it is often not easy to decide in the concrete whether such a group is really schismatic in the sense defined. But the important point in this connection is the one which we have already briefly laid down, namely that the formation of a formal group of this kind from below – in other words independently of any prior authorization on the part of the official authorities is in principle perfectly legitimate, and must not be suspected from the outset of being schismatic in tendency merely on the grounds that it has not been formed by the official authority, or that its aims are not *a priori* brought into positive conformity with those of the official authority. In order to justify this statement reference must not simply be made to the rights of the individual to freedom, to the right and duty of every Christian actively to co-operate in the life of the Church, to the necessity for public opinion to be expressed in the Church, or to similar fundamental considerations. Nor must the proof from tradition be adduced by appealing to the fact that there always have been such groups in the Church, even though they have appeared under different labels and often with a less social formulation. In order to justify the position we have adopted reference must be made to one point alone: if there necessarily is a charismatic element in the Church, if a charismatic dynamism cannot and should not be achieved by the official institutions in the Church totally and of themselves, and if, furthermore, in the very nature of man himself and of society it is quite impossible for the charismatic element to exist or to function efficiently without any kind of concrete social embodiment, then 'spontaneous groupings' from below of the kind we are speaking of are in principle perfectly legitimate even if, under certain circumstances, the form in which they arise may be startling and uncomfortable to the Church's officials.

Side by side with the official institutions, therefore, and independently of them, there should also be those through whom a certain formation of will should be manifested, canonized and made effective in the contemporary scene from the grass roots upwards, as for instance in councils of priests, pastoral councils etc. Just as in the secular sphere, side by side with the parliaments, despite them and at the same time for them, there are parties, and in a more complex society it is quite inevitable that there should be such if a parliament is to be set up which is really capable of its work and genuinely democratic, so too in the supremely complex society of the Church such 'spontaneous groups' formed from below, and having a certain similarity to political parties, are perfectly legitimate and necessary. Hence they should not from the outset be suspected of being schismatic in tendency.

A schismatic tendency would only be present in cases in which a group of this kind, without regard to the wellbeing of the Church as a whole, sought to uphold merely its own special interest, if it employed unfair or unChristian means in order to make its will effective, if it worked against the official authorities in the Church as a special group and with the threat of schism, if it conducted itself in such a way as no longer to make it apparent that it was sustained by that eschatological hope against all hope which to earthly man must appear as folly, but rather sought to achieve its aims by human cunning and human force *alone*. We in the Church of today have to accustom ourselves still more than in former ages to such 'spontaneous groups' arising from the grass roots, and we must learn to accord due scope to such groups in a spirit of fairness and brotherly openness. We have still to find, and still to discover again and again the happy medium between a revolutionary sectarianism which all too easily asserts itself in such groups, and that attitude of mere pious devotion towards the Church's officials in which we do not have the courage to hold our own opinions and to bring influence to bear at the social level.

Incomplete Identification

The problem of schism, or alternatively merely of the presumption of schism, must be approached from yet another angle. The phenomenon we have in mind here is the fact that many individual Catholics identify themselves only partially with their Church. The phenomenon in question is extremely complex and exists in very many forms, which are also essentially different from one another. To speak quite simply what we mean is that a Catholic remains in contact with his Church in his life, continues to 'practise' (at least in a certain, although it may be a very restricted sphere of that life) but in any case never thinks of separating himself from the Church at the manifest and social level, yet at the same time retains certain notable reservations in his attitude towards his Church. Such reservations may be of the most varied kind. They may be such as are positively recognized as perfectly legitimate by the official institutions of the Church in their understanding of her essential doctrine, and hence too do not properly speaking affect the theological attitude of the Catholic involved towards his Church even though he has these reservations. For instance the individual has a perfect right to hold the opinion that this Pope is not a saint or not a skilful and wise ruler. He has a perfect right to consider many of the man-made laws of the Church as deficient in wisdom, as antiquated, or even as unjust and inhuman. In themselves such reservations do not affect the theological attitude of the Catholic concerned towards the Church. In fact, however, many Catholics of the present day do have reservations, and very far-reaching reservations at that, affecting the very substance of the Catholic faith and the nature of the Church herself, calling them in question or unequivocally rejecting them in themselves without the Catholic concerned feeling compelled on that account to separate himself from the Church even though he does not stand apart from it in this way, and in such cases his reasons for not separating himself from the Church, for continuing partially to identify himself with the Church, can in their turn be very varied, ranging from a bourgeois conformity to convention to motivations of a genuinely religious kind.

Now with regard to this incomplete identification with the Church as it bears upon our present theme we shall only be putting forward a few observations which in no sense constitute an exhaustive treatment of this subject of merely partial identification. An initial point to be laid down: reservations of the second kind which we have mentioned above do in themselves amount to a state of objective heresy, and thereby of a partial apostasy from the faith of the Church, and so too of an interior schism even when this is not made manifest at the social level. But so far as the concrete instances of such an attitude are concerned we will have to be cautious in arriving at such a judgement, in which we actually conclude that the cases concerned do amount to heresy and schism. Very often, or even in the majority of cases, a reservation of this kind which seems to be heretical does not entail any subjective guilt. This means that in judging of the individual who makes these reservations we should have to apply all those principles with regard to membership of the Church which apply to merely material heresy and the heretic at the merely material level, and that too even in the sort of case in which a heresy of this kind is far from being manifested at the level of public and social life, and in which he who makes the reservations is not for one moment deliberately separating himself from the Church and her life. In such cases a situation that has really arisen in the concrete is simply one which has constantly arisen and constantly will arise everywhere in the Church in innumerable instances, a situation namely in which some individual at once wills to adhere to the Church and so to attain to salvation, maintaining a *fides implicita* in the full and orthodox faith of the Church, yet at the same time upholds opinions which objectively speaking are in contradiction to the faith of the Church. If therefore we assume *bona fides* to be present in such a reservation, and if this reservation is not manifested in the public and social life of the Church (for instance through the heretical preaching of an individual priest in the public services of the Church) then he who makes a reservation of this kind, despite the fact that he is in a state of only incomplete identification with the Church (at the level of conscious awareness) is, nevertheless a good Christian and Catholic. There would be no need to cause him any special 'disquiet', especially as after all there are precisely many cases in which psychologically speaking it is in practice often impossible within the limited time available to arrive at any *positive* synthesis and reconciliation between the statements of the Church's faith on the one hand (which are not always easy for every individual to understand) and the opinions and attitudes of the Catholic involved on the other, which are in themselves justified. Here too we find ourselves faced with that phenomenon which can only very unsatisfactorily be characterized by the traditional term 'schism'.

A further possibility is that the reservation which seems to be heretical does not truly represent a judgement on the part of the Christian who holds himself apart in this way, but is merely an expression, to some extent primitive and not fully worked out, of the fact that the Catholic concerned has failed to achieve any *positive* harmonization of the proposition of faith which has been called in question with the remaining tenets which he holds according to his own individual lights. In a case of this kind it is even less possible to say that schism and heresy are present in any objective sense. Of course for all that we have said we are not denying that the official authorities in the Church have the right and duty to guard the unity of the creed and the full purity of the Christian faith, and to conclude that heresy and schism are present in those cases in which an attitude of unequivocal separation from the Church's doctrine is made manifest at the social level. It is clear that in such a case he who really makes reservations of *this* kind can no longer be tolerated as a teacher and director in the Church at the public level. Now between these two extremes constituted

by the first-named kind of reservations and the second kind many intermediate attitudes of reservation, and so too of partial identification of this
sort are to be found, which vary in their nature and are difficult to analyse.
They may entail dangers of schism or heresy while still not as such having
to be qualified as *ipso facto* being schismatic or heretical in themselves. Not
every theological opinion which is not already positively declared to be
legitimate or admissible by the Church, yet which does run counter to
some currently received opinion on the part of her teachers, *ipso facto*
constitutes a heretical reservation contrary to the teaching of the Church.
Not every individual act of disobedience against the man-made juridical
dispositions of the Church implies a partial non-identification with the
Church of such a kind that we would be compelled to judge it as schismatic, or would be forced to regard it as entailing a real danger of a schism.
Indeed certain forms of partial non-identification with the Church in the
concrete are recognized in her doctrinal tradition, and these have a positive
function to perform. What we are referring to here are 'customs contrary
to the law' which can be legitimate and concerning which it cannot
genuinely be maintained in every case that they owe their origins to an
initially immoral transgression of the law. A partial non-identification with
the Church in *one* respect can therefore in some *other* respect perfectly well
constitute an identification with her Spirit, with other concrete realities in
her, and with her future.

All these considerations serve to bring out situations and problems
which cannot be coped with by means of formal rules alone. There are
many cases in which it cannot be established solely on the basis of the
Church's doctrine whether they are heretical or schismatic or non-heretical
and non-schismatic in character. There are conflicts between directives on
the part of the Church's authorities and the resistance that is offered to
them, which cannot be definitively ruled out even by the application of
the principles of formal justice, since even juridical authority on the one
hand and the obedience due to it on the other are not simply or exclusively
the principle which dominates all else in the Church, but merely constitute
a partial principle, the precise force of which in a specific case can perfectly
well be an open question which cannot in its turn be decided unequivocally
by this authority itself. In other words there are cases of conflict in the
Church which cannot be solved simply by the rational application of
theoretical and general principles to one individual case, but which can
only be solved by the practical reason, i.e. *in concreto* by patience, modesty
on both sides, efforts to overcome that intolerance which is to be found
among both conservative and progressive Christians, humility and charity

which are capable even of surrendering a right, faith and hope which are able to overcome in weakness by keeping their gaze fixed upon the Cross of Christ.

Is it really so very surprising that there should be a situation of conflict of this kind in the Church? After all according to our Christian convictions the abiding nature and the power of the Church ultimately derive not from the univocal significance of propositions of faith formulated by human minds or from inflexible juridical rules (however true it may be that both have their necessity and their justification) but from the power of the Spirit who makes use of many human means and does not totally identify himself with any one of them. If we really believe this then we shall no longer be so very surprised at the fact that for many of the conflicts in the Church there are no smooth ready-made solutions. Admittedly in a conflict of this kind each individual, whichever side he is on, must (in a 'discerning of spirits') put to himself the critical question of whether his own attitude in the conflict really leaves sufficient room for the sway of the Spirit or is after all, in the last analysis merely governed by self-will. Often it is in fact impossible to solve such conflicts by the application of formal principles or merely at the level of rational argument. But often too it can plainly be recognized which side has more faith, hope, and dedicated love, humility and readiness for genuine *metanoia* in a spirit of self-criticism. Given this discerning of spirits we can after all arrive at a decision as to which 'party' in a conflict we should support. Even in a case such as this God is not simply and exclusively on the side of one party alone, but brings his own work to fruition according to his own good will by means of all the parties to the conflict. Our task, however, is not to seek to be God, but rather to seek out our own decision and our place in such conflicts in whatever direction a Christian discernment of spirits guides us.

7

HERESIES IN THE CHURCH TODAY?

W HAT we shall be attempting here is to state certain points of fundamental importance with regard to 'heresies in the Church'.[1] The theme has certainly become vitally relevant since the Council. The Christian in the Catholic Church who grew up in the pre-conciliar age and felt himself at home in this pre-conciliar Church not infrequently has the impression that the old faith is wavering, and that today even in the very pulpit itself doctrines and opinions are put forward which are claimed to have validity in the Church, yet which such a Catholic feels to be in contradiction to his own faith, to constitute heresy. He hears that in Holland an Adult Catechism has been published with the approval of the united Dutch episcopate which is at the same time denounced by other Dutch Catholics to the Pope at Rome on the grounds that side by side with much that is good it contains heresies or doctrines suspected of heresy. Again such a Catholic hears of the Doctrinal Letter of the German Bishops,[2] in which those entrusted with the task of preaching are warned

[1] On the basic problems involved cf. also J. O. Sanders, *Heresies Ancient and Modern* (London, 1948); K. Rahner, *Gefahren im heutigen Katholizismus* (Einsiedeln, 1950); W. Philipp, 'Irrlehre', *RGG* III (3rd ed., 1959), 898–901; J. Trütsch, 'Glaubensabfall', *LTK* IV (2nd ed., 1960), 931–934; J. Brosch, 'Häresie', *LTK* V (2nd ed., 1960), 6–8; K. Rahner, 'Häresiengeschichte', *ibid.*, 8–11; *idem*, 'On Conversions in the Church', *Theological Investigations* III (London and Baltimore, 1967), pp. 373–384; *idem*, 'Some Remarks on the Question of Conversions', *Theological Investigations* V (London and Baltimore, 1966), pp. 315–335; *idem*, 'What is Heresy?', *ibid.*, pp. 468–512; A. Böhm, *Häresien der Zeit* (Freiburg, 1961); U. Ranke-Heinemann, 'Die Kirche und die christlichen Konfessionen', *Handbuch der Pastoraltheologie* II/2 (Freiburg, 1966), esp. pp. 84–87.

The chapter which follows is a very much abbreviated version, and an excerpt from a larger treatise entitled 'Häresien in der Kirche heute?' which the author prepared for publication in the series, 'Quaestiones Disputatae' (Verlag Herder, Freiburg). For a more detailed exposition of the arguments presented here the author may refer to this projected study.

[2] *Schreiben der deutschen Bischöfe an alle, die von der Kirche mit der Glaubensverkündigung beauftragt sind* (Treves, 2nd ed., 1968). In this connection cf. also the

against false doctrines, attitudes at variance with the Church, wrong interpretations of the gospel, of the Resurrection of Christ, of the Eucharist
etc. Such a Catholic has experience of apostasy on the part of priests who
give up their priestly calling not merely because the duty of celibacy seems
unbearable to them,[3] but also by reason of an interior apostasy from their
very faith. And such a Catholic then feels oppressed by the further question of whether other priests too, even though for various reasons they
still continue at their posts, may not fall away in their faith in a similar
manner. In questions affecting his own moral life, especially with regard
to married ethics,[4] such a Catholic hears of differences of opinion among
moral theologians and confessors, and indeed among bishops, even concerning doctrines which as recently as a decade ago seemed to him to be
put forward by the Church's official teachers as uncompromising and
beyond all doubt. In short such a Catholic asks himself whether today
doctrines are not emerging unchallenged, and even being put forward
within the Church herself, which, measured by the teaching traditionally
upheld up to the present, would simply have to be rejected as heresies, as
errors against the faith.

I

The question we are raising here is not concerned simply with heresies in
the full sense. The fact is that individuals come forward in the Church proclaiming an opinion or upholding a doctrine which is then declared

encyclical of Paul VI, 'Mysterium Fidei', *AAS* 57 (1965), pp. 753–774, and also the
Letter of Cardinal Ottaviani to the Universal Episcopate, *AAS* 58 (1966), pp. 659–
661 and on the latter, K. Rahner, 'Theology and the Church's Teaching Authority
After the Council', *Theological Investigations* IX (London and New York, 1972),
pp. 83–100.
    [3] On this cf. F. Wulff *et al.*, 'The Discussion on Celibacy, France, Germany and
the Netherlands', *Concilium* 3/5 (Pastoral), 1969, pp. 86–90.
    [4] In this connection the practice in mixed marriages and the question of birth-
control occupy a central place in the discussion. On this cf. J. M. Reuss, 'Eheliche
Hingabe und Zeugung', *T.Q.* 143 (1963), pp. 454–476; T. Roberts, *Empfängnisverhütung in der christlichen Ehe* (Mainz, 1966); F. Böckle, *Das Problem der bekenntnis-
verschiedenen Ehen in theologischer Sicht* (Freiburg, 1967); further, E. McDonagh,
'The Moral Theology of Marriage: Recent Literature in English', *Concilium* 1 (Moral
Theology, 1965), pp. 70–82; J. David, *Neue Aspekte der kirchlichen Ehelehre* (Ber-
gen-Enkheim, 2nd ed. 1966); B. Häring, *Moralverkündigung nach dem Konzil*
(Bergen-Enkheim, 1966), and also K. Rahner, 'On the Encyclical "Humanae Vitae"',
Theological Investigations XI (London, 1973), pp. 263–287.

irreconcilable with the Christian and Catholic faith by the Church's official teachers, with the result that the upholders of any such doctrine must either submit to the pronouncement of the Church in the obedience of faith or alternatively depart from the Church in a way that is manifest even at the level of her social and public life. But this is something which has always happened again and again in the course of the Church's history, and it is not this that constitutes the subject of our considerations. What we are treating of, rather, is the phenomenon that Catholic Christians uphold opinions of this sort in the Church, deviating from the Church's faith in a way that is in some degree manifest and public in her social life without on that account then departing from the Church. Indeed their way of upholding such opinions may actually be such that the ecclesiastical authorities, with the doctrinal authority vested in them, may not even take proceedings against them in a sufficiently clear manner. In speaking of heresies within the Church in this way we are of course not referring to variations of opinion on theological questions such as there have always been in the Church, without prejudice to her one faith and her one creed. Admittedly we are also aware of the fact that it is not always easy to establish the line of demarcation between such variations of opinion in theology on the one hand, freely existing side by side with one another, and heresies which are hostile to the faith on the other. In other words it is not always easy to say whether a given opinion really does constitute a heresy, and radically calls for the intervention of the Church's *magisterium*.

Nor do we intend here to investigate the question of the extent to which anything which has to be called heresy within the Church really is present in the Catholic Church of today, and if so how great or how small the threat that this represents for her is. All that we are assuming is that the threat is present in some degree, and that it is such that a consideration of this phenomenon does not merely constitute the heart-searchings of a reactionary Catholic who is the prey of anxious nightmares. The fact that this phenomenon is present in some measure, at least as a genuine danger, is in fact apparent from the Doctrinal Letter of the German Bishops mentioned above, and also from the warning words of the Pope. In other words it has been pointed to by individuals in the Church who certainly are not struggling against mere nightmares. What we intend, rather, is, without adopting any more precise or in some sense statistical position with regard to the phenomenon of heresies in the Church of today, first and foremost to enquire what the reasons are for this state of affairs, which is, in a certain sense at least, a new manifestation. These reasons are certainly complex and together constitute a unity, and it is only by taking them together as a unity that we can to some extent explain this phenomenon. Catholics who are over-anxious and conservative in a sense that is not altogether above suspicion have already laid the blame for this manifestation at the door of the Council itself.[5] This is of course mistaken. First the Council has never in any sense cast doubt upon, or even merely obscured, any of the real doctrines of faith hitherto upheld by the Church. Perhaps, however, it is possible to say that the Council has in some respects acted as a sort of catalyst through which the true origins of this phenomenon have been set in motion and have brought these heresies within the Church to the surface at the level of the Church's public life as well— heresies which were already present previously, albeit *in radice*, and only in a latent form. For the Council realistically and boldly faced up to the intellectual and social situation in which the Church has to live today, and this situation, in which all of us as individuals and so the Church too have to live, is the real cause of this phenomenon.

Faith recognizes its own nature in relation to a great number of sciences, intellectual disciplines and branches of the natural and sociological sciences which have become autonomous and which show the widest possible variations. And in the questions they raise, the conclusions they arrive at, and the aims for which they strive all these have an ideological relevance.[6] Faith as it exists today lives in a world which is intellectually and sociologically speaking pluralist in character. Every believer comes continually into contact with men who have different philosophies of life, amounting in extreme cases to a dedicated and militant atheism. Even on the most basic questions of human existence there is today no one homogeneous public opinion in which the conviction of the individual could find support in virtue of their self-evident truth and universal acceptance. The world has become *one* in such a way that the individual has been brought to close quarters with cultures which were formerly very remote, and has become

---

[5] In this connection we should notice the criticisms which the French episcopate put forward on the 27th June 1966 with regard to various articles in the periodicals, *Itinéraires, Défense de Foi, Lumière* and *Le Monde et la Vie*. Cf. also in the German-speaking sphere, *Nunc et Semper. Eine katholische Korrespondenz für Kirche und Papstum* 1 (1966) and ff.

[6] On this cf. K. Rahner, 'A small Question Concerning the Contemporary Pluralism in the Intellectual Situation of Catholics and the Church', *Theological Investigations* VI (London and Baltimore, 1969), pp. 21–30; *idem*, 'Reflections on Dialogue Within a Pluralistic Society', *ibid.*, pp. 31–42; *idem*, 'Reflections on the Contemporary Intellectual Formation of Future Priests', *ibid.*, pp. 113–138; *idem*, Theologische Deutung der Gegenwartssituation als Situation der Kirche', *Handbuch der Pastoraltheologie* II/1 (1966), pp. 233–256.

familiar with their interpretations of existence and modes of living. The world which was once static has become dynamic. The changes it undergoes, planned and carried through by man himself, are becoming ever swifter, and in this world which is the creation of man himself, or seems to be so, it is not so easy to discover God. In a world of this sort it is obvious that faith is much more threatened and assailed in the individual than in an earlier static or homogeneous society, the ethos of which first bore the stamp of Christianity and in which any view that deviated from the publicly accepted and homogeneous Christian opinion immediately met with resistance from society itself.

Now in a situation of this kind, in which faith is threatened, it is obvious that more inroads will be made into the faith of the individual, and even more inculpable breakdowns of faith at this level, than in an earlier age. A further point is that in a new situation of this kind the ancient faith, precisely in order to remain the ancient one, must learn to interpret itself afresh. It must surrender old patterns of interpretation which are not identical with itself, and seek for new ones. It must express itself in new forms in order to make itself understood in the contemporary scene, and manage to make contact with findings arrived at in other branches of human knowledge and human life in such a way that it does not cause the tension inherent in the very nature of faith in relation to the rest of human experience to become too great for the individual to sustain. The root causes of the phenomenon we are considering as indicated above are still, however, insufficient of themselves, for the only effect it could produce, and in fact to a considerable extent does produce, is that those who find themselves opposed in their convictions to the faith as it has existed hitherto either cease to be members of the Church even in the external sense, or alternatively become so remote from the Church at least in virtue of ceasing to take any active part in Church life or any interest in the Church's doctrine that it is hardly possible to speak of any heresy within the Church at all. There must be some further cause besides the one which we have mentioned, and in fact there is such a cause.

Modern man is, from a certain point of view, man in a strange state of transition.[7] One of the dominant characteristics of him is a kind of

[7] For a description of modern man's social situation cf. H. Freyer, *Das soziale Ganze und die Freiheit der Einzelnen unter den Bedingungen des industriellen Zeitalters* (Göttingen, 1957); K. Mácha, *Individuum und Gesellschaft* (Berlin, 1964); R. Linder, *Grundlegung einer Theologie der Gesellschaft* (Hamburg, 1960); K. Rahner and N. Greinacher, 'Grundzüge der Gegenwartssituation', *Handbuch der Pastoraltheologie* II/1 (1966), pp. 188 ff. (A further bibliography is to be found here, cf. pp. 178 ff.).

individualism which has arisen in recent times such that it is only with the greatest difficulty that he can reconcile himself to any authority imposed upon him from without so far as his understanding of existence and his mode of living is concerned. Now certainly among the elements that go to make up this modern form of individualism there is one which we must want to endure, and that too precisely as Christians: the right to freedom of conscience and of personal decisions, which must neither be directed nor replaced by any external compulsion from the society in which we live. At the same time, however, it seems to me that contemporary man, characterized as he is by this modern form of individualism, is also in a strange way already one who belongs to a future era. Man as we envisage him here is aware of the fact that any absolute individualism is not only unrealistic and futile, but also, so far as knowledge is concerned, leads to what is merely arbitrary and capricious. He already feels, albeit not in any very explicit way, that truth itself is somehow bound up with society and institution. Unlike the man of the age of upper-class individualism, he is no longer assured of the fact that one can discover one's religion for oneself according to one's own opinions and inclinations. There is a certain scepticism in his attitude which he directs against himself, and which makes it less easy for him to regard his own philosophy of life as the only true one.

Now a man of this kind, standing as he does at the point of transition between a modern form of individualism and a new experience of the importance of the collective discovery of truth (to express it vaguely) is thereby exposed to the temptation of opposing his own views, drawn from his own personal philosophy of life, to the collective awareness of faith upheld by the Church as a whole, and yet even while doing this of continuing to claim his place in this community, constituted though it is by a body of religious convictions which cannot hastily be worked out afresh. He wills to be a heretic within the Church. He wills to remain within her in order to avoid simply degenerating into scepticism and relativism, yet without unreservedly submitting to the claims which his community makes to be in possession of a collective truth, and he does this in the *hopeful* conviction, which he strives ever afresh to realize, that it is possible to achieve harmony between his own individual sense of truth and the convictions upheld by the believing community.[8]

[8] On this cf. also K. Rahner, 'On the Theology of Hope', *Theological Investigations* X (London and New York, 1972), pp. 242–259; *idem*, 'A Small Fragment "On the Collective Finding of Truth" ', *Theological Investigations* VI (London and Baltimore 1969), pp. 82–88.

In addition to this there is a further fact which, though correct in itself, has the opposite effect to what might be expected in its bearing on the case we are considering. The Council itself has recognized that in the totality of the Christian and Catholic faith there is a hierarchy of truths,[9] in other words that even though the binding force of all the doctrines of the Church (which really are such) is formally speaking the same, nevertheless there are extraordinarily wide differences between the individual doctrines in respect of their importance and the weight they carry as applied to objective situations and particular concrete circumstances. Not all the statements of the Catholic faith are equally important or central. Hence it is all too easy for an individual caught up in this state of transition to arrive at the opinion that he can preserve those truths of the Christian faith and those fundamental practices of Christian life which really are most central, in other words belief in God, prayer and hope of eternal life, and thereby remain in the Church and hold firm to the practices of Christian living, and nevertheless, with regard to the less central teachings of the faith, form his own opinion in contradiction to the official teaching of the Church.

In addition to all these other causes there is finally one further cause for the phenomenon we are considering. There are many questions which are matters of dispute in theology.[10] As the German bishops have explicitly recognized, there are *de facto* propositions which, though not defined, have nevertheless been authoritatively taught in the Church up to now, which have turned out to be either erroneous or at least susceptible of legitimate doubt. This applies not merely, for instance, to the sphere of biblical studies, but also to the sphere of morality in questions which have a wholly practical significance for the life of the individual Christian.[11]

[9] Decree on Ecumenism, No. 11.

[10] On this cf. n. 4, and further the discussions concerning the relationship between nature and grace, between the Pope and the College of Bishops, and also concerning questions bearing upon Jesus' awareness of himself, the relationship between scripture and tradition, the Virgin birth, the precise nature of transubstantiation, original sin etc. In these respects, however, our situation is not essentially different from that of earlier ages in which the Church likewise had to endure sharp differences of opinion (Thomists, Scotists, Suarezians, Augustinians) and had to bridge the gulf between them (Bánez-Molina, the Contritionists-Attritionists).

[11] As an example from an earlier age we might mention the following: Innocent VIII on the question of the burning of witches, Gregory XVI on the question of the press and freedom of conscience (DS 2730), Pius IX in The Syllabus of Errors (DS, 2977–2980). In this connection cf. R. Aubert, 'Religious Liberty from "Mirari Vos" to the "Syllabus" ', *Concilium* 1 (1965, Church History), pp. 49–57.; H. J. Zwetsloot,

Finally it is not always easy to draw any exact line of demarcation between that which constitutes the true doctrine of the Church, which is irreformable, and those opinions and interpretations which are open to discussion, but which have hitherto to some extent been amalgamated with this essential doctrine without sufficient conscious discrimination. In the light of this it is, once more, understandable that a Christian who legitimately rejects views which have hitherto been current in the Church may without noticing it, and indeed even while intending to achieve a new and better understanding of the Church's doctrine, overstep the limits and contest or throw doubt upon doctrines which have an absolute dogmatic binding force as well, without thereby either entertaining or enunciating any intention of separating himself from this fellowship of the believing Church.

II

We shall now attempt to formulate certain rules for a right understanding and a right attitude towards the phenomenon with which we are concerned.

1. There is both a legitimate and an illegitimate way of distinguishing between the individual and the collective conviction of faith. Not every distinction between the conviction of faith entertained by the individual and that of the Church is legitimate, for otherwise there would in fact be no heresies in the Church such as are obviously to be rejected. Conversely, however, not every distinction is illegitimate. If we were to overlook the fact that there both can be and is a legitimate way of distinguishing between the individual and the collective conviction of faith, we would not merely be overlooking the situations which de facto exist, but also failing to adopt a right attitude to that element of concern inherent in the heresies within the Church which is justified.[12]

'Witch-Hunting', *Sacramentum Mundi* 3 (London and New York, 1968), pp. 143–145. On the question of usury, J. T. Noonan, 'Die Autoritätsbeweise in Fragen des Wüchers und der Empfängnisverhütung', *Diakonia* 1 (1966), pp. 79–106; *idem, The Scholastic Analysis of Usury* (Cambridge, 1957); *idem, Contraception. A History of Its Treatment by the Catholic Theologians and Canonists* (Cambridge, 1965).

[12] On the distinction between the individual and the collective awareness of faith cf. M. Löhrer, 'Überlegungen zur Interpretation lehramtlicher Aussagen als Frage des ökumenischen Gesprächs', *Gott in Welt* II (Festschrift für K. Rahner) edited by J. B. Metz, W. Kern *et al.* (Freiburg, 1964), pp. 499–523; K. Rahner, *Bemerkungen*

The truth which this is intended to express is this: there is an illegitimate way of distinguishing; it is found in the heresies in the Church which arise in connection with some truth of the faith in the strict sense, for which the official teaching authority of the Church claims an absolute assent of faith through a definition of the Pope of the Council, or else through the ordinary channels by which doctrine is promulgated. Such heresies arise when a Catholic unequivocally denies, or of his own free decision casts doubt upon truths of the faith of this kind (though obviously the difficulties which we may feel with regard to some doctrine of the faith promulgated by the Church do not of themselves entail any such doubt or denial), and arise above all in those cases in which this denial or voluntary questioning of a truth of faith also becomes a factor in the public life of the Church. When he does deny a truth of the faith in the strict sense in this way, or at least when his denial becomes a factor in the public life of the Church, a Catholic separates himself from the Church even though juridically speaking, and so far as external Church membership is concerned he still continues to belong to her. For instance he may continue to pay the Church dues or attend Church on Sundays or send his children for religious instruction. Even so he is separated from the Church, and that too even though the Church's officials may not have laid down that he is separated from her by a distinct and specific juridical enactment. Such a Catholic is separated from the Church because the Church is a spiritual community united by all her members holding the same faith, and not merely an external juridical organization. Now a Christian of this sort separates himself from this one unified community of the faith as a matter of his own personal decision by rejecting a doctrine which this community adheres to with an absolute assent of faith, and in virtue of the fact that by his denial of such a specific truth he is also rejecting, at least by implication, the doctrine of the infallibility of the Church's faith in the strict sense and of her teaching authority. Of course in defining the general principles according to which heresy is judged to involve separation from the Church we have still not decided the practical question in the individual case of where in the concrete such heresy is to be found. For manifestly a

zum Begriff der Offenbarung, Quaestiones Disputatae 25 (Freiburg, 1965), pp. 11–24, esp. pp. 11/12 (with reference to Modernism); idem, 'Theoretische und reale Moral in ihrer Differenz', Handbuch der Pastoraltheologie II/1 (Freiburg, 1966), pp. 152–163; idem, 'Questions of Controversial Theology on Justification', Theological Investigations IV (London and Baltimore, 1966), pp. 189–218; idem, 'Theology and the Church's Teaching Authority After the Council', Theological Investigations IX (London and New York, 1972), pp. 83–100.

denial of a doctrine of the Church only constitutes a heresy that separates the individual concerned from the Church in the sense we have defined when it is posited with sufficient freedom and responsibility, when this denial really signifies a grave fault in God's sight, when the denial is really directed against a doctrine of the Church and not merely against some misinterpretation of such a doctrine.[13] Very often we are far from being able to establish all these conditions exactly in the individual case. Besides this a distinction which we shall not be entering into any more fully at this point should be drawn between heresy which is merely objective and that which is subjective too according to whether in the particular case supposed the denial of some defined doctrine of the Church is culpable or inculpable.

But there is also, as has already been stated, a perfectly legitimate distinction between the individual's own convictions of faith and that of the Church as a whole. Heresy in the true sense often emerges precisely through the failure to recognize this legitimate distinction and to be bold enough to apply it to one's own case, with the result that then, when difficulties arise in understanding the faith, we go beyond the prescribed limits, not knowing how to resolve our difficulties except by specifically denying some defined doctrine of the Church.

In what does this legitimate distinction consist? First and foremost it is clear that at the level of his own personal convictions of faith an individual Christian does not have to be in possession of all the doctrines of the Church's faith with complete clarity and in a fully explicitated and developed form as these doctrines are present in the convictions of faith of the Church as a whole. The catechism or concrete body of convictions present in the mind and heart of any one individual believer is in most cases much smaller and more modest than the printed catechism or the compilation of all the doctrinal decisions officially laid down by the Church. This is not merely *de facto* the case – something which no-one surely will deny – but it actually should be the case. Precisely today, when it is man's most ultimate decisions with regard to God, Jesus Christ, and the hope of eternal life that are in question, it is quite impossible, and moreover not for one moment to be supposed in the case of an average Christian, even one who is interested in religion and well instructed, that his personal commitment of faith will be equally alive and vigorous to every truth without exception. It is perfectly legitimate for him to con-

---

[13] On the concept of heresy cf. K. Rahner, 'What is Heresy?', *Theological Investigations* V (London and Baltimore, 1966), pp. 468–512; J. Brosch, 'Häresie', *LTK* V (2nd ed., 1960), 6–8; H. Flatten, *Der Häresieverdacht im CIC* (Amsterdam 1963).

centrate his personal will to achieve the truth on the most central questions of the Christian faith and the Christian way of life, in other words upon a living and prayerful relationship with God in his history, upon Jesus Christ, upon the task of bravely enduring his life and the demands it makes upon him, upon the hope of eternal life, and all this within the Church of Jesus Christ and in the fellowship of those who do believe in this way and celebrate the memory of their Lord. Provided he does have a conviction of faith of this sort, orientated towards the most central realities of the Christian message, the Christian of today can freely leave unexplored much else that belongs to the convictions of faith upheld by the Church as a whole. He must not deny it. He will maintain an openness in the convictions of his personal faith and the development of his own religious experience to this more ample fulness of the Christian faith in the Church as a whole. But he does not need to act as though he were obliged to maintain an equally intensive attitude in his own concrete personal circumstances towards everything which the Church proclaims as pertaining to the faith, and in doing so to overstrain the capacities of his personal religious life. With regard to the less central truths of the faith, for instance the position of Mary, the number and importance of the sacraments, and other matters, it is perfectly legitimate for him to say: 'I do not deny all this; in principle I fully acknowledge that all this pertains to a legitimate explicitation of the basic reality of Christian revelation as upheld in the universal convictions of the Church. But here and now in the concrete situation of my own religious life I cannot take any special interest in these matters. I leave all this more or less on one side. My personal conviction of faith is not simply a repetition of the total convictions of the Church, but merely a legitimate part of those convictions arrived at by a certain process of selection and individual arrangement'.

Once the Christian recognizes this legitimate distinction between his own individual convictions of faith and those of the Church as a whole, once this distinction is not merely *de facto* present but also boldly and freely invoked, then many difficulties are avoided in a perfectly reasonable and harmonious way which in other cases lead to heresies within the Church, because in these other cases the individual supposes that as a matter of his own personal conviction of faith he has always and in every case to achieve an explicit and conscious appropriation of any and every truth of faith in his own personal life. And this may be impossible in the here and now precisely in the individual's own case. A further point is that in the contemporary scene modern man has a lively awareness of the difference between accepting a given doctrine merely at the conceptual

level and making it his own at a genuinely personal level in such a way
that the truth concerned really does achieve a genuine effectiveness and
force in his own life. Now because of this the attempt to achieve a personal
appropriation of this kind of a given doctrine of the Church, such that it
becomes a force in the individual's own personal life, can easily lead to an
over-straining of the will, and then this over-straining can lead precisely
to the heresies in the Church of which we have been speaking. These are
the difficulties which we would be able to avoid if we were clearly and
freely to allow for the fact that there is a legitimate difference between the
message which we hear or can hear in the official preaching of the faith and
that in this message which we effectively appropriate in our own personal
lives, without thereby denying the rest of the message.

The situation here is the same as in other departments of life. When we
demand more of ourselves or believe that we have to demand more of
ourselves than we are actually capable of we do not even manage to
achieve that which really is within our capacities In other words with
regard to many individual truths of the Church a Catholic of today,
especially an educated one, can perfectly well say: 'I do not understand
this or that point. It raises difficulties for me. I cannot cope with it at all.
Any genuinely personal understanding of it is simply not given to me or
accessible to me here and now. But on the other hand I do not deny it. I
set it on one side. I have a perfectly genuine right as a human being to do
this, and in principle it has nothing whatever to do with cowardice or
dishonesty', because in other spheres of individual experience and the
development of ideas in his personal life every individual is aware that
the totality of objective truth, of the values and benefits for human life
which a given culture, or even humanity itself, has to bestow is too great
for the individual to be able positively to appropriate this totality for himself at the level of his own personal understanding.

2. The justifiable pluralism arising from the theological freedom within
the Catholic Church must freely be accepted as a given fact.[14] In the last
century Catholic theology bore a neo-Scholastic stamp and exhibited a

[14] On the concept of freedom in the Church cf. K. Rahner, *Das freie Wort in der
Kirche* (Einsiedeln, 2nd ed., 1954); *idem*, 'Freedom in the Church', *Theological
Investigations* II (London and Baltimore, 1966), pp. 89–133; *idem*, 'Dialogue in the
Church', *Theological Investigations* X (London and New York, 1973), pp. 103–123;
idem, 'Do not Stifle the Spirit!', *Theological Investigations* VIIA (London and Balti-
more, 1971), pp. 72–87; *idem*, *Das Dynamische in der Kirche*, Quaestiones Disputatae
5 (Freiburg, 3rd ed. 1965). With regard to the statements of the Council cf. the
Dogmatic Constitution on the Church, 'Lumen Gentium', No. 37 and the Decree on
Ecumenism No. 4.

great uniformity, and if we abstract from relatively few exceptions, it was regarded as obvious that it was simply *the* predominant theology in the Catholic Church, even though in principle it had always been recognized that there should be various schools in theology. Now in the last few decades the situation has been very considerably changed, and this change has been accelerated by the Council. As a result of bolder confrontations with the modern sciences, with the problems and findings of exegesis, with Protestant theology, with all the questions which are raised by the contemporary climate of ideas, Catholic theology has become far more varied than we could have imagined a few years ago. Even in those cases in which we are willing to accord an unreserved respect to the defined doctrines of the Church there are, in contemporary theology very great variations of opinion even on important questions, very great differences between the perspectives in which the reality of the faith is viewed, between the philosophies and terminologies which theology employs in its attempt to master and express its subject-matter.

The increasing pluralism in Catholic theology which has come about in this way cannot be depicted at any greater length here. Nevertheless it has a very great significance for the question with which we are here concerned. It is in fact not always easy to distinguish between a body of doctrine which all hold in common and the various theologies which interpret it. Indeed any absolutely clear-cut division between the common stock of dogma on the one hand and its more detailed theological interpretations on the other is quite impossible, since every theological statement of a given dogma necessarily and of its very nature involves a certain element of interpretation[15] without thereby being absolutely identical with it, yet at the same time without being able to be set apart from it by any absolute process of separation either. This situation gives rise to a danger of heresies in the Church. It is necessary constantly to reinterpret dogma afresh, though of course this does not mean to alter that essential content of its message which has a permanent validity. In order to be assimilated to the living faith of believers a dogma must again and again be brought into confrontation with the totality of the overall intellectual climate in which man lives today taken as a whole, and this is changing ever more swiftly. But precisely this necessity inevitably produces a wealth of varied interpretations of the dogma in the contemporary situation

---

[15] Cf. also K. Rahner, 'Theology and Anthropology', *Theological Investigations* IX (London and New York, 1972), pp. 28–45; *idem*, 'Philosophy and Philosophizing in Theology', *ibid*, pp. 46–63. On the historical development of the dogma itself cf. *Mysterium Salutis* I (Einsiedeln, 1965), pp. 727–782.

even in those cases in which what is aimed at is the *one* essential point which the dogma is intended to convey, and even in those cases in which these varied interpretations do not necessarily simply contradict one another, but merely exhibit a certain disparity and incommensurability among themselves.

Hence it can come about that even with the best intentions, the most whole-hearted willingness to be loyal to the faith, and genuine obedience towards the Church's *magisterium* the interpretations of official doctrine put forward in theology are either irreconcilable with that doctrine as a matter of objective fact, even though their irreconcilability has not been realized, or, even when they are in conformity with that doctrine and indeed may be necessary for any genuine understanding of the faith in the contemporary situation, they are still wrongly rejected by other believers or theologians as irreconcilable with the Church's doctrine. Thus over and above the differences of opinion between the various schools which have always existed, in the pluralism of theologies as it exists today doctrines are put forward within the Church which either really are heretical or are unjustly suspected of being so. In this situation it is not always easy to distinguish between these real heresies and those which are merely presumed to be so. The task of distinguishing between real and merely presumptive heresies in these new interpretations of the ancient and abiding doctrine of the Church may require long and toilsome efforts on the part of theologians, the official teachers of the Church, and in the developing awareness of the Church's faith. For this task there is need of patience, self-criticism on the part of individual theologians and of theology in general, and on the part of the Church's official teachers generosity and patience on the one hand and vigilance on the other.

What takes place at the level of specialist theology clearly also exists at the level of the less consciously and methodologically worked out theological development of the convictions of faith of those Christians who are to some extent instructed and religiously awake. At this level too real and also merely presumptive heresies are to be found as personal interpretations of the Christian faith. All, Christians and theologians alike, must be aware of the fact that it is necessary to achieve a lively understanding of the faith in the context of an ever-renewed confrontation with the climate of ideas in general, that the danger of mistaken interpretations of the official doctrine cannot be avoided merely by monotonously handing down the traditional formulae of faith, and that therefore, in a pluralism of theologies which cannot be overcome[16] (and, it may be

[16] On this cf. no. 6.

said in passing, is already present in holy scripture itself) real or merely presumed heresies may arise in the Church, that it takes time to distinguish between the two, and requires patience on the part of the official teachers as well as of theologians and believers, and that for this reason we should not be too hasty to throw suspicion upon either side with regard to an interpretation of this kind, accusing it either of being stupid and old-fashioned or alternatively as *avant-garde* and heretical. Again the official teaching of the Church is subject to a living process of historical development, and at a time when the history of human ideas is undergoing swift transformations it too must critically, boldly and confidently accept and endure these historical conditions to which it is subject.

3. This inevitable pluralism of theologies which exists today must not and need not surrender the unity of the Church's creed even at the verbal level.[17] In the theology of the Church and in the mind and heart of the individual believer there must be a pluralism in the interpretation of any given dogma. Otherwise it is quite inconceivable that there can be any lively understanding of the Church's message such as can become a force in human life. Indeed in a situation in which each individual retains his own radical individuality, even though there may be a genuine verbal intercommunication between men, it is quite impossible, even in respect of truth itself, to establish empirically with absolute certainty whether two individuals pronouncing and accepting in common the same proposition really think and mean the same by it.[18] But all this does not exclude the fact that there must be unity of creed within the Church and, moreover, that this can be established in sufficient measure. On any Catholic understanding of the faith this unity cannot consist merely in the unity of that reality which is ultimately signified but is beyond words, and to which the various theological statements refer. There must also be a unity in the verbal creed itself within the one Church. So as to ensure a sufficient possibility and certainty of achieving and establishing this it is necessary that we both believe and express in words the same truth even though in doing so it must be recognized that differences do incontestably exist in the concrete between individuals according to their own personal conditions in their individual interpretations of what they all assert in common.

In order to ensure that there shall be a unity of one and the same creed

---

[17] On this cf. also K. Rahner, 'The Need for a "Short Formula" of the Christian Faith', *Theological Investigations* IX (London and New York, 1972), pp. 117–126 and the study entitled 'Reflections on the Problems Involved in Devizing a Short Formula of the Faith', *Theological Investigations* XI (London, 1973), pp. 230–244.

[18] On this cf. K. Rahner, 'A Small Fragment on "The Collective Finding of Truth" ', *Theological Investigations* VI (London and Baltimore, 1969), pp. 82–88.

within the Church in a context of insuperable pluralism with regard to the understanding of the faith, and in order to uphold the verbal expression of the truth in its presentation at the social level, it is inevitable and legitimate to have a certain linguistic norm.[19] There are also unjustified deviations from such a linguistic norm as laid down by the Church which are illegitimate (even though they do not necessarily and in all cases *ipso facto* also have to deviate from what is signified in the Church's official formulation) at least in those cases in which the formulation that deviates from the linguistic usage of the official Church is presented not as a possible interpretation of this official statement of the Church, but rather itself, either explicitly or in practice, rejects this official formulation. Again a proposition which is merely presumed to be heresy though in fact it is not can in its turn have to be rejected on the grounds that it itself rejects the verbal formulation of the official Church and departs too far from it in its own formulation, so that in practice it is in danger of arousing in the hearers of such an interpretation opinions which really are heretical even though they were not intended as such by the original upholders of this interpretation. The Christian and the theologian must adopt a policy which has nothing to do with any cowardly or facile ecclesiastical conformism, namely to strive in a spirit of sincerity and self-criticism to ensure that a verbal formulation of the creed expressing the one faith of the Church is really preserved. And to this end they must ever anew bring their own interpretation of the faith (however justified or indeed necessary it may be in itself) into conformity with the one creed of the Church, and help to promote this one creed. Otherwise in the long run the danger of real heresies arising in the Church can no longer be excluded.

4. There is a possibility – indeed under certain circumstances a necessity and a duty – for the Church to reject a doctrine arising within her as heretical.[20] Such a statement is distasteful to modern man. He feels all too easily, although ultimately speaking unjustly, that any condemnation on the part of the Church's official teachers of a doctrine upheld by an individual Christian is an attack upon the freedom of conscience and opinion. Ultimately speaking there can be no question of this, although it must be conceded that a non-definitorial rejection of a theological opinion on the

[19] This requirement is emphatically laid down in 'Humani Generis' (DS 3881–3883). Cf. also on this *Mysterium Salutis* I (Einsiedeln, 1965), pp. 693–696.

[20] On this problem cf. the following further articles by the author: 'Membership of the Church according to the Teaching of Pius XII's Encyclical, "Mystici Corporis Christi" ', *Theological Investigations* II (London and Baltimore, 1963), pp. 1–88; 'Kirchengliedschaft', *LKT* VI (2nd ed., 1961), pp. 221–225.

part of the official teachers can be, and in fact often has been in the past, over-hasty, lacking in charity, or erroneous. When the Church rejects the doctrine of a theologian or the opinion of an individual Christian within her midst as heretical she is in no sense asserting that the case involved necessarily constitutes a subjectively culpable error. Nor does she deny the possibility that an individual may be unable to extricate himself from his error, which subjectively speaking is invincible and inculpable, even though it leads the individual concerned out of the Church. On the contrary the following principles apply:

a) In any definitorial rejection of a given doctrine put forward by one of her members the Church states that such a doctrine is absolutely irreconcilable with the Church's own convictions of faith, and on these grounds the conscience of the individual concerned with regard to truth is confronted with the alternative either of abandoning this view or, if such a measure is irreconcilable with the subjective conscience of the individual involved with regard to truth, of separating himself from the Church in an attitude of mutual respect because the Church is a free community constituted by the unity of her faith, and the individual involved is precisely in the position of no longer sharing in this faith as a whole. The sphere of freedom of conscience and opinion which the Church herself protects and recognizes is not simply coterminous with the sphere of that which can be believed and taught in the Church.

b) In any non-definitorial rejection of the doctrines or views of one of her members the Church states that having examined such doctrines or views to the best of her ability with the means at her disposal at the given point in time, and while retaining all respect for it and all charity towards its protagonist, she cannot see how this doctrine or view can be reconciled with her own faith. In such a case, in which a truly authoritative but non-definitorial rejection of a doctrine of this kind has been pronounced by the Church's *magisterium*, the individual who has been 'censured' in this way must examine his own conscience as to how, in the concrete case, he can reconcile his own subjective convictions with the respect and the obedience due to the authority and the competence of the official *magisterium* of the Church. In such cases, in which the Church has taken up an authoritative but not irrevocable position with regard to certain theological opinions (which incidentally can have an effect on practical life) various possibilities are conceivable according to the circumstances involved in each particular case, none of them necessarily provoking either an internal or still less an external breach with the Church. In this connection, and for a better understanding of what has been said, reference may be made to the

Doctrinal Letter of the German Bishops, in which, perhaps for the first time in an official ecclesiastical pronouncement, this point is treated of in a realistic and genuine manner. In this we find the following passage:

'On this point a difficult problem arises calling for realistic discussion, and one that in the case of many Catholics of today, and to a greater extent than formerly, threatens either their faith or their free and trustful attitude towards the Church's *magisterium*. We refer to the fact that errors can and do infiltrate into the *magisterium* in the exercise of its official functions. The fact that this sort of thing is possible is something of which the Church has always been aware and which she has actually stated in her theology, and she has developed rules of conduct to cater for such a situation. This possibility of error does not apply to those statements of doctrine which are proclaimed by a solemn definition of the Pope or the universal Council, or through the ordinary channels of official teaching as requiring to be received with the absolute assent of faith. It is also historically incorrect to maintain that an error of the Church has subsequently been brought to light in such doctrinal definitions. This is of course not to contest the fact that even in the case of a dogma, while its original meaning must be maintained, a development in the understanding of it is always possible and always necessary provided due safeguards are observed to avoid misinterpretations which may formerly have been current. Nor should the question which has been raised be confused with the manifest fact that side by side with the divine law, which is immutable, there is also a human law in the Church which is subject to change. Such change has from the outset nothing to do with error, but at most raises the question of the opportunism of the earlier or more recent juridical decision concerned.

'With regard to error or the possibility of error in non-definitorial statements of doctrine of the Church, which themselves in turn can vary greatly in their degree of binding force, it must be first recognized realistically and decisively that human life, even taken quite in general, must always be lived with the utmost conscientiousness according to those lights which on the one hand must be recognized at the speculative level as not absolutely certain, and yet at the same time which have to be respected 'here and now' because provisionally speaking they cannot be bettered as valid norms for thinking and acting. Every individual is aware of this from his own concrete life. Every doctor in his diagnosis, every statesman in his evaluation of political circumstances and the decision he bases upon them is aware of this fact. The Church too in her doctrine and practice cannot always and in every case allow herself to be faced with the dilemma of either imposing a doctrinal decision carrying ultimate binding force or simply being silent and leaving everything to the opinion of the individual to decide in any way he likes. To preserve the true and ultimate substance of the faith she must, even at the risk of error in some point of detail, put forward doctrinal directives which have a specific degree of binding force, and yet, since they do not constitute a definition of faith, carry with them a certain element of the provisional even amounting to the possibility of error. Otherwise she cannot proclaim or interpret her faith at all or apply it as a decisive reality of life to each new human situation as it arises. In a case of this sort the position of the individual Christian with regard to the Church is analogous to that of a man who recognizes that he is obliged to accept the opinion of a specialist even when he knows that this is not infallible.

'In no case can there be any place for an opinion opposed to the provisional doctrinal pronouncements of the Church in preaching or catechetics even when, under certain circumstances, the faithful have to be instructed concerning the nature and the limited range of any such provisional doctrinal decision. This is a point which has already been discussed. He who believes that he has to hold his own private opinion and that already here and now he is in possession of that better insight which the Church will arrive at in the future must ask himself in the sight of God and his own conscience, and in a spirit of realistic self-critical evaluation, whether he has the necessary breadth and depths of specialized theological knowledge to be in a position to deviate from the current teaching of the official Church in his private theory and practice. In principle it is possible to conceive of such a case. But subjective arrogance and over-hasty self-opinionatedness will have to answer to the judgement of God'.[21]

However clear it may be that all this has to be borne in mind by a present-day Catholic and, in appropriate circumstances, put into practice as well, the fact still remains that one harsh truth which is still more radical must not be obscured, namely that under certain circumstances the Church must recognize her duty and have the courage unequivocally to reject specific teachings if and to the extent that they are irreconcilable with the Church's own convictions of faith. And this is true today even of those teachings the champions of which do not simply leave the Church of their own initiative because of their opinions, but suppose that an opinion of this kind has a right to be at home in the Church and is reconcilable with

---

[21] Letter of the German Bishops, *loc cit.*, 12/13; cf. also B. Schüller, 'Bemerkungen zur authentischen Verkündigung des kirchlichen Lehramtes', *Theologie und Philosophie* 42 (1967), pp. 534–551.

the Church's doctrine as rightly understood, and indeed may be the only practicable interpretation of this doctrine at the present day. It is true that for very good reasons the Church has refrained from pronouncing anathemas of this kind at the Second Vatican Council. But this does not mean that the Church either must not or *cannot ever again* pronounce such an anathema in the future.

Certainly in a situation of pluralism in language and in the conceptual apparatus by means of which theological realities are expressed today it is often very difficult to bring different statements into confrontation with one another, to translate them, as it were, into another language and transpose them into another conceptual world, and so to come to a position where it can be recognized whether a given statement is in conformity with or in contradiction to the faith of the Church. It can also be the case – and this precise point is emphasized by the bishops in the same Doctrinal Letter – that the Church either fails to form any opinion at all or forms one only with great difficulty as to whether a specific conception as enunciated by its original learned authors is or is not reconcilable with the faith of the Church. But in this passage of their Doctrinal Letter the bishops explicitly emphasize that the Church has the right to intervene with her anathema once she establishes that in the majority of her adherents or among the faithful of the Church in their existing concrete situation and according to their present understanding a conception of this kind will be understood in such a way that at least in what is, perhaps, its over-primitive formulation of the relevant doctrine it is no longer reconcilable with the faith of the Church. The Church would betray her gospel and the *magisterium* of the Church would betray its task if from the outset they no longer had the courage under certain circumstances to pronounce an unequivocal 'no' to a doctrine which arose in the Church and attempted to achieve a legitimate footing there.

Very many theological questions – for instance with regard to what is meant by the Resurrection of Jesus Christ – may be open questions and remain obscure, and various answers to them may be found within the Church. But when someone disseminates a doctrine in the Church which, so far as the Church's conscious faith is concerned constitutes in practice a simple denial of the Resurrection of Christ, then the Church can and must respond with an actual definitorial anathema. Perhaps in certain circumstances it might still be possible to say that in such an anathema the relevant doctrine has been misunderstood. But in that case it would still always be the duty of the teachers of such a doctrine, if they wanted to put it forward in the Church, to formulate it, expound it, and remove all dangers from it in such a way that this misunderstanding on the part of the faithful in the Church and her official teachers would not arise. On any showing the unity of the creed of the universal Church takes precedence in value and importance in the Church and for her over the theology of an individual or of individual groups.

Even though in a specific case the Church may recognize the necessity for such an anthema, and may pronounce a condemnation of this kind, still it does not *ipso facto* follow that the condemnation will be successful in all respects. He who in a spirit of genuine faith assents to the Church and to her *magisterium* is indeed aware that the Church has pronounced right judgement (subject to the distinctions already touched upon in the Doctrinal Letter of the bishops). He is aware that teaching cannot be put forward in the Church or for her in the way that the condemned doctrine is put foward. But in a twofold respect the real success of such a condemnation is still not assured. For *in the first place* it can be the case, and that too for the reasons already mentioned when we were considering the causes of heresy in the Church, that those who incur condemnation in this way may perhaps indeed be silent or more subdued in the promulgation of their opinions, yet at the same time will be willing neither to depart from the Church nor to give up those opinions. Against this position the Church has only very limited possibilities at her command. *Secondly* it is possible that the real success of such a condemnation, namely the preservation of the faith from corruption or injury and the genuine and joyful willingness to believe on the part of the faithful are only achieved when the doctrines safeguarded by this condemnation are themselves thought out in a new and living way, and formulated in a way that can be assimilated and preached from an attitude of personal conviction. A mere condemnation taken by itself is still not enough to assure that all this shall be the case.

In certain circumstances the only way for effectively safeguarding an irreformable doctrine of the Church is – to express it paradoxically – to reform that doctrine in a forward direction. In other words while preserving that in its message which has an abiding validity, to express it in fresh terms which have a living relevance, and to set it in broader and more comprehensive contexts.[22] To put the point in what is perhaps a somewhat exaggerated form, we might perhaps imagine that in not a few cases an

[22] On the basic principles involved cf. *Mysterium Salutis* I (Einsiedeln, 1965), pp. 696–698, 756 ff., 771 f. Besides this we can see this demand fulfilled on a right understanding of the definition of the definition of 'Pastoral Aims' by the Council, cf. K. Rahner, 'On the Theological Problems Entailed in a "Pastoral Constitution" ', *Theological Investigations* X (London and New York, 1972, pp. 293–317.

anathema of this kind pronounced against individuals who do, after all, at least in principle intend to be Christians, is actually a sign of theological petrification and ossification on the part of the Church's *magisterium*. At the same time, however, even though in all realism this point may be conceded, it should not in its turn be regarded as amounting to an obligation imposed upon the Church such that she cannot reject any interpretation of the faith which she recognizes as clearly contradictory to her own faith by an unequivocal 'No', for she can do this even before she has achieved this positive task of arriving at a living and freshly acquired understanding of her faith.

5. A point which has to be borne in mind throughout the whole question which we are considering is the difference between pulpit and seat of learning, between the preaching of the faith and theological speculation.[23] Certainly close connections do exist between the preacher authorized by the Church and the theologian engaged with his problems. What the theologian is reflecting upon in his scientific study is in fact the conscious faith of the Church as it is present in and expressed in the Church's preaching and the Church's life under the direction of the official doctrinal and pastoral authorities. And conversely the preacher must be theologically educated. He must have studied before he preaches in order that he may preach the word of God in a way that does justice to his subject-matter and to the circumstances in which he preaches. At the same time, however, there is an essential difference between the pulpit and the seat of learning. The message which the preacher utters from the pulpit must be neither in contradiction to the teaching of the Church nor something that runs counter to his own personal sense of truth as a serious student of theology. At the same time, however, the pulpit is not the place in which abstruse points of theological controversy should be canvassed. The reason for this is not that Christians, and especially educated ones, must be shielded from the problems of theology, or that in the pulpit it is a 'simple faith' that should be put forward such as the learned theologian in his study or in his professorial chair feels himself superior to. The real reason why such problems should not be canvassed in the pulpit is that here it is the word of God as guiding and vivifying that must be preached, the word that is intended to touch our consciences and hearts and change our lives. For in the pulpit it is God's truth, albeit expressed in human words, that must be imparted, and not human problems concerning this word of God. Certainly it is very often difficult to maintain this distinction in the concrete

[23] On this point cf. the author's article 'Demythologization and the Sermon'> *Concilium* 3/4 (1968, Pastoral), pp. 12–20.

individual case. Nevertheless it is in principle valid. When the preacher fails to respect it in a spirit of self-effacement and submissiveness to the truth of God and the Church the pulpit is turned into the place where heresies arise in the Church. Problems are then raised which have not yet been coped with even by scientific theology, and it is quite inevitable that the believer who is not a theological specialist, and moreover, does not need to be so, misunderstands these problems in his turn, receives a crude and inaccurate impression of the attempts that are made to solve them, fails to recognize what may be a possible way of reconciling theological positions of this kind with the substance of the Church's faith, and then supposes that in order to be 'modern' he has to surrender the Church's own statement of faith rather than the interpretation of this statement which has been offered to him and misunderstood by him.

It would be false to suppose that today it is impossible to make any statement of the Christian faith from the pulpit without explicitly embarking upon theological problems of this kind. In certain circumstances the preacher must be aware that such problems exist. He must pay due heed to them in his preaching, but in interpreting the text of holy scripture he must concentrate on a central content of faith, and for this he does not need to enter into exegetical problems in the passages concerned which are ultimately unimportant. Certainly however by keeping his eyes fixed on the essence of the Church's faith in a spirit of modesty and responsibility he will be able to express the faith as found in the gospel and the Church without thereby being false to his own conscience as a serious student of speculative theology, and without preaching in such a way that his message is no longer 'brought home' to his hearers because it sounds old-fashioned, stereotyped, and cliché-ridden. To reiterate: when we fail to observe the difference between the pulpit and the chair of learning the pulpit becomes the place at which heresies arise in the minds of the hearers, often against the will of the preacher. A situation may arise, however, in which an educated Christian who is not a professional theologian nevertheless wishes to be instructed as to the current theological problems and in which he has very solid grounds, over and above a general and praiseworthy spirit of enquiry, for wishing this. In such a case there are sufficient opportunities elsewhere for him to receive such instruction: in lectures, in conferences arranged by the Catholic academies, on the radio, in books and so forth.

In any case, however, the preacher must avoid giving any 'scandal' to believers from the pulpit such as can be provoked from both sides. The preacher can preach in such a way that he fails to do justice to the demands of a hearer who may under certain circumstances be theologically very well educated. He may maintain propositions which he has no right whatever to impose upon his hearer as binding in faith. But the preacher can, however, take the opposite line by presenting a so-called modern theology which is either objectively irreconcilable with the Christian faith or at least is such that the hearer fails to understand how it can be reconciled with that which a Christian must on any showing believe and hold firm to, so that in this way he takes scandal. Even today there still exists a middle course between these two possibilities of scandal. This does not mean that the preacher has to take into account any and every conceivable difficulty which may arise, or that every sort of 'pious' prejudice entertained by a narrow-minded man has to be sanctioned from the pulpit. Under certain circumstances theological findings also emerge which are sound and, subject to the guidance of the Church's *magisterium*, genuinely received in Catholic theology. And it is in the interests of a genuine and free faith on the part of this same modern man than these should be stated simply, even though here and there there may be some old-fashioned listeners who will take scandal at them.

III

Paul himself already recognized that divisions, 'heresies' as he puts it arise again and again in the Church. And it is even less surprising that divisions of this kind should exist today at a time of immense spiritual upheaval. Today more than ever before the ancient faith is confronted by fresh questions, so that it is not surprising to find that not infrequently even genuine questions meet with poor answers since the process by which a good answer is arrived at to such questions is inevitably only a slow one. Nevertheless even today the situation is not such that a sincere Christian with a ready will to listen to the word of God in the mouth of the Church no longer knows what he may and should believe, or that the word of the Church has become ambiguous or obscure. Certainly it is true that faith always involves a self-commitment to the incomprehensibility of God, and so to a truth which is and remains a mystery. But if we say: 'We believe in God, in his forgiving compassion and his love; we believe in Jesus Christ our Lord, the crucified and risen one; we believe in the grace of God and in eternal life, in the community of those who believe in Jesus Christ as their Lord and Redeemer and are united among themselves in hope and love', then while it is certainly true that such statements still always remain mysterious and again and again provoke fresh theological speculations as to how they should be understood, still it is nevertheless true at the same time that in such statements we know what we intend to say, and we know that that truth which is mysteriously pointed to in such statements constitutes our life and our assurance in death.

Certainly our faith is not simply identical with a fixed sum of statements which have been formulated once and for all. Our faith, suffused as it is by the grace of God, ultimately speaking bears not precisely on the statements but on the reality of God himself who through Jesus Christ and in his grace has drawn near to us in forgiveness and divine self-bestowal. Hence our faith is constantly to be conceived of as the faith of men who are still on their way, making pilgrimage towards eternal life. It is a faith that is open to the future. And whatever propositions it may be formulated in it is committed ever anew to the living mystery of God himself. It endures its own imperfections and the contradiction which it experiences, but even as such it is also a faith of the holy fellowship of the Church borne up by the assistance of her Spirit in a single creed. Yet for this very reason it should also have the humility and the courage to say 'No' to heresies which contradict it. In such a 'no' it does not condemn men, but neither does it allow itself to be drawn away by human opinions from committing itself to the truth of God which it has received from God through Jesus Christ and in his Church.

8

CONCERNING OUR ASSENT
TO THE CHURCH AS SHE EXISTS
IN THE CONCRETE

IF I am to discuss the nature of the assent to the Church as she exists in the concrete two preliminary observations must first be made in order to understand what this theme involves and to define the area within which it falls. The assent of which I am speaking is an assent to the Church in the *concrete*. This means that what is being treated of is not, or at any rate not primarily, the Church as she is envisaged in a presentation of fundamental theology or in a dogmatic treatise on ecclesiology. In other words it is not so much the Church in her abstract theological nature, but rather the Church in the concrete, with those special characteristics which derive from the historical conditions of the present age, the Church as we find her in the contemporary situation in which she stands – in brief the concrete Church in that form which has been conditioned by the age in which we live and in which she represents at once a challenge and a burden to us.

The precisions and restrictions which we are thus imposing upon the subject-matter are not invalidated by the fact that here once more, and in the context with which we are concerned, we cannot speak of this Church in the concrete otherwise than at a very general and abstract level. In spite of this the fact still remains that it will be the Church in the concrete that we shall be referring to, the Church as we experience or even suffer her in our everyday human and religious lives. Now in speaking of the Church in this way we are speaking of Catholics, and not to those others, whether Christians or non-Christians, who do not belong to this Church and are, for that reason, quite incapable of experiencing her so immediately as we Catholics do as a burden and a challenge. We are speaking, therefore, to Catholics who are Catholics not merely as defined by the sort of rules which a state official might devize in determining a specific social group, but who will to be Catholics on the basis of a commitment of faith even though this is something which they may have to achieve again and again and only at the cost of toil and pain. It has been necessary to introduce what we have to say with these brief preliminary remarks in order that the nature of our theme should be understood and that its limits should be defined.

I

If we are honest and recognize not merely that we should be honest but also that we have to be Christians, since otherwise we cannot truly be believers at all, then we must say that to us of today the assent of faith, hope, and charity to this Church as she exists in the concrete does not come easily. At this present moment it makes no difference whether there was some other time at which this was not the case, or whether in every age the Church has always been something more than merely the sustainer of faith and the sphere within which our Christian lives are lived, namely, albeit in ways which constantly vary according to the historical circumstances, a harsh burden and a challenge that threatens our faith as well. In any case this is the situation today, and that too for many reasons which derive – at least for the most part – precisely from the situation in which willy nilly we have to live today in terms of the development of ideas, of civilization, and of society. Some brief indication, albeit a very general and abstract one, must be given of what these reasons are.

Before we can arrive at a position to evaluate causes of this kind we must consider that a Catholic Christian feels himself confronted by his Church in her doctrine and in her life as an entity that imposes demands and exacts duties from him. Of course within this Church there are wide areas, both in her theology and in her living practice, in which the individual Catholic is left free to decide for himself, so that in these areas no absolute obligations are imposed even upon one who wills to be a Catholic Christian. His personal methods of prayer, how often (within an area defined by a minimal demand) he takes part in Church activities, attends divine service, or receives the sacraments, whether, for instance, he does or does not gain indulgences, what personal opinion he holds with regard to the traditional theology of the Church while respecting her essential dogmas – all this and much else besides is left to his own free decision even though this still does not imply that he can be arbitrary or capricious in arriving at it. But this does nothing to alter the fact that to the Catholic the Church as she exists in the concrete is an entity that makes demands upon him and exacts obligations from him. So far as the individual Catholic is concerned this Church is not the sort of authority which he can accept or reject as he likes in any given case, so far as her effective reality and the decisions she takes are concerned, provided only that he maintains his ultimate commitment of faith to her. This Church has a body of dogmatic teaching which is enduring and binding. She has a specific concrete life within which the individual Catholic must lead his own personal religious life and work out his salvation. She is made up of concrete individuals, and the qualities which these possess in the concrete, and the historical conditions to which they are subject, inevitably have their effect even in the most supreme exercises of authority and the decisions of this Church, which are authoritative and binding upon the individual Catholic.

Once we have recognized that the relationship between the Church and the individual Catholic is of this kind, then it becomes easy to see what those factors are in contemporary life which makes his assent to the Church as she exists in the concrete so difficult and which represent a danger to it. It is because he cannot simply adopt an attitude of critical detachment to her, or reject these concrete factors in the Church from his own personal life precisely at that point at which the teaching and way of life proper to this Church become difficult for him to understand. Today the individual lives amid a vast multiplicity of opinions, ways of life, social groupings with the most varied characteristics and tendencies. In the milieu in which his life is passed there is virtually nothing which can simply be taken for granted and would be disputed by no-one, nothing which can find a sufficient justification simply in our personal life alone without itself in turn having further to be justified by our own personal decision. In such a situation, from which we cannot escape, even the faith which the Church herself teaches us, and even the essential nucleus of that faith as presented to us as absolutely binding dogma, can no longer appear to us simply as something that is unassailable and to be accepted without question. This is all the more true in view of two other factors bearing upon the Church's own awareness of her faith. First in the course of almost two thousand years of history this has undergone enormous developments and an immense multiplicity of further distinctions. Second it is in practice still to a large extent formulated in terms of concepts and viewpoints which are not in any simple or obvious sense those of our own age.

Hence it is quite inevitable that much even of that which is most proper to the essence of the Church's message of faith shall strike us as strange, so that it is only with difficulty that we can bring it into a reasonably harmonious synthesis with what we experience elsewhere and with the findings of the contemporary sciences which we accept and regard as established. In this present-day situation it is quite impossible wholly to avoid a position (even though there is very much that could and should be avoided) in which the Church's teaching of the faith strikes us at first sight and at a first trial of it as in some sense impracticable, old-fashioned and, so far as the concrete life which we have to lead is concerned, irrelevant.

The extremely complex distinctions in the Church's doctrine, then, combined with our failure to synthesize this doctrine in any adequate way with the rest of our attitude to life is one of the factors which make our assent to the Church as she exists in the concrete difficult. An additional point of difficulty arises from the aspect of the individuals belonging to the Church and especially those who hold official positions of authority in her. If we are Catholics we have to live in a society with which, however possible and justified it may be to maintain certain reserves, we must after all ultimately identify ourselves, a society made up of individuals and official authorities which all too often appear pitiful, narrow-minded, old-fashioned and out of date. Humanly speaking they often strike us as under-developed, restricted in outlook and pettifogging, and yet they confront us with demands and requirements which on the one hand are put forward in the name of the enduring gospel and the enduring nature of the Church herself, and yet on the other hand are all too clearly stamped with the personality precisely of these individuals, and of the historical and human modalities to which they are subject. All too often they may receive the impression that the Church has been too old-fashioned to overcome the burden of her own past, that she preaches her message in a way in which it is simply no longer possible for us to put it into practice, that what she regards as important is in fact secondary and insignificant, and that at the same time she is overlooking points which are of decisive importance for our present age. Alternatively it may seem to us that she is merely paying a hasty lip-service, which she herself does not take altogether seriously, to these points of decisive importance, and that even after the Second Vatican Council, and in spite of all the concessions which have been wrung from her in the way of *aggiornamento*, she still prefers anxiously to build upon the past which she feels to be true and trusted, rather than upon a creative future which is still unsure; that she is truer to the letter than to her own Spirit. This portrayal of the factors which make our assent to the Church as she exists in the concrete so burdensome, and which represent a danger to it, is only a very pale and abstract one. But we have sought to point to precisely those factors which should recall to our minds what we ourselves experience every day in our concrete lives as Catholics.

II

We must now ask ourselves how it is that the Catholic Christian, despite all those factors in his experience of the Church which he finds burdensome and oppressive, nevertheless finds it possible to give a whole-hearted and honest assent to this Church as she exists in the concrete. Before entering upon this question, however, we must begin by pointing out the following factors: viewed from a purely formal standpoint these same oppressive difficulties are also to be found in other departments of human life even apart from the Church. In all departments a tension arises between freedom and society which can never be so completely solved at the theoretical level that all the difficulties arising from this tension are eliminated from the outset. Everywhere in the world, and in all the group-ings that exist within society, the degree of social organization *and* the desire and will for freedom are both increasing at the same time. We all recognize that today and in the future it will be impossible for the indivi-dual taken in isolation to live outside the kind of society which is some-thing more than a mere pre-existing entity which is taken for granted, which raises no problems and therefore is never felt to represent a burden to him at all. Today and in the future, rather, the kind of society in which the individual will be forced to live is itself highly planned, institutional-ized and controlled. It is a society which imposes demands and certain inevitable compulsions upon the individual. On the other hand we also recognize that we are becoming more individualistic and more critical in our attitude towards society, its institutions, its patterns of behaviour and taboos, and its frozen ideologies. Indeed our reaction to all this is one of protest. Now the question of how these two factors can be reconciled on the one hand with the greater degree of social organization and on the other the greater degree of individualization is a problem which exists every-where in the world today, and not merely in the Church, a problem for which there is no patent solution such as can eliminate all the conflicts which arise in the concrete from the outset, a problem in which we cannot short-sightedly opt for either the one or the other of the two alternatives, even though we do not find, and in the concrete may be destined never to find, any completely satisfactory synthesis between them anywhere in the world. Thus we place the question with which we are concerned within this broader perspective. While it still does not lose the difficulties with which it is burdened, still in the light of this we are reminded of the need for that patience, prudence, and courage without which we cannot endure all these tensions in the living of our lives either at the secular or the Christian levels.

I believe that in seeking the *point of departure* for a hopeful and committed assent to the Church in the concrete we can to some extent show where this lies in three ways or from three distinct aspects:

a) Human living in the concrete is not artificially developed by a process of speculation as though in a test-tube. Certainly the power to speculate is a part of human nature, the capacity to experience the question of human existence, to adopt a critical standpoint towards, and to enquire into, that state in which all unquestioned we have been placed. Certainly there is nothing in this existence such that it either should or even may seem to be excluded from the outset from this process of critical speculation. But after all this is only one side of human existence.

We never wholly include ourselves in our critical speculation. In it we take as our starting-point again and again presuppositions which we have not subjected to our critical questioning in their own right or in the same way. Constantly we find ourselves already embarked upon a course the starting-point of which already lies behind us. In our critical evaluations we proceed from certain standards and intellectual perspectives, and even though we certainly could subject these in turn to our process of critical questioning, *de facto* we have failed to apply this process in their case. We never really begin from zero. Indeed we are incapable of doing this because otherwise we would be standing outside our own course of history and the historical mode which is proper to us, and this is impossible for us. Even the most radical revolutionary in his quest for an ideological critique which is unconditioned, cannot achieve this without in turn, whether he is aware of it or not, beginning from some point which he himself has not determined and upon which he has not reflected in any adequate sense.

The will to achieve a critical standpoint which is absolute, which in its concrete exercise has refused to commit itself by an act of trust to any prior assumptions, would lead only to a state of absolute immobility, to total sterility, to a radical neurosis of existence such as would incapacitate its practitioners for living. It is a fact that nothing comes from nothing. Where there is real and genuine life at the intellectual level, such as is capable of surviving and taking responsibility, there will also be an attitude of trustful and willing commitment in which that which is inevitable is accepted and accorded its due force. And for this reason anyone engaged in genuine living freely accepts, by an ultimate act of trust in life itself, the impossibility of totally comprehending life in his own speculative processes and in the process of critical enquiry precisely into this life. And this remains true even though it does not mean that any one specific factor should from the outset be excluded from this process of critical speculation. Man as a being endowed with critical faculties calls all things in question, and man as finite, and as a being who exists in a specific pre-existing situation which he himself has not created is himself in turn critical with regard to his own critical faculties, and for all these critical attitudes of his, in an absolutely ultimate sense he proceeds in his life from an unreserved act of trust in the fact that however true it may be that any individual factor can be destroyed, that which is prior and given would ultimately speaking and taken as a whole stand up to his critique even at those points at which that critique can no longer in practice be applied to it in any adequate sense. We are speaking of a certain unity between an attitude of radical criticism at the fundamental level on the one hand, and a spirit of unreserved trust in that which is untested by criticism on the other. Now this is not something which man could control for himself in his practical life (different in this from theory which remains at the merely formal level). It is not something which he himself in his turn could master or bring within his control by achieving a standpoint of trans-cendence at some high level from which he could subject it to a concrete critique. Rather it is something which is bestowed upon him as that in-comprehensible reality of his life which is called grace, though admittedly this must also be accepted and can be refused. The actual situation is this: the concrete human life which a man lives is not created in the test-tube of speculation. It is not first dissected by his critique down to the point of an absolute void, so that subsequently it can be artificially built up by specula-tion, criticism and theory.

Now so far as the Catholic is concerned one of the factors in his concrete human life is his membership of the Church and his life in and with her. For him this state of belonging to the Church is not some kind of minor incidental factor in his life which can even disappear without his life as a whole being thereby altered, as though it were like a man buying a new suit or going to live in another district. This assent to the Church as she exists in the concrete has already permeated our entire life. We have prayed, supplicated for the eternity of God in his holiness. We have heard the words of eternal life from the mouth of the Church, experienced the grace which she has imparted to us through her sacraments. Again and again we have been roused by her from the inertia and apathy of our everyday lives. Through her we have experienced the eternal in ourselves. Already in our lives we have lived, and in this sense uttered, an assent in the concrete to the Church in the concrete. This assent has truly been made at the very centre of our personal human existence. Hence we also have the right and duty, precisely on the basis of intellectual honesty, freely and unreservedly to commit ourselves to this assent, to let it stand even though in doing so we are constantly aware of the fact that we have still not mastered all the reasons for this assent which have unconsciously asserted themselves in us or all the implications which it carries by our speculative processes; even though we are aware that this assent can be confronted again and again with fresh critical questionings, and that the relationship between the free and trustful prior decision governing our lives on the one hand and the process of critical speculation on the other is constantly shifting and constantly bringing us fresh surprises. Certainly even our relationship with the Church is something that we subject again and again to critical questioning. But we have the right and the duty, until the contrary is proved beyond all doubt (and this is something which we do not fear) to assume and to live by the fact that these critical questionings do not destroy this relationship of ours with the Church, just as in other ultimate commitments and attitudes of our lives, commitments to loyalty, love, integrity without thought of reward or trust, or commitments to our neighbour, again and again through life itself and through the processes of our critical speculations we experience the fact that these commitments are under assault and yet, so long as we do not fall into a neurosis of criticism and doubt, we are aware that these basic commitments endure throughout all the purgatory of doubt and questioning.

We have already said at the outset of these remarks that we are addressing ourselves to Catholics. Now these have experienced the fact that their assent to the Church is not some kind of incidental option which they have taken in their lives, but in a true sense is to be numbered among the basic attitudes which sustain those lives. But if this is true then they have the right to commit themselves to this assent in a spirit of trust, to nourish ever fresh hopes that the inner spiritual continuity of their lives will endure throughout all the manifest and painful vicissitudes in the unfolding process of their lives as spiritual beings, whether these be great or small. We cannot allow ourselves to be manoeuvred into that kind of questioning which is destructive of our lives, and we would be doing this if we were suddenly to notice at some point that after all the ultimate grounds on which our assent to the Church was based had given way as a basic reality of our personal lives and that our existence had become a bottomless abyss into which we had been cast. This is a situation in which we do not stand, and we must not allow ourselves to fall into it. And hence it is

meaningless when faced with the possibility (absolutely speaking conceivable) of a kind of doubt which of itself does not admit of any further
answer already in the here and now to react to this with a universal doubt
of the kind that negates our assent to the Church. Otherwise we would be
in the position of men who for fear of death already did themselves to
death in the here and now. We must recognize the fact, therefore, that
human life in the concrete cannot be constructed by any absolute process
of reflection. And for this reason it must not feel itself to be called in
question at the ultimate level by these particular critical questionings
which may arise on individual points even if there are such. Now the
perception of this fact is the first aspect of the point of departure at which
we must take our stand again and again in critically re-appraising our
assent to the Church in the concrete in the manner that is legitimate and
prescribed. The true process of critical re-appraisal is itself in turn subjected to its own critique, and with regard to our experience of the
realities of life *in globo*, which, even though we do not subject it to speculative analysis is nonetheless genuine and sustaining, this genuine process
of critical re-appraisal trustfully allows this global experience the chance
to endure and again and again to prove itself genuine.

b) This brings us to a second aspect of the point of departure for
arriving at a correct answer to our basic question. Global decisions of life,
which affect the totality of our human lives and which are therefore incapable of ever being totally subsumed under our critical speculations,
should endure throughout those unresolved tensions which arise between
the decisions themselves and our critical reflections upon them. Newman
pointed out long ago that a thousand difficulties of faith such as we obviously experience still do not constitute a doubt of faith such as constitutes
a negation of our commitment to faith. In view of the finitude of their
intellectual resources in the concrete, the finitude of their knowledge and
the brevity of their lifespan, neither the average Christian nor yet the
learned theologian are in any position to solve for themselves in any
positive and clear way all the difficulties which can be raised against the
convictions of faith in critical questions. We are confronted with the
immense complexity of our existence, with an immense pluralism among
the philosophies of life and the problems and findings of the sciences, such
as cannot be mastered by any one individual. We are confronted with the
multiplicity of our personal experiences of life, which can never wholly be
reduced to a synthesis at the level of theory. And in view of all this it is
obvious from the outset that our ultimate commitment of faith is always
surrounded by an incalculable range of questions which we have not yet

positively solved, mastered, or reduced to a positive synthesis within this commitment of faith in any effective sense.

But we must and can in all calmness achieve the perception that this is also something which is not for one moment to be expected, because it is impossible that this tension between question and answer can be solved in any direct and definitive manner. On the contrary it has constantly to be endured in a spirit of confidence and patience in our lives until one day the eternal light illumines us. Even the Catholic Christian can say: 'When an individual genuinely and inculpably comes to grief as a result of this tension, when he is genuinely *incapable* of enduring it any longer, he is guiltless and hence even in these circumstances he has not lost the true substance of his faith at all'. But in a spirit of self-criticism we must guard against the danger which arises in the concrete circumstances of our lives of supposing that we have arrived at a state in which we 'cannot do any more', when in reality the point that we have arrived at is one in which an 'acquittal from guilt' of this kind is merely serving to cover up an ultimate cowardice of life which is no longer *willing* to endure these unreserved tensions. In other departments of life too the situation that arises is in fact this: We have enough harsh and disappointing experiences of ourselves and our fellow men to have seemingly good grounds for adopting an attitude of doubting scepticism towards humanity. Now we can never solve such grounds as these by any process of theoretical reasoning in such a way that they no longer represent a threat to our ultimate and basic attitude towards humanity, no longer bring it ever anew into mortal peril, that basic attitude which consists in trust, reverence, and love. And yet at the same time we are aware that we must maintain this affirmative and loving attitude towards humanity right to the end. In the same way many temptations, questionings, problems and objections obviously arise on the personal, historical, and theoretical planes against our assent to the Church, her truth and institutions, objections which it is not given to us to work out in any positive and direct way until we have arrived at a complete solution to them. But the attitude of trustfully enduring unresolved tensions even in our relationship with the Church is only one instance of a reality which is actually a factor inherent in our lives. We cannot overcome such tensions by running away from them.

c) This leads us on immediately to the third aspect of the right point of departure for finding the answer to our basic question. It is only in the act of striving for that which is greater, more enlightening, a greater force for life, that man has the right to relinquish something that belongs to his life, to surrender it. And it is only for the sake of a greater meaningfulness that he has the right to abandon that which has hitherto been meaningful to him as meaningless. Perhaps this statement will not enlighten a sceptic who has allowed mistrust, and that doubt which calls everything in question, to penetrate into the innermost centre of his life. But nevertheless this statement is true, and without it life cannot endure. Indeed the radical sceptic recognizes the truth of this statement even though in doing so he contradicts his own position when he achieves the courage to embrace a scepticism which on his view is devoid of illusions as the highest meaning of his existence. And most average men are quite unaware when they adopt a sceptical attitude of this kind, of how much in the way of meaningfulness, in the way of that which is unquestioningly taken for granted and made the basis of their lives, they are still constantly allowing to remain. But he who, as a Catholic Christian, takes this statement as the standard by which to evaluate the question of his assent to the Church in the concrete can in all intellectual honesty justify this assent of his ever afresh despite all difficulties and temptations. For he can see what it will mean to depart from the truth of the Church, from her essential message, from the living and protecting mystery which we call God, from the hope of eternal life, from a hopeful sharing in the death of Jesus who, in a spirit of hope and love, allowed himself to fall into this mystery of God, from the fellowship of love called the Church, from the acceptance of forgiveness for the guilt of our lives, in brief from all that which the Church signifies. To depart from all this would not bring the individual concerned into a greater sphere of meaningfulness, of light, of freedom or of hope. Instead such a departure could only lead to one of two consequences: either an attitude of surrendering oneself to a lethal darkness of scepticism and of unworthy relativism or to the dubious attempt to live in isolation by the impoverished remnants of meaningfulness, light and courage which still remained, without really being able to see why these remnants deserve more assent or trust than that fulness of meaningfulness which is present and living in the Church.

III

Taking this as his point of departure the Catholic can raise the question ever afresh of what the Church means for him, seeing that in spite of all temptations which persist he can give a bold assent of faith to her. Clearly she presents too complex a picture for him to comprehend in its entirety. How could it be otherwise seeing that she is intended to be the historical and social embodiment of the truth and grace of God in man's personal life and in society and history, the sacrament of salvation for the whole of man and for humanity. But if in virtue of this she necessarily constitutes the most complex, the most manifold, and the most variegated entity, extending into all levels of man's existence and of society, then, from this point of view, it must be the most difficult task of all for the individual man to come to terms with her.

a) But let us take the three aspects we have mentioned, and which belong to that point of departure which any man must take in arriving at an ultimate commitment of his life, and consider her under these aspects. It may be obvious to the individual, or gradually become so, that when confronted with the ultimate realities of life, he cannot select or discard any one he likes, that there are realities in life which he will either achieve or lose as a whole, and towards these we can only adopt a critical attitude in that we commit ourselves to them immediately without reservation. Now if we recognize all this then, in spite of all, the Church, who of her very nature is too much for our comprehension, can nevertheless once more become a simple and self-evident fact for us. We who have already had a positive experience of this Church are familiar with not a few aspects and realities in her, of which we are aware that we cannot give them up, that they are in the heart and centre of our lives, even though much else in her, her doctrine, her official authorities, her institutions, her way of acting in the concrete in our own time, may seem strange, alienating and difficult to endure. Our relationship with her is similar to our relationship to a specific individual to whom we entrust ourselves and whom we love. Much in him may continue to be alien and incomprehensible to us. But nevertheless we have found a way of access to him. We have experienced what he is, and this justifies us and obliges us to accept and love him as a whole, to entrust ourselves to him as he is even in those factors in his nature which are alien and incomprehensible to us. And we know that we only have him and live with him when we do accept him and entrust ourselves to him in this way even in respect of those aspects of him which we do not understand.

So too it is in our relationship with the Church. We have never wholly understood her, and certainly in specific points we have fully justified objections to raise against much that exists within her in the concrete. We can have such objections and must have them, though admittedly they are objections which have to be endured in the Church and as an intrinsic factor in our membership of her, and not from an attitude of withdrawal or detachment from her such as would lead us to relinquish our grasp upon her as a whole. We have had sufficient experience of her to give us the right to accept her as a whole in a spirit of hope, love, and intellectual honesty. In her we have achieved the experience of God, of prayer and of hope in an absolute future. In her we have encountered Christ the crucified one who gives us the ultimate trust to accept our own death and all the futilities in our lives as a means of entering upon eternal life. The Church has given us the scripture as her own book which, after all, we can read as the word of God only within the sphere of her own faith. And this is the only way in which we can approach the scriptures unless we are merely seeking to come face to face with ourselves and the unanswered questions which we represent once more within their pages.

A man cannot do away with his parents once he is born. The very fact that we are and that we continue to exist assures us of the fact that they continue ceaselessly to be our parents. Hence we cannot be Christians with these ultimate Christian experiences by quitting the Church which has been, and remains, once and for all the mother of this Christian existence of ours. Otherwise all that we have, ultimately speaking, is an abstract God and an abstract Christ who continues to exist merely as the projection of our own subjectivity, a projection which is merely resolved into this subjectivity once more, and hence fails to escape from it. By way of analogy we may take our relationship to another man whom we have unreservedly accepted. In such a case even though there are elements in him which remain alien, so that we are constantly on the way to over-coming this alienation, nevertheless from the first we have accepted these alien elements in a spirit of trust, because we have already experienced in him that which we have at once understood and recognized as meaningful for us. It is the same with our relationship with the Church. The positive experience of this Church which sustains our life gives us the promise and the hope that that in her which is still alien and incomprehensible as well can be meaningful for us and can gradually, albeit always in an asymptotic process, be assimilated by us. Admittedly this can take place only if we constantly proceed from that threefold starting-point of which we have spoken, and which is legitimate, because even in other contexts it is prescribed and imposed upon us beforehand by life itself.

b) In this connection, and in order to understand the nature of our assent to the Church in the concrete, we must now enter in somewhat greater detail into a more specific question which bears upon our relationship with the Church as the accredited messenger of God's revelation, and as such endowed with authority to teach. For the Catholics who believe in her the Church has an authority to teach. This statement cannot be denied by the

Catholic, however true it may be that the forms and ways in which this teaching authority finds expression are also constantly subject to the laws of history and change, and influenced by the need to orientate the message to the particular climate of ideas prevailing at any given time. There is no doubt that precisely in respect of the binding doctrinal authority of this Church contemporary Catholics find that their assent to the Church in the concrete again and again entails a heavy burden.

There is much in relation to this question which we cannot enter into at this point. In particular we cannot treat of the question of how the immutability of a defined dogma can be reconciled with the necessity for re-interpreting this dogma ever afresh in the light of the climate of ideas prevailing at any given time. Nor can we describe the very different degrees of binding force which are to be ascribed to this authority which the Church possesses according to whether in any given case it is a dogma in the true sense that is being treated of or merely an officially promulgated doctrine which, though authentic indeed, is nevertheless in principle capable of reform. There is a further question into which we cannot enter, and which though difficult is, after all, an obvious one in view of the difference which cannot be overcome between knowledge as initially acquired and theoretical reflection upon that knowledge. This further question then is that which concerns the boundary line (which is always somewhat imprecise at the level of conscious awareness) between dogma in the true sense and other kinds of teaching put forward by the Church or by theology. Again we do not intend explicitly to discuss the question of what, in the particular concrete case, the relationship should be between the individual Catholic's personal conscience with regard to truth (something which must never be passed over) and the teaching authority which in principle is assented to by Catholics. For the decision taken by this teaching authority may vary greatly in degree in a specific instance and again the degree of binding force to be attached to such a decision may vary greatly. But my purpose here rather is simply to formulate and explain a single specific statement which can throw light upon this assent of ours to the Church as she exists in the concrete in this respect, and justify it for us in all intellectual honesty while safeguarding our conscience with regard to truth. The statement I am referring to may be expressed as follows: Truth, and that truth precisely in its specific force as illuminating and sustaining human existence as a whole has something to do with institution. It is not possible at this point to reveal the full and exact significance of this statement in existential and ontological terms, or to show its precise application and justification. In order to make it intelligible

we shall confine ourselves merely to a few simple observations.
I am not infrequently surprised at how individuals in my own milieu
give voice to their personal opinions with the utmost emotion, as though
they were absolutely obvious. They call these their convictions and proclaim them as manifestly correct even in those cases in which they are
either really (or often presumably) in contradiction to some doctrinal
declaration on the part of the Church. It is indeed obvious that an opinion
of this sort which is binding upon the individual concerned in his conscience with regard to truth can be inculpable even when such an opinion
or conviction involves a rejection of some dogma (though admittedly in
that case, according to Catholic convictions, it is objectively erroneous).
It is inculpable even though it may be that an individual of this kind, who
is led by his own conscience with regard to truth to a position in which he
firmly believes that he has to reject a dogma of the Church, can no longer
be called a Catholic in a theological sense. It is also obvious that any
proposition which contradicts a doctrine of the Church which though
authentic has not been defined and is therefore in principle reformable can
objectively speaking even have a chance of being materially correct. But
even while conceding and explicitly stating all this I am still amazed at the
degree of naïve self-opinionatedness and emotional aggressiveness against
the Church's official teachers that not a few Catholics are accustomed
emphatically to evince in contradicting the teaching of the Church
whether defined or not.

The present age is characterized by a pluralism of ideas, of experiences
of life, of systems and theories, questions and problems, together with the
constant temptation to relativism and scepticism which these entail. It is
true that underlying this tendency towards relativism and scepticism there
is a good and necessary attitude of openness to a truth which is broader
and richer than that which we already explicitly possess. Nevertheless the
attitude itself should really be directed against our own persons, and
should cause us to question our own opinions in a spirit of self-criticism.
Even in the purely human sphere in general it is dangerous and oddly
naïve to regard one's fellows more or less from the outset as less intelli-
gent or having less good with than oneself. Now this is far truer of our
relationship to the teaching Church.

We of today, with that strange 'later individualism' of ours in thought
and opinion which is, at bottom, no longer modern at all, stand in danger
of being dominated by our emotions and trapped in our own subjectivity
by over-valuing our personal opinion, our theological knowledge, and
our capacity for theological thought in terms of analysis and synthesis

alike, when our opinion comes into conflict with some doctrine which is
proposed to us from the Church and by her official teachers, which at
first sight strikes us as alien. It is manifestly true that our personal subjectivity and our own moral and inalienable responsibility for the truth
is something which we can never neglect. We must attempt subjectively
to appropriate the truth of the Church and to make it our own in a process
which is never completed. And we have not achieved the true obedience
of faith so long as we merely repeat theological formulae, or simply
leave them unexplored in a spirit of total indifference. But nevertheless it
is the part of every true man to allow the truth to be borne in upon him,
that truth which on his first encounter with it – and this after all is something seriously to be taken into account – strikes him as alien, difficult to
understand, startling and forcing him out of his former finite subjectivity.
Where there is no readiness to do this this man remains trapped in the
capriciousness of his own subjectivity. He experiences himself only within
the limitations of his own individual human nature and his personal experience. He is incapable of transcending this subjectivity and taking into
himself that which is really new. Of course this applies primarily to those
cases in which what is in question is not the particular findings of the
so-called exact sciences, evidence for which can be acquired by experi-
ments which can be repeated, but rather that truth which applies to man
as a whole, that truth which imports salvation. In this quest for truth we
rightly demand an authority which cannot simply be manipulated by our
own subjectivity, one which, while we neither possess it nor can possess
it otherwise than in the form of an utterance of our own personal and
inalienable conscience with regard to truth, is nevertheless capable in
particular cases of genuinely confronting us and laying demands upon us,
an authority, therefore, which is something more than merely the projection of our own personal opinion. Only so can we manage to escape from
the capriciousness of our own subjectivity. Only so can we strive for that
freedom in which we are set free above all from ourselves.

Now this authority, this archimedian point outside ourselves, on the
basis of which we can overcome our own narrow subjectivity, will vary
according to the particular truth arising in the concrete circumstances of
our lives that is involved in any given case. Now the truth of salvation
precisely demands an archimedian point of this kind outside ourselves.
With regard to this authority in which the truth of salvation resides, and
which frees us from our own subjective capriciousness, we may ask how
it is to be determined in more precise theological terms. Are we to say that
it is the historical experience of faith of the Church as a whole? Or that it

is scripture? Or that it is the official authority to teach instituted by Jesus Christ? We may further enquire how these various elements, which constitute this one authority, are related to one another. But for the moment it is not these questions that concern us. However there must be such an authority in order that salvation may be bestowed upon us and liberate us from our personal subjectivity. And the only real way in which such an authority is no longer liable to be subordinated to our own subjectivity is if it is upheld by other subjects existing in the concrete and capable of acting in the concrete within our own historical situation.

Even though we have only been able to indicate these considerations above, nevertheless they do surely enable us to realize the meaning of the statement that truth, when it applies precisely to man as a whole, man who can never exist in the 'splendid isolation' of his own subjectivity without being entrapped in it – that truth, I say, has something to do with institution. We do not need to be communists in order to understand this, although sometimes we may have the impression that this statement is better understood among them, albeit in a perverted application, than among us 'later individualists' with our liberalist mentality, which calls everything in question, and can still continue to do this for a whole epoch until the last remnants of what is valid from the past have been worked over.

But let us understand this statement that truth has something to do with institution, and that it is not the case that it is our own only when it is emancipated from this. On the contrary it is our own when we have grasped this statement and made it our own truth. Once we have understood this, then it can be that a radical assent to the Church as she exists in the concrete, even in respect of her teaching authority, will no longer be so difficult for us as it may sometimes seem. Obviously the difficulties which arise in points of detail, and with regard to specific individual doctrines of the Church, are still not wholly eliminated thereby. But nevertheless it has perhaps been made a little more intelligible why, and with what right, the individual Catholic conducts his dialogue with the Church (a dialogue which is always necessary and never concluded) from within the Church herself, recognizing her in principle as a binding authority for his convictions of faith.

c) For all that has been said so far, the Church still always remains – however much she may constitute the sphere of our life and our hope – a fearful burden upon us. We can neither cast this burden aside nor pretend to ourselves that it does not oppress us. The burden of the human factors in her to which we ourselves too make our own pitiful contribution. The burden of traditions for which it can in no sense be claimed that they share in the promise of eternal assistance to the Church. The burden of the difference between the formulae and that which is expressed in them, the burden constituted by the fact that she falls short of the immeasurable grandeur of her task. The burden of the difference between the official and institutional element and the charismatic one. The burden of the difference between the peoples and civilizations which have to live together within her. The burden constituted by the fact that the measure of living faith, of creative hope for the future, and of selfless love is always too small. If anyone feels this burden, which always represents an assault on our assent to the Church in the concrete and makes it difficult for us, let him consider that he too plays his own limited part in increasing this burden. Let him consider above all that the Church is always the Church who wearily seeks her way through history, that she and we ourselves are on the way, and have not yet arrived at that goal at which all will be reconciled.

And finally: all that the Church is, all that she does, all that she seeks to help us in with all her statements of faith, her sacraments and institutions, all this has after all one single significance, namely that by loving our neighbour, by hoping and working to make this life bearable, we let ourselves fall through that death which is being died throughout the whole of our lives in a spirit of submission and adoration into the incomprehensible mystery; that we achieve this in faith, hope and love in that creed of ours which runs counter to all that our experience suggests to us, telling us that this mystery is the mystery of freedom, of truth, of love and of forgiveness, and is addressed to us as such in Jesus Christ who was crucified and definitively received by God.

But because we really do find this too within her, because in her, in the hard and often harsh concrete forms of her reality the real message achieves concrete embodiment in our own lives, therefore, rising above all the burdens and tensions of our relationship with her we utter our assent to the Church. We do not take refuge from her everyday manifestations, however pitiable these may often be in ideals which are all too facile and which would merely deliver us up to ourselves in our own narrow, sinful, and pitiful limitations. We endure her in faith, hope and love precisely because so far as we are concerned, while still existing in her dimension of divine truth, she is the Church of those individuals who, as the people of God on pilgrimage, have embarked on that course in which the history of mankind opens up into the blessed mystery of God which is our own hope, but even as such the sustaining force of our life as well. We are critical in our attitude to the Church because this critique belongs to the very nature of our faith itself since in union with the faith of the Church it is on the way to the eternal light. But this means that the critique itself derives its life from an assent to the Church as she exists in the concrete which is ever renewed in hope, causing our faith to rise above all temptations and constantly to renew itself.

9

ANONYMOUS CHRISTIANITY AND THE MISSIONARY TASK OF THE CHURCH

I T is important to emphasize right at the outset that the following considerations do not, properly speaking, refer to that which we have for some time been accustomed to call 'anonymous Christianity',[1] nor yet to the missionary task of the Church as such,[2] but merely to the relationship which these two entities bear one to another. Nevertheless it is obvious that something must be said at least very briefly concerning the two realities, the relationship between which is intended to constitute the proper subject of these considerations.

In speaking of the universal missionary task of the Church as a right and a duty of the Church herself this is taken to include the basic duty of every man to become a Christian in an explicitly ecclesiastical form of Christianity, because it is quite impossible to separate these two entities from one another. The reason that this needs to be emphasized is that the objections raised against the doctrine of the anonymous Christianity of the

[1] The author has already given his views on this theme at length in other contexts On this point cf. also the bibliography supplied by K. Riesenhuber, 'Der anonyme Christ nach K. Rahner', *ZKT* 86 (1964), pp. 286–303; in addition to this now cf. K. Rahner, 'Anonymous Christians', *Theological Investigations* VI (London and Baltimore, 1969), pp. 390–398, and further *idem*, 'On the Theology of the Ecumenical Discussion', *Theological Investigations* XI (London, 1973), pp. 24–67; *idem*, 'Atheism and Implicit Christianity', *Theological Investigations* IX (London and New York, 1972), pp. 145–164; *idem*, 'Church, Churches and Religions', *ibid.*, pp. 30–49; *idem*, 'Salvation of the Non-Evangelized', *Sacramentum Mundi* 4 (New York and London, 1969), pp. 79–81.

[2] On this cf. K. Rahner, 'Grundprinzipien der heutigen Mission in der Kirche' *Handbuch der Pastoraltheologie* II/2 (Freiburg, 1966), pp. 46–80, esp. 55 ff.; further. *idem*, 'Mission dringlicher denn je!' *Die katholischen Missionen* 86 (1967), pp. 3 ff.; B. A. Willems, 'Who Belongs to the Church?', *Concilium* I/1 (Dogma, 1965), pp. 62–71; M. J. Le Guillou, 'Mission as an Ecclesiological Theme', *Concilium* 3/2 (Pastoral Theology) (1966), pp. 43–61; J. Schütte (ed.), *Mission nach dem Konzil* (Mainz, 1967); S. Brechter, 'Kommentar zum Dekret über die Missionstätigkeit der Kirche "Ad Gentes"', *LTK* Suppl. III (1968), 9–125.

162   ANONYMOUS CHRISTIANITY

Church's universal missionary task[3] can likewise be raised and *de facto* ar raised in virtue of the basic and indisputable vocation and duty of ever individual to become a Christian in a sense that is manifested at the histori cal level, having an explicitly credal force and social dimension. The fact therefore, that the following considerations refer more explicitly to th possibility of reconciling the doctrine of anonymous Christianity with th doctrine of the universal missionary task of the Church in itself also in cludes an enquiry into the question of why the doctrine of anonymou Christianity is reconcilable with the doctrine of the duty of every man to become a Christian in an explicit sense.

In discussing the question of anonymous Christianity here, therefore we must begin by emphasizing that this subject implicitly involves two different questions: first the question of the inadequacy or appropriateness of the terminology under various possible aspects involved in the subject-matter, second the question of the objective reality referred to by this terminology independently of the problem of whether this reality is itself adequately described by this terminology.

So far as the terminology is concerned the question has already been raised of whether in enquiring into whether the choice of terms is adequate a further distinction should not be drawn between the concept of the 'anonymous Christian' and the concept of 'anonymous Christianity'. The well-known theologian Henri de Lubac, for instance, rejects the concept of 'anonymous Christianity' but has no objections to the term 'anony-mous Christian'.[4] Perhaps in order first to settle this ancillary question it might be pointed out that in German the term *Christentum* (= 'Christen-dom' or 'Christianity') can be used in at least two fairly distinct senses. *Christentum* can simply signify the sum total of real Christians. Hence anyone who concedes that there are anonymous Christians should not raise any objections against the point that in that case there is an anonymous *Christentum* (or Christendom) in this sense as well. The question becomes more difficult if by the term *Christentum* we understand that which con-stitutes a specific individual as a Christian ('Christianity'). For in that case it could be argued that one of the factors belonging to Christianity in this abstract sense is precisely its manifestation in history in the explicit

[3] On these objections cf. also A. Schmied, 'Prozess gegen den impliziten Glauben?', *Theologie der Gegenwart* 13 (1969), pp. 103–107, and the article 'On the Theology of the Ecumenical Discussion', *Theological Investigations* XI, pp. 24–67, esp. nn. 14, 15.

[4] H. de Lubac, *Geheimnis aus dem wir leben*, Kriterien 6 (Einsiedeln, 1967), pp. 131–154, esp. 149 ff.

Christian creed, in a Church that is constituted as a society, in the fact that membership of the Church comes through baptism, and in all those other elements which go to make up full membership of the Church. On this basis the following argument might be put forward: if this explicit Church membership belongs to the very nature of Christianity, i.e. to that which constitutes an individual as a Christian in the full sense of the term, then there is no anonymous Christianity because the term 'anonymous' is precisely intended to exclude that historical and social manifestation which belongs to the essence of Christianity. But if we adopt this line of argument, basing it on this second sense of the term, then to be consistent we should also reject the concept of an 'anonymous Christian', because the objection mentioned above applies just as much to this. In our enquiry into the opportunism of this terminology, then, we can set on one side the distinction between the concepts of 'anonymous Christian' and 'anonymous Christianity' as being unimportant, and assume that for practical purposes and in the concrete we must either accept the possibility of using both terms or else we must reject both.

Even in the light of the foregoing observation it is certainly to be conceded that a certain difficulty is entailed in both concepts. For Christianity in the full sense of the term does involve as one of its factors a conscious awareness of faith, an explicit Christian creed, and a constitution of the Church as a society. And it is precisely these factors which are once more eliminated by the term 'anonymous'. This reservation is openly to be conceded. But before rejecting these terms on the grounds mentioned certain points still remain to be considered.

First the term 'anonymous' is certainly a term that, understood absolutely and in a general sense, does not provoke any special misunderstanding, and therefore is in itself legitimate. Yet the term 'anonymous' precisely expresses the fact that the individual thus designated is devoid of a name. For what leads to the naming of something is a process of explicitly reflecting upon a nature that is de facto real and existing, the explicit and public recognition of the fact that this nature is present in a specific existing individual. Now manifestly there can also be the sort of anonymity that is envisaged here, and it can be designated by the term 'anonymous' when the nature of the reality referred to is such that it makes a difference whether this state of conscious self-realization is or it not present in the anonymous being concerned, his conscious awareness of his own nature and his recognition by a distinguishing name. The term 'anonymous', therefore, is fully capable of expressing the fact that the state of anonymity is in a certain sense a state that is contrary to nature, that should not be because there is an inherent tendency in the very nature of the being involved to overcome this state of namelessness. When we consider these possibilities latent in the term 'anonymous', a term which certainly contains a paradox, then the objection against the idea of 'anonymous Christianity' loses its force. 'Anonymous Christianity' serves precisely to express the fact that in the case of a Christianity asserted to be present in this way something is missing from the fulness of its due nature, something which it should have and towards which the nature already present is tending. A consideration of this kind does of course presuppose that the term 'Christianity' designates an extremely complex reality in which very many differing elements are contained, elements which do not as a matter of necessity simply have to be present at the same time, or which are removed altogether at one blow. But once we do make this assumption (and unquestionably it does apply to the term 'Christianity', as will be argued in fuller detail at a later stage from the very nature of the case) then the term 'anonymous Christianity' does not involve any intrinsic contradiction. It is not 'wooden iron' (to borrow a phrase from Hegel), for in that case this term signifies precisely the fact that while it is true that Christianity is already present in an incipient state it has not yet developed to the true fulness of its nature, not yet come to be expressed in its historical and social modality and visibility, and hence that it is precisely anonymous.

Two final points must be made with regard to this merely terminological question. First, concepts involving the use of two terms always entail a certain difficulty and obscurity. Language is never wholly precise. Concepts which are intended to express something more than the rudimentary data of sense experience, and which stand for extremely complex realities can hardly ever avoid a certain ambiguity and possibility of misunderstanding. In them we sum up an extremely complex reality for the sake of expressing it briefly. But in using a concept of this sort we omit certain aspects which are not unimportant for a right understanding of the concept involved. (As examples of this we might adduce such terms as original sin, infused virtue etc.). In such terms the adjective is precisely something more than a mere supplementary specification of the term which stands for the substantive. For it supplies a very important modification of this term (the *peccatum* referred to in the phrase '*peccatum originale*' is not the same *peccatum* as in the phrase '*peccatum personale*', and again the word 'virtue' as used in the phrase 'infused virtue' in its own intrinsic meaning stands for something different from virtue as used in the phrase 'acquired virtue'). So too the word 'Christianity' as used in the phrase 'anonymous Christianity' is far from signifying exactly and totally the same reality as

'Christianity' as used in the phrase 'Christianity as explicitly manifested in the Church'. And this means that a linguistic process is being applied which is often found in other contexts as well, and which should not give rise to any misgivings.

To this a second point must be added: ultimately speaking it is not this terminology that is the essential point at all. Anyone who recognizes the existence of the realities signified by these terms and has a brief practical term of his own expressing these realities just as clearly or more clearly, and that too briefly enough for this term of his to be used in other contexts as epitomizing in brief the outcome of a long consideration can readily dispense with the terminology we are considering here.

We now come to the realities themselves. We will start with a brief word on what is meant by 'anonymous Christianity' or 'anonymous Christians'. What they signify is nothing else than the fact that according to the doctrine of the Church herself an individual can already be in possession of sanctifying grace, can in other words be justified and sanctified, a child of God, an heir to heaven, positively orientated by grace towards his supernatural and eternal salvation even before he has explicitly embraced a credal statement of the Christian faith and been baptized. What 'anonymous Christianity' signifies first and foremost is that interior grace which forgives man and gives him a share in the Godhead even before baptism[5]. Considered in its formal essence this concept still leaves open the question of which man can be thought of as justified before baptism, whether for example they are only the catechumens or – in accordance with Heb 11:6 – those who believe in the existence of God as the guarantor of the moral order, or even, over and above these, those too who have not arrived at any explicit acknowledgement of God or of their own guilt but nevertheless are striving to live good lives even without God's grace (as is stated in the document of the Second Vatican Council, 'Lumen Gentium', No. 16). In the concept of anonymous Christianity formally as such nothing is decided with regard to this question. Of course in practice it is only meaningful to speak of anonymous Christianity if we assume that justifying grace can be present even in those cases in which there is no explicit orientation to Christianity and its official verbal revelation at the historical and conceptual level. Indeed as the Second Vatican Council explicitly teaches, it can even be present in those cases in which God has not yet been discovered at the level of conscious thought or as the subject of any explicit statement, and in which at

[5] Cf. K. Rahner, 'Universal Salvific Will', *Sacramentum Mundi* 5 (New York and London, 1969), pp. 405–409.

this explicit and conscious level the individual concerned believes himself to be an atheist.[6] The proposition being put forward here is that in this broadest sense there can be anonymous Christianity, i.e. justifying grace, even apart from any explicit Christianity. In other words that even in this infralapsarian order at least in the case of mature individuals no other limits can be set to salvation than those of grave subjective guilt. And this is something which cannot be established merely by the fact that in the course of his life the individual concerned has failed to arrive at any explicit Christianity. At this point we cannot embark upon any fuller justification of this thesis.

Obviously a long history lies behind the point at which it has come to be recognized. We might say that that history began with the recognition, already present in the New Testament, that under certain circumstances God imparts his Spirit even before baptism.[7] As stages in this history we might point, for instance to the teaching of Ambrose that even the cate-chumen who dies before baptism can attain to salvation,[8] or again the mediaeval doctrine of the *votum baptismi* or baptism of desire, through which the individual can be justified even before the sacrament of baptism,[9] a doctrine which was confirmed by the Council of Trent,[10] or again we

[6] The relevant texts of the Council are discussed at length in K. Rahner, 'Atheism and Implicit Christianity', *Theological Investigations* IX (London and New York, 1972), pp. 145–164.

[7] Cf. Acts 10:47, with the explanations of this passage by M. Barth, *Die Taufe – ein Sakrament?* (Zürich, 1951), esp. pp. 154–159 and G. Beasley-Murray, *Baptism in the New Testament* (London, 1962).

[8] PL 16, 1374. Still more ancient is the doctrine of the power of martyrdom to justify. Taken together the two doctrines represent the counterpoint in scholastic theology to the thesis of the necessity of baptism as a medium (*necessitas medii*) of salvation: *PSJ* IV (Madrid, 3rd ed., 1959), pp. 147–170. Instructive for the whole range of problems entailed is E. Schillebeeckx, 'Begierdetaufe (asl aussersakramentale Heilsweg)', *LTK* II (2nd ed., 1958), 112–115, and *idem*, *Christus, Sakrament der Gottbegegnung* (Mainz, 1960). On the radical turning-point which arose on this question at the Council through the doctrine of degrees of membership of the Church cf. A. Grillmeier, 'Einführung zur geschichtlichen und theologischen Problematik von Art. 14 (der Kirchenkonstitution)', *LTK* Suppl. I (1966), 194 ff.

[9] On this cf. A. M. Landgraf, *Dogmengeschichte der Frühscholastik* III/1 (Regensburg, 1954), pp. 210–253. This author is struck by the fact that the very nature of the question is such that the doctrine of 'sacramentum in voto' was formulated significantly earlier than, for instance, that of the causality of the sacraments. Indeed it must actually be acknowledged that precisely from the recognition of the *sacramentum in voto* which had already been achieved great difficulties arose for an understanding of the effectiveness of the sacraments (*op. cit.*, p. 211).

[10] DS 1524, 1604, 1677.

might point to the doctrine of the mediaeval theologians that in the normal cases the renewal of justification in one who has fallen into sin after baptism takes place even before priestly absolution has been given, indeed that properly speaking it must take place before this.[11] Or again we might point to the controversy among the post-Tridentine moralists as to which truths of faith have to be believed as a necessary means for being able to be justified. Those involved in this controversy were forced to arrive at ever milder and more generous solutions.[12] A further stage in the history leading up to this recognition is the teaching of the Holy Office (of the 8th August 1949, against Leonard Feeney)[13] that even a merely implicit *votum ecclesiae* could be sufficient for justification, and a final stage is the teaching of the Second Vatican Council which in a note-worthy departure from established tradition holds that not even every kind of atheism (even when it is of a positive nature and of long duration) is *ipso facto* gravely sinful, but rather leaves this question open to be decided in each individual case and does not deny that the atheist who unequivocally follows his own conscience can obtain salvation.[14]

[11] Cf. K. Rahner, 'Bussakrament', *LTK* II (2nd ed. 1958), 826–838, esp. 832 ff.

[12] Admittedly the whole question, right down to the present day, is overshadowed by the subject of the relationship between nature and grace, a subject which is very difficult to define. The post-Tridentine theology, in which there is a widespread tendency to identify faith in its explicit form more or less with supernatural grace in general, does at first seem to leave no possibility of salvation for the individual in the non-Christian sphere who cannot give his faith any expression ('implicit' here signifies the truth which is contained but not expressed in a given statement). The whole question, therefore, is brought to a head, however strange this may sound, by the problem of unbaptized children who now appear as a prototype example of the un-believer in general. As a logical outcome of this Billot develops the idea of a limbo for the pagans.

On the way in which the question was framed by post-Tridentine theology on this point cf. S. Harent, 'Infidèles', *DTC* VII/2 (Paris, 1923), 1726–1930. Now however it is coming to be recognized that the state of 'pure' nature never exists in the concrete at all. Rather man is placed all along in the sphere of history and it is here that he is summoned by God. Now if this is true then it also necessarily follows that 'historical' man *as such* and 'historical' revelation are in a positive sense mutually conditioning entities. The offering of salvation by God is already in existence prior to the practical proclamation of it, and is the intrinsic factor that makes it possible.

[13] DS 3866–3873. A historical survey of the whole affair is to be found in C. Goddard Clarke, *The Loyolas and the Cabots* (Boston, 1950).

[14] Cf. n. 6. A similar development is also to be traced in other problematical areas. Thus the Second Vatican Council declares that man has the right to religious freedom (Decree on Religious Freedom No. 2), that God 'in ways known to himself can lead those inculpably ignorant of the gospel to that faith without which it is impossible to please him' (Decree on the Missions, No. 7), that the other 'ecclesias-

Only a few remarks will be made concerning the missionary task of the Church. According to the evidence of the New Testament itself this task is in principle universal, i.e. fundamentally it is directed to all men in the sense that there is no *a priori* principle laying down that from the outset (for instance because of a specific nationality, a specific form of civilization, a specifically different religion) specific individuals are excluded so far as this missionary task of the Church is concerned as in principle and from the outset not being included in the offering of grace and the duty to become Christians. The universality of this missionary task does not mean, however, that this positive obligation of divine law for the Church must be actively pursued to the same extent at every moment in every situation or for every individual. The same of course applies too to the basic duty of every individual to become a Christian. This too varies greatly in its degree of actuality in each individual case according to the individual involved and the situation in which he stands.

There is a further question, that namely of whether right from the initial promulgation of the gospel and from the first Pentecost this objective duty has been laid upon all men, and whether the history of this obligation is merely the history of how they come to recognize it in practice. Or alternatively whether the objective duty as such itself arises only in a process of historical development to which all men are subject, though obviously in that case the duty, the right and the dynamic force needed to engage in this historical process in order to bring it to the universal state which is proper to it are themselves subject to a process of becoming which is far from complete. But these are questions which can be passed over here.

Now that we have briefly described the two entities involved what is their relationship one to the other? It is only at this point that we come to our true theme. The crucial question, which is important for practical purposes as well, is whether these two entities can exist in unison or whether the one removes the other. There is a practical problem implicitly contained in this question, that namely of whether the will to fulfil the universal missionary task of the Church is not deprived of its force in the case of one who is convinced of the possibility and the existence of an anonymous Christianity. Of course this question can also be put the other way round, and we can approach the question from the opposite point of view by asking whether any genuine missionary energy is conceivable, at any rate today, otherwise than by assuming that an anonymous

tical communities' have in principle a saving significance (Decree on Ecumenism, Nos. 19–24). On this cf. also the literature adduced in n. 2.

Christianity of this kind is already present as an enabling condition for a preaching of the faith in that individual to whom this missionary preaching is addressed.

It is clear that to supply an answer to these questions which would be satisfactory in every respect would require a whole theology of mission, its nature and its ultimate justification.[15] And this is something which can neither be prescribed or assumed here for the very reason that there is no such theology at all of a completely satisfying kind or as generally accepted.[16] What we shall have to say with regard to our present problem, therefore, must be presented and understood with this reservation.

First we may surely say that in order to be possible or to have any hope of success missionary preaching necessarily presupposes that which we may call by the name of anonymous Christianity or by some other name. On any right understanding of the nature of the Christian faith it is clear that a missionary preaching is possible only if we presuppose the grace of faith (at least as offered). The word of God as preached can only be heard and received as the word of *God* through this grace of faith.[17] Obviously however this should not be taken to signify merely some kind of psychological assistance provided by God in order to overcome the intellectual or emotional obstacles involved, which derive from the nature of the hearer, his cultural situation, the kind of personal history he has undergone etc., and which always make it difficult to understand or accept any kind of teaching that is hard. The object of faith as such can itself be recognized and accepted only with the help of supernatural grace imparting a share in the divine life. Now at least according to the Thomist doctrine, which after all is relevant to this point and which has the weight of ancient tradition behind it, this grace is precisely something more than

[15] On this cf. also the Decree on the Missions of the Second Vatican Council, which in its first chapter attempts to lay down the basic principles governing missionary activity, and cf. also the relevant commentary in *LTK* Suppl. III (1968), 9–125; J. Hampe (ed.), *Die Autorität der Freiheit* III (Munich, 1967), pp. 518–573; E. Dhanis and A. Schönmetzer (edd.), *Acta Congressus Internationalis de Theologia Concilii Vatican* II (Rome, 1968), pp. 340–442; Y. Congar, 'Theologische Grundlegung', *Mission nach dem Konzil* edited by J. Schütte (Mainz, 1967), pp. 134–172.
[16] In fact the missionary decree likewise has avoided attaching itself to any of the theories of mission developed hitherto.
[17] This idea is more fully presented in the section entitled 'Wort Gottes', *LTK* X (2nd ed. 1965), 1235–1238. In this connection cf. also K. Rahner, J. Ratzinger, *Revelation and Tradition*, Quaestiones Disputatae 17 (Freiburg, 1966); K. Rahner, 'Scripture and Tradition', *Theological Investigations* VI (London and Baltimore, 1969), pp. 98–112; *idem*, 'Scripture and Tradition', *Sacramentum Mundi* 6 (London and New York, 1970), pp. 54–57.

what it was maintained to be by a Molinist school of thought against Thomism and against Suarez, namely a mere ontological and subconscious alteration of the act of faith. Rather it also implies a genuinely conscious alteration and imparts a dimension of understanding which cannot be attained to by any merely natural act, having a formal object which is specifically supernatural.[18] Only in the light of grace can we recognize and accept the light of the gospel. The grace of faith is the necessary prior condition for the teaching of the faith. But it would be to suppose the miraculous, almost to indulge in mythological ideas, if we were to hold that this grace of faith was conferred only at that moment at which the preaching of the gospel actually reached the ears of those to whom it was addressed. In this moment it does indeed become actual, effective and demanding, but this is precisely in virtue of the fact that it has been present all along and belongs to the enduring existential modalities of man, albeit at the level of the supernatural, in the same way as the natural spiritual faculties are present all along in man even though they only become actual and effective when they encounter an external object of experience which corresponds to them.

For our present purposes we cannot provide any more detailed justification for this conception of grace as involving a unity of so-called habitual and actual grace.[19] From the point of view of dogmatic theology, however, it cannot be contested, and is at basis already contained in the Thomist doctrine laying down that the act by which justification is appropriated takes place in the power of the habitual grace which is already present. Now if we accept this classic Thomist conception we need only to go on to consider a further point with regard to that habitual grace which is offered as the condition enabling the subject to act for his own salvation, and which, according to Thomas, is logically prior to the free act by which salvation is appropriated in the subject's own personal life. There is no longer any difficulty in regarding this grace as constituting, even from the temporal point of view, an abiding grace-given existential modality. Then

[18] A more detailed treatment of this point is to be found in K. Rahner, 'Concerning the Relationship between Nature and Grace', *Theological Investigations* I (London and Baltimore, 1961), pp. 297–317; *idem*, 'Reflections on the Experience of Grace', *Theological Investigations* III (London and Baltimore, 1967), pp. 86–90; *idem*, 'Nature and Grace', *Theological Investigations* IV (London and Baltimore, 1966), pp. 165–188; *idem*, 'Gnadenerfahrung', *LTK* IV (2nd ed., 1960), 1001–1002; *idem*, 'The Existential', *Sacramentum Mundi* 2 (New York and London, 1968), pp. 304–307; J. Alfaro, 'Formalobjekt, übernaturliches', *LTK* IV (2nd ed., 1960), 207–208.

[19] On this cf. the expositions of K. Rahner under the heading 'Gnade', *LTK* IV (2nd ed., 1960), 991–1000.

without further consideration it can be assumed that the preacher of the gospel who seeks to impart faith as an appropriation of grace addresses himself, and must address himself (since it is impossible to preach the faith without the grace of faith) to an individual who already possesses justifying grace at least as offered, and indeed, it may be, as already freely accepted in an implicit way. The individual concerned would in this sense be an anonymous Christian. The missionary task, therefore, must be one that can exist together with anonymous Christianity because on theological grounds we must hold that this missionary task presupposes the existence of the anonymous Christian as the only possible hearer of the gospel message.

But we can view this possibility of union and mutual interrelationship between the missionary task and anonymous Christianity from the aspect of anonymous Christianity itself. Even though anonymous Christianity is prior to explicit Christianity it does not render it superfluous. On the contrary, it itself demands this explicit Christianity in virtue of its own nature and its own intrinsic dynamism. In order to achieve a clearer recognition of this point we may begin by stating the following general thesis:

In the general economy of salvation it is a perfectly logical process for the grace that creates salvation, and indeed constitutes the individual as saved, to be both logically and temporally prior to the sacramental act which signifies it. Yet as such and in virtue of its own intrinsic dynamism it itself demands to be realized in this visible sacramental mode and in the dimension of the Church. It presses forward towards this sacramental incarnation of itself, and thereby ensures that it is not impossible for this effective sacramental symbol of this same grace to be itself a cause of the grace and not merely an outward expression of it such as ultimately speaking would make no difference.

This thesis requires a little further explanation. But if it were not correct, then basically speaking it would no longer be possible to explain how in that case Paul can sometimes attribute justification to faith without baptism, and elsewhere attribute it to baptism alone. We have already emphasized above that on the occasion of the baptism of Cornelius Peter insists upon the fact that Cornelius can and indeed must be baptized *because* he has already received the Holy Spirit.[20] The thesis we have put forward is simply an application of the fundamental doctrine concerning salvation history as a whole to the salvation of the individual, the doctrine, namely, that the grace of Christ, as that of Christ himself, was temporally present throughout the whole of salvation history and was prior to its

[20] See n. 7.

manifestation in the *Ursakrament* of history which is Christ himself, and that it is precisely in virtue of this fact that it issued in the fullness of time in the eschatological victory of the crucified and risen Lord.[21] This basic thesis is also to be found in many of the more particular doctrines of sacramental theology.[22] Properly speaking, when we come to baptism we must already have faith, hope and love, in other words the state of justification. It is meaningless in the context with which we are concerned to seek to raise the value and significance of the sacrament itself by saying that a sacrament can justify even one who only possesses imperfect repentance and so has not yet received the grace of justification. This may be correct, although a point that would still have to be considered is that according to Thomas it is precisely this sacramental grace that raises man in his personal life from being an 'attritus' to being a 'contritus', in other words that after all what is bestowed upon man is not that deed of salvation in virtue of which he justifies himself in an *opus operantis*.[23] Abstracting from this, we must say in all realism and against all the strangely heated controversies between contritionists and attritionists in post-Tridentine theology that while it is true that we can distinguish between imperfect and perfect repentance, in practice this distinction has no special significance since he who by an act of perfect repentance has achieved an unequivocal rejection of sin (something that must also be present in imperfect repentance) no longer has any difficulty in loving God with his whole heart, or in choosing him as the goal of his own personal life in an act of true charity, since he necessarily must have a freely determined goal for his personal life of this kind. Yet *ex supposito* he no longer seeks it in any finite good which he has sinfully made his absolute goal. Even in baptism, then, the situation is that through it an anonymous Christian becomes an explicit Christian, and in any case through such a baptism he may indeed be validly baptized, but

[21] On this conception of saving history cf. K. Rahner, 'History of the World and Salvation History', *Theological Investigations* V (London and Baltimore, 1966), pp. 97–114; A. Darlap, 'Fundamentale Theologie der Heilsgeschichte', *Mysterium Salutis* I (Einsiedeln, 1965), pp. 3–156; K. Berger and A. Darlap, 'History of Salvation (Salvation History)', *Sacramentum Mundi* 5 (New York and London, 1970), pp. 411–419; E. Klinger, *Offenbarung im Horizont der Heilsgeschichte* (Zürich, 1969).
[22] The interpretation of what is meant by sacrament presupposed here is presented more fully in K. Rahner, 'Personal and Sacramental Piety', *Theological Investigations* II (London and Baltimore, 1963), pp. 109–133; *idem, The Church and the Sacraments*, Quaestiones Disputatae 9 (Freiburg, 1963); *idem*, 'Sakramente als Grundfunktionen der Kirche', *Handbuch der Pastoraltheologie* I (Freiburg, 1964), pp. 323–332.
[23] On the series of connected questions here a more detailed treatment is to be found in K. Rahner, 'Problems concerning Confession', *Theological Investigations* III (London and Baltimore, 1967), pp. 190–206; cf. also n. 11.

not justified. In the case of adult baptism the justification is prior to the baptism itself, and it is precisely in baptism that it achieves its manifestation at the ecclesiastical and social level. This does not entail any denial of the efficacy of the sacrament as conferring grace, or make it impossible.[24] For first we can and must say that on any showing the sacrament increases the justifying grace even though this increase in its turn is mediated through the personal intensification of the subjective act in the reception of the sacrament. And secondly it must be pointed out that as 'causa finalis' of the history of a dynamic grace, as the incarnation and effective symbol of this grace, the sacrament can constitute one side of a mutually conditioning relationship being the effect and the cause at the same time of the original grace.

All that we have stated above finds expression once more, and that too in a way that is commonly even more emphatic, in the teaching concerning the sacrament of penance. For Thomas Aquinas and the whole of theology prior to him (Scotus was the first to introduce any change) it was regarded as obvious that when the sinner came to the sacrament of penance he had already been justified once more (through penitence), and indeed in normal cases actually had to be justified in order to approach the sacrament of penance. And the theologians did not feel the smallest difficulty in regarding the sacrament of penance for all this as a sacrament that was necessary for salvation. They did not in the least feel it to be any objection to ask how in that case the sacrament was still necessary and meaningful, seeing that the *res sacramenti*, the justification, is already conferred even before the reception of the sacrament.[25] Manifestly in their theology of saving history and grace at the collective and individual levels it was obvious to them that the signs of grace as found in the historical dimension and in the Church were not rendered superfluous and meaningless by the fact that grace is already prior to them, for there is an incarnational order such that this grace itself of its very nature seeks its historical embodiment in the

---

[24] This causality is investigated more fully in the author's studies, 'The Theology of the Symbol', *Theological Investigations* IV (London and Baltimore, 1966), pp. 221–252 and 'Sakrament', *LTK* IX (2nd ed. 1964), 225–230.

[25] In this connection the theology of penance of the very recent past has provided a new development of the ancient conception of '*reconciliatio cum ecclesia*' considered as an essential element (*res et sacramentum*) in the sacramental process. On this cf. amongst others K. Rahner, 'Penance as an Additional Act of Reconciliation with the Church', *Theological Investigations* X (London and New York, 1972), pp. 125–149. This idea could have significance for the future from the standpoint of general ecclesiology as well. For at the Second Vatican Council the Church as a whole is interpreted as the sacrament of salvation for the whole world.

word and above all in the sacrament, so that it itself would be denied if an individual sought in principle to frustrate this incarnational dynamism inherent in grace itself.

What is so much taken for granted in all the traditional theology concerning the relationship between grace and sacrament can unhesitatingly be extended to the relationship between grace and the word. For we also have need of grace in order to hear the word of the gospel, and even this word of the gospel can and must be conceived of as a kind of incarnation of grace at the level of human conceptualization in its objectifying and speculative function. For if grace consists in the self-bestowal of the triune God which of its own intrinsic nature seeks for the historical incarnation of the Logos and is, for that reason everywhere and in all cases a grace of Christ,[26] then it follows that the total reality which faith as articulated in words expresses is already present in this grace considered as the self-bestowal of God. And from this we can understand why it should be a property inherent in the very nature of this grace to press forward to this state of conceptual objectification which we call the doctrine of the faith at the level of the collective history of revelation and the personal history of faith. For it is in this explicitation as the doctrine of the faith that he who has been endowed with grace and the grace itself achieve a state of full and conscious self-possession. Grace, therefore, presses on to its state of conceptual objectification in the preaching of faith and is prior to this as its enabling condition. The explicit preaching of faith is not superfluous, because the grace which is preached is prior to this preaching as the condition of it and as the content of its preaching. Precisely because it is prior to the preaching the grace itself demands that it shall be preached. Now to say this is *ipso facto* to say too – for it is only expressing this in different words – that anonymous Christianity does not render explicit Christianity superfluous, but rather itself demands it, and that there would no longer be any anonymous Christianity, or at most it would only continue to exist as a judgement against the individual concerned, if he upon whom it is bestowed as offering were radically to close himself to any explicit Christianity.

In the light of the consideration so far put forward it is valid to hold that the theology of mission, of the meaning of and the necessity for mission, requires in part to be interpreted afresh. In former times the

---

[26] For fuller details on this point cf. K. Rahner, 'Der dreifaltige Gott als transzendenter Urgrund der Heilsgeschichte', *Mysterium Salutis* II (Einsiedeln, 1967), pp. 317–401, esp. 369 ff.; *idem*, 'Die Kirche als Präsenz der Wahrheit und Liebe Gottes', *Handbuch der Pastoraltheologie* I (Freiburg, 1964), pp. 121–131.

necessity for mission was regarded more or less explicitly and radically from the point of view of the personal salvation of the individual, and the reasons for this necessity were sought here. Mission was regarded as necessary on the grounds that those individuals to whom no mission was directed would be lost. It is true that even in former times certain theories were adumbrated in order to be able to explain God's infralapsarian will to save all men universally, such theories as that of the private enlightenment of a particular individual or that of an original revelation handed down to later ages. By these means it was sought to explain how, at least in certain instances, a real faith in a supernatural revelation (taking this to be the necessary prior condition for justification) was at least in principle possible, and so too how justification itself was possible in principle, even without the explicit message of Christianity. But it was held that in practice this sort of situation arose only in a few exceptional cases, and these exceptions were explained by referring to original sin or to the universality of the breaking of the natural moral law, this being taken, even in the infralapsarian age, to justify the withholding of the supernatural grace of faith on God's part despite the conditional will of God to save all men.

In this connection, and in order correctly to evaluate such ideas, it must be realized that prior to the modern age European theology had no true idea of the enormous numbers of individuals outside Christianity or of the immense length of non-Christian history. Thus in arriving at the basic ideas of the traditional theology of mission the following assumption was conceivable: Mission is aimed at the salvation of individuals who otherwise simply could not avoid being lost, and that too with a necessity which is properly speaking prior to any question of the grace of faith as offered being rejected in any individual case. Today we can recognize the full length and breadth of non-Christian human history, and evaluate the power of the Cross of Christ at its true worth, and in view of this we can no longer assume that a majority of mankind is destined to perdition. Formerly this was assumed, and that too not merely on the grounds that they refused the grace of faith as offered to them – in other words not on the grounds that they had specifically rejected Jesus Christ – but for different reasons. And conversely today we are in a position to consider more clearly and with a deeper theological insight the question of how an individual who is not brought face to face with the explicit preaching of the gospel can still be brought, albeit at a quite unexplicit level, to an authentic decision of faith, and how he can thereby attain to a state of justification through faith (a theme which obviously cannot be developed in any fuller detail at this point). Now in view of all this we can and must take it as established that it is possible for all men, including non-Christians, to arrive at a state of justification by having supernatural grace conferred upon them. But if this is the case then we cannot deduce the meaning and necessity of the Church's missionary task primarily or exclusively from the salvation of the individual, as though apart from this (abstracting from a few special cases) he would be lost unless he were subjected to the preaching of the gospel and baptism.

A positive evaluation of the meaning of mission is both possible along these lines, and in a true sense already given in what has been said so far. The grace of God which is intended effectively to redeem all has an incarnatorial character. It wills to extend itself into all the dimensions of human life, and in other words to take effect and find expression in the historical and social dimensions of this as well. This grace is intended of its very nature to be constitutive of the Church. Mission and the missionary actively contribute to this incarnatorial dynamism of grace. Of course this represents only a brief indication of the theology of mission, which could and should be supplemented and deepened on the basis of scripture, and also, for instance, in the light of the missionary decree of the Second Vatican Council by the insight that mission is directed not exclusively to the individual in his own personal quest for salvation, but no less primarily to peoples and civilizations as such. Mission consists in a sending out to all people. It has the task in saving history of making Christ, his gospel and his grace present among all peoples as such in their own specific histories and cultures, and thereby of achieving a quite new incarnatorial presence of Christ himself in the world. Once and for all Christianity is not intended merely to assure a salvation conceived of embryonically and almost in abstract terms for the individual in the other-worldly dimension, but is rather intended to make God's grace manifest here below in all its possible forms and in all historical spheres and contexts. The palpable dimension of the present world itself is intended to be made Christian to the utmost possible extent, because it is precisely not merely the other world that belongs to God and his Christ, as though he secretly rescued a few isolated individuals out of a merely secular world. On the contrary this world too belongs to him, the earthly dimension, history, the peoples, and also the history which present-day humanity itself sets itself actively to shape, instead of merely passively enduring it.

This new interpretation of the theology of mission in no sense involves any assertion that mission has no connection whatever with the personal salvation of the individual. Even if it is maintained that there is a basic possibility of salvation and a genuine opportunity of achieving salvation for all at all times, and even outside the sphere of any explicit preaching of the gospel (an opportunity which is lost only through the personal fault of the individual), still this is in no sense to assert that the salvific situation and the opportunity of achieving salvation constitute an entity that is undeviatingly the same, equally present at all times, and for every individual man. It is obvious that mission improves the situation in which salvation can be achieved and the opportunity of salvation for the individual, even though at the same time it must be recognized that according to the New Testament the situation in which salvation can be achieved is also rendered more radical thereby, and so in a certain sense more dangerous too. In principle and quite in general the following statement may be applied to the conscious objectification of the existential modalities of human life, even though in principle these can be freely realized at a quite implicit and unconscious level: the conscious objectification of these modalities, while it does not necessarily or as a matter of compulsion bring about the actual realization of them or the radical modification of personal human life which such realization entails, still does induce conditions which are very favourable to this realization. Otherwise any metaphysical anthropology, for instance, would have no significance for concrete personal living whatever, but would simply be of concern to those who had a purely speculative interest in metaphysics for its own sake. If man is consciously aware of who he is and what he is making of himself of his own freedom, the chance that he will succeed in this self-achievement of his and arrive at a radical self-fulfilment is greater than if he merely possesses and fulfils his own humanity at a merely inert and unconscious level. Hence the conscious self-realization of a hitherto anonymous Christianity brought about through missionary preaching implies on the one hand the achievement of a more radical dimension of responsibility and on the other a greater chance of this Christianity interiorly bestowed by grace being brought to its fulness in all dimensions precisely as an explicit Christianity and in a state of radical freedom. Nor let it be said that if the only difference between explicit Christianity and anonymous Christianity is that the opportunity of achieving salvation afforded by the former is greater (instead of saying that salvation is initially bestowed by that explicit Christianity), this must after all have the effect of weakening missionary zeal. It is perfectly possible for there to be an absolute duty in human life to offer one's neighbour a greater chance of freely achieving the fulness of himself even when in principle the chance of such full self-realization was present all along even without offering him this further opportunity.[27]

[27] A similar line of argument is to be found in chapter II of the Decree on the Missions.

No father questions the fact that he is still far from being dispensed from the duty of giving his child the opportunity of having the most favourable start in life that he can merely because his child is already assured a minimal opportunity in life. Love strives for what is greater, and this striving is not to be accounted as greed. In fact it is precisely this striving which constitutes that love which is an absolute duty. This also applies to mission, for it is in this that love for God and neighbour is realized. The doctrine of anonymous Christianity as applied to the theology of mission does not exclude, among other things, a right understanding of the reference which mission has to the personal salvation of the individual.

PART TWO

Church and Society

10

THE QUESTION OF THE FUTURE

A'POLITICAL THEOLOGY', whatever more precise interpretation we may place on such a phrase, implies a certain understanding of the questions of whether and how an individual can know something of the future. This surely calls for no further explanation. It can therefore represent a contribution to the discussion of 'political theology' if the question of what the future holds is considered precisely *as a question*. In adopting this approach we must emphasize right from the outset that we can only discuss this question from the viewpoint of the theologian. This means that our enquiry into the future cannot be presented from the viewpoint of the futurologist,[1] the practitioner of cybernetics, the politologist, or even the philosopher. By comparison with all these the theologian is certainly the one who knows the least of all with regard to any 'this-worldly' future, and is indeed the one who, as we shall shortly have to explain more fully, makes this ignorance of his the true pith and essence of his message, regarding it not as a mere afterthought or peripheral phenomenon by comparison with some knowledge of the future, but rather as that which as a theologian he is striving precisely to bring and to keep before men's eyes. *Docta ignorantia futuri* is from the outset the theme that is proper to the theologian, which he must put forward in season and out of season, and whether it is attended to or falls on deaf ears. In these preliminary remarks it must first be emphasized simply by way of warning that the theologian is no futurologist.

[1] The concept of futurology was applied for the first time in 1943 in the United States by O. K. Flechtheim as a characterization of the work of systematically coping with the problems of the future. The programme for this science of the future can be summed up in a few key-words: research into the future, shaping of the future, and interpreting the future. An initial introduction to the range of problems involved together with a comprehensive bibliography is supplied by O. K. Flechtheim, *Futurologie – Möglichkeiten und Grenzen*, Projekte und Modelle No. 3 (Frankfurt, 1968).

I

The moment the precise terms are adverted to of the title to this study, 'The Question of the Future', it is immediately apparent that the point of concern is not to define in terms of actual content what actually can or will be the case in the future. The question of the future is to be considered, rather, precisely as a *question* – indeed as *the* question which man himself constitutes and which he is impelled to pose to himself from something more than mere curiosity. What we are enquiring into, therefore, is the question of the future and not the actual content of the future. If the theologian is he who inculcates that *docta ignorantia futuri* spoken of above, then an enquiry of this kind into the question itself is certainly appropriate to him, because he, if anyone, is most of all in a position to say something about this.

It is proper to Christian theology of its very nature, and in virtue of its contemporary state, that it should be concerned with a question of this kind. It is proper to it of its very nature because that Christian faith which is the subject of theological speculation, the recognition in hope of that absolute future of man which is God, lays down that this absolute future of the world is not simply offered as a mere open possibility, but in Jesus Christ is infallibly and victoriously promised. And this is something that man himself confesses. Finally it is appropriate to Christianity of its very nature to concern itself with this question because however true it may be that this absolute future is constituted by God and by his activity it still remains true that the acceptance of it on man's part is undertaken only in his own personal history when he adopts a right and responsible relationship to that future of his which has to be wrought out by himself in this present world.

It is true that in Christian theology eschatology is treated as a special branch falling at the end of dogmatic theology. But for the reasons we have indicated above eschatology also constitutes the whole of Christian theology or at least a formal structural principle for all theological statements.[2] For regardless of whether this is explicitly adverted to or not we only know what is meant by God if we recognize our own state as being orientated towards an absolute future. We only understand what saving history and revelation history mean if we live through them and recognize

---

[2] This point has long been treated of clearly and thematically in its own right in the work of H. Cox, W. Pannenberg and J. Moltmann, where theology is actually interpreted *as* eschatology. The most recent presentation of this position is to be

them as the history of the promise of salvation extending more and more to the very roots of our being. We only understand what it means to say that Jesus Christ is the incarnate Word of God if we believe in him as the one who will 'come again', in other words as he who belongs to the future and *as such* constitutes the Word of God's absolute promise of himself to the world. We only understand what faith is if we recognize clearly the edifice of hope that is built upon it, in which it accepts God's revelation as promise. We only value the Christian sacraments at their true and intrinsic worth if we also understand them as *signa prognostica*, to adopt the parlance of Thomas Aquinas. If we define the essence of Christianity as consisting in love of God and of man then we cannot overlook the fact that this love lives by, and necessarily must live by, the expectation in hope that that which is the counterpart to this love has still to come in the future which belongs to the God whom we love and the humanity that we love. And it is this that renders this love authentic, definitive, and blessed.

It is in the very nature of theology as such, therefore, that the question of the future belongs to it as one of its basic questions. But this question is rendered still more urgent in the light of the contemporary state of faith and of theology. The world in which man lives has been set in motion. It has become possible to plan and shape it. Man himself is no longer merely one who puts up with himself, makes himself the subject of his own metaphysical speculations or religious contemplations in the sphere of his theoretical reason, no longer one who 'works' himself *in the same way* as he might work a machine already in existence and working properly until it was worn out. On the contrary man is, at least in the first instance, the one who has made something of himself, one who at the individual and collective levels alike, makes plans and projects for himself – in a certain sense takes control of himself, not merely drawing out what is already there, but creatively discovering that which is not there, that which belongs to Utopia. And it is in this way that man shapes the present in the light of the future. However incipient all this may seem to be,

---

found in J. Moltmann, 'Die Zukunft als neues Paradigma der Transzendenz', *Internationale Dialog-Zeitschrift* 1 (1969), pp. 2–13. From the Catholic side the author who has probably followed this position most consistently is J. B. Metz who, in view of the primacy of the future in our contemporary world, conceives of theology primarily as providing an eschatological and social critique. A survey of this point which is concerned with the range of problems we are discussing, and which at the same time includes a *prise de position* with regard to the problems of futurology, is provided by W. D. Marsch, *Zukunft* (Stuttgart, 1969).

however true it may be that even today man still constantly has to endure himself and the world in which he lives instead of only shaping it creatively, the prospect is still opened up to him of a future which can be shaped, and does not merely have to be endured. The future is no longer *merely* something which he has to wait for, something which is merely hoped for, merely dreamed about. Instead it is a reality which has achieved power to influence the present itself and in that sense has become the real.

There is such a reality as cybernetics; it is possible to develop complicated computer-programmes and the planning of the futurologists has its validity. For Christian theology this raises the question of what the relationship is between modern futurology and Christian eschatology. In earlier times what entered into the present was an eschatology and a hope for that which was not the outcome of man's planning, not capable of being developed by man himself. Today there is a future into which the designs of the futurologists enter, one which is orientated towards that which can be planned and developed. And this gives rise to the question of whether this present-day futurology has replaced the old eschatology, whether the old eschatology constitutes merely the obsolete mythological form or the preliminary adumbration of present-day futurology, or *alternatively* whether this futurology is embedded in the 'this-worldly' sphere of human living in such a way that this earthly sphere itself taken as a whole, despite the radical changes which it has undergone, still constantly remains circumscribed by that which constitutes the goal of Christian eschatology and hope. In any case Christian theology as eschatology has arrived at a state in which quite new demands are made upon it precisely in respect of its special and peculiar role as eschatology. Moreover it is obvious without any further discussion that a 'political theology' regards these questions as questions which essentially belong to the subject-matter which is most proper to itself.

II

Before applying ourselves directly to a theological enquiry into the question of the future certain conceptual distinctions have to be drawn which, for the sake of clarity, must be considered first even though the objective justification for them will appear only when we come to treat directly of the theme which is the proper subject of these considerations. We have to distinguish between the absolute future which is God himself and another future, whether more proximate or more remote, which belongs to this world. It is self-evident that *precisely at this stage* we cannot supply any answer to the question of what right we have to assume at this point that the term 'God' is understood, or to introduce it into our considerations in order to define what is meant by the phrase 'absolute future'.

Nor must it be denied that under certain circumstances a 'political theology' must proceed and is justified in proceeding in the opposite direction, in other words precisely from the experience of being orientated towards an absolute future. Taking this experience as its starting-point, therefore, a theology of this kind must undertake a radical critique, and one that has to be achieved ever afresh, of the present and future with which we are confronted at any given stage, for it is only so that we can arrive at an understanding of what is meant by God, and precisely in this way that such an approach becomes a political *theology*.

With the proviso that even when we have drawn this distinction between the two kinds of future we have still not arrived at any unambiguous conclusion with regard to the mutual relationship between them,[3] we may define this distinction as follows: the *absolute future* is God himself or the act of his absolute self-bestowal which has to be posited by him alone. The effect which this produces does not constitute any specific event within the world, representing one particular element in it such as can be defined in 'this worldly' categories. Rather it is a specification of the world as a whole, comprehending the whole of reality and determining where its consummation is to be achieved. To this extent it has a transcendental character. Properly speaking, therefore, it cannot be planned or brought about by man either, because as the total consummation of reality as a whole it cannot *per definitionem* be brought about by any one particular element within this reality. This is neither to exclude nor to deny a further point regarding the subjectivity of man through which he is confronted with himself and with the whole of reality in knowledge and freedom. In virtue of this subjectivity of his he can and must accept this

---

[3] This proviso must be especially emphasized here because it is important to guard against the misunderstanding that here a 'transcendence-immanence' theology is being restored as a separate polarization in each case. What we are concerned with here rather is precisely to overcome this opposition by means of an orientation towards God as coming, and as already present in Jesus as the future of *this* world. This idea, and the question of the necessity for a process of mediation, are also factors of decisive importance in the author's earlier studies. Cf. K. Rahner, 'Das Christentum und der "neue Mensch" ', *Schriften zur Theologie* III (7th ed., 1967), pp. 159–179; 'Marxist Utopia and the Christian Future of Man', *Theological Investigations* VI (London and Baltimore, 1969), pp. 59–68; also the articles on eschatology, *Theological Investigations* X (London and New York, 1972), pp. 235–291.

totality of the consummation of the finite reality of the world, in other words the absolute future (with the spontaneous power that is proper to this), and in this sense the absolute future will be brought about by man's own act.

The 'this-worldly' future of man signifies that which at any specific moment, conceived of as the present, remains to be achieved, but which will come about within this world and within the dimensions of space and time belonging to it as a particular event or a specific state of this world. 'This-worldly' futures of this kind, which per definitionem always remain open to a further future, are themselves in turn radically distinct from one another. There are such futures or elements in such futures which can and must be thought of as conforming to the pattern of an evolutionary process determined by merely casual factors. In these that which belongs to the future simply constitutes the succession of the series of situations prevailing at any given time as determined by natural law, and the content of the future unfolds from the correlation of these succeeding elements. In such futures or elements of the future the content of the future is the slave who is governed by strict laws, the sheer outcome of present and past. Such futures are to be thought of not in eschatological terms but rather in protological or archaeological ones. The law of the beginnings is the law of the end. The future is the return to the arche, to paradise. Then, inasmuch as any element of personal history can still be discerned in such a process the watchword can only be: 'Back to the sources', for there that which the future is capable of producing is already implicitly contained in its pure and original form. In the sphere of the biological the potential immortality which the process of reproduction through the adult's act of generation is intended to assure would constitute one kind of a future conceived of in terms such as these. And yet a conceptual image of this kind would no longer possess any clarifying force even so far as a trans-specific process of evolution is concerned.

But there are quite different futures or elements in such futures, the special quality of which cannot be conceived of in terms of any such mechanistic or evolutionary conceptual pattern: future as that which is radically new, as the creative factor which is brought about in the process by which man freely shapes his own history without having simply been contained from the first in hidden form in the origins, or consisting in a mere variation of constitutive elements present all along from the origins, a variation which is ultimately indifferent and to be conceived of simply in spatial and quantitative terms. It is a fact that there can in this sense be an element which is genuinely and radically new in such a future, and that taken by itself any evolutionary conceptual pattern as characterized above would fail to do justice to the realities. It is a fact that it is this element of the radically new that provides the truly qualitative transition, and that at least the history of personal development implies a process of genuine self-transcendence. But all this cannot be considered here in its own right, and must be taken as recognized.[4] A further point which must likewise remain undiscussed here is whether, how, in what sense, and why even a future that is brought about creatively in this sense nevertheless still has a cause in its turn and is not generated simply from the void, from nothingness. On this point we must confine ourselves to stating quite briefly on the basis of a Christian understanding of God that the Christian calls this cause the origin of a future of this kind which is brought about by a free and creative process, by God, recognizing that it cannot come from mere empty nothingness. It must further be stated that the Christian, precisely in order to allow this genuine kind of future to emerge and to achieve its own authentic reality does not regard God as an element in the unfolding process of personal history, but precisely as the condition for any genuine future such that it does not reduce this to a mere process of evolution. It does not reduce it in this sense even in those cases or at those points at which this future is not identified with God himself as the absolute. The distinction within the 'this-worldly' future between that which is evolutive and that which is free and creative, is of course not intended to be conceived of as though in the sphere of the human these two futures simply existed side by side as two separate entities. On the contrary they are elements in the 'this-worldly' future of man which mutually demand, and dialectically condition one another. For this future of man constantly depends upon previously existing factors from which it derives by a process of evolution, *and at the same time* always contains also a creative and utopian element which is underivable, in virtue of which man does not merely achieve a further extension of his own past and present, but in a real and radical sense surpasses it.

III

The *first thesis* which we propose to establish runs as follows: The content of the Christian preaching consists in the question, which we maintain

[4] For the significance of self-transcendence in the total process of evolution cf. the article by K. Rahner in K. Rahner and P. Overhage, *Das Problem der Hominisation*, Quaestiones Disputatae 12/13 (Freiburg, 1961); *idem*, 'The Unity of Spirit and Matter in the Christian Understanding of Faith', *Theological Investigations* VI (London and Baltimore, 1969), pp. 153–177.

open, into the absolute future, and properly speaking in nothing else besides. One point is very remarkable: Christians and non-Christians alike have the impression that in its doctrine and practice Christianity is an extremely complicated affair, a highly developed system including a multitude of factors, a doctrine which far exceeds any other philosophy of life in its claim to knowledge and the ability to supply answers.

The true position, however, if we pay close attention to the preaching of the Christian message and really allow it to impart its own message to us, is quite otherwise. Of course Christianity is an extremely complex reality, and ultimately speaking no one individual can achieve a comprehensive view of it as a whole. Nevertheless it is such only because Christianity neither omits nor neglects anything in the complex reality of man and his world whether at the individual or at the collective levels of human life, whether of the body or of the spirit, whether of the past or of the present. At the same time, however, the message which Christianity has to convey to this infinitely complex reality of man *precisely as such*, and the manner in which it lives in and through this reality, in other words that which alone constitutes what is specific and proper to Christianity, is something utterly simple, namely the question, maintained in openness, of the absolute future which is God or – which is saying the same thing – the question of God who is the absolute future.

In order to understand this statement we must achieve an overall view of many manifestly basic assertions of Christianity, subsuming them all in a single ultimate basic statement: the world and man have a history which God himself has made his own history. This one history of God, the world and man is, on any real understanding of its nature as history, ultimately speaking only intelligible and realizable from the standpoint of the future to which it tends. Now this future is the self-bestowal of God upon the world as radically consummated, and is not merely some kind of property of the finite world as distinct from the absolute and infinite God. This God, however, who is the absolute future of man and the world, is the absolutely incomprehensible mystery which remains, and which is now bestowed upon man in the radical openness of his knowledge and freedom and in a mode that transcends any one specific definable factor. In other words it is bestowed in the mode of the radical question as such and only in this mode, and not in the form of an answer supplied from without to this question which, supposing that this were the case, would represent only a partial fulfilment. Only when the question is posed in its radical openness do we know at all what is meant by God. We do not know this until every idol is shattered, the idol of an answer which fails to meet the question in all its radical breadth, and yet at the same time seeks to bring the question to an end. Properly speaking Christianity states merely that all that we are still awaiting as our future is that this God, as the true fulfilment of the question in all its absolute extent, shall come in that which we call 'visio beatifica' and 'eternal life'. And even when he comes to us in this mode he will still always remain the eternal mystery[5] to which man commits himself in the ecstasy of love. In a real sense, therefore, Christianity in its true essence is the state of radical openness to the question of the mystery of the absolute future which is God. All individual statements in Christianity, in its knowledge and its life, therefore, can be understood only as a modality of this radical commitment to refuse to call a halt at any point and to seek the fulfilment of its life, its 'salvation' in something to which no further name can be assigned,[6] something which still lies in the future and remains an eternal mystery, something which love alone can receive.

To understand Christianity in its truest essence in this way is neither to omit nor to overlook Jesus Christ. It is no self-evident truism to say that God himself intends to be the absolute future of man in a free act of self-bestowal, or above all that this self-bestowal of God is not merely one of the possibilities to which history is open, but also *de facto* imposes itself as the future end of history. On the contrary, this is something that was only promised to us precisely in Jesus Christ in whom alone, as the crucified and risen Lord, God has entered into the world as absolute future. If we seek to understand how it is that in the incarnation of the Logos God has not ceased to be the promised future of the world as still outstanding, we must consider that for a true understanding of the Incarnation of the Logos which has made itself to be history, this history is precisely the history of him who has to come again, or, to put it better, his coming has only begun, and is still moving towards the future consummation of his

[5] For an understanding of the sustaining and sheltering function of the mystery cf. K. Rahner, 'The Concept of Mystery in Catholic Theology', *Theological Investigations* IV (London and Baltimore, 1966), pp. 36–73.

[6] We cannot enter any more fully here into the discussion concerning the word of God or into a critique in terms of language and logic. Cf., amongst others, G. Ebeling, *Gott und Wort* (Tübingen, 1966); K. Rahner, 'Meditation über das Wort Gott', *Gnade als Freiheit* (Freiburg, 1968), pp. 11–18; 'Gott ist keine naturwissenschaftliche Formel', *ibid.*, pp. 19–23; E. Jüngel, 'Gott – als Wort unserer Sprache', *Evangelische Theologie* 1 (1969), pp. 1–24; C. A. van Peursen, *Das Wort Gott* (Göttingen, 1969). As used here this formulation is intended to emphasize that God is not a name in the sense that through this naming the object so named has come to be unequivocally available to the investigations of the namer.

advent. We must consider that this incarnate Logos has entered precisely into the death of man, and we achieve a share in his salvation and his promise only in virtue of the fact that we die with him, i.e. that in knowledge and still more in the act of living, precisely with him we break through all provisional answers or cause ourselves to break through to that expectation which looks for nothing more and hopes for nothing more than the future of God who is the eternally incomprehensible salvation of man through his self-bestowal. Despite the many branches into which Christianity has spread, the manifold forms in which it has articulated itself, and the manifold distinctions which have been introduced into it over two thousand years of its history, it can be expressed in very brief formulae. One formula, which could in a certain sense be called a futurological one, would be this: Christianity is the attitude of abiding openness to the question of the absolute future which seeks to bestow itself, which has definitively promised itself as coming in Jesus Christ, and which is called God.

IV

The *second thesis* which we propose to put forward runs as follows: The 'this worldly' future of man always constitutes an open, and abidingly open, question.

No long explanation is required to define the formal meaning of the phrase 'this worldly future': it is that which man discovers by his own creative powers, sets before him as his Utopia, plans for and realizes, and thereby draws down into the world of space and time in which he finds himself placed in such a way that it continues to be subject to this world and its laws. This still remains valid even though it must not be denied that a future of this kind, definable in 'this worldly' categories, makes retrospective impact upon the conditions already existing in the world, and plays its part in altering them in such a way that, without man being able clearly to recognize or manipulate it a variable balance is struck between the previously existing conditions which make such a future possible and the future itself.

We have no intention here of treating at any length the theological question, in itself fundamental, of what in more precise terms the mutually conditioning relationship consists in between man's orientation towards his 'this-worldly' future and his orientation towards the absolute future. We must confine ourselves here to asserting without any more detailed supporting arguments, that these two orientations, towards the 'this worldly' future and the absolute future, mutually condition one another in such a way that the Christian attitude towards the absolute future which is God neither diminishes nor eliminates the responsibility it entails for a 'this worldly' future, but rather imparts a radical dimension to it.[7] The reason is that the only genuine way in which man can achieve this state of readiness to hold himself open to the absolute future in his personal life is for him to adopt an attitude, at once positive and critical, of responsibility and active engagement leading to the achievement of an ever-fresh future within this world.

After these brief preliminary remarks let us consider our second thesis in itself. The 'this worldly' future always remains an open question. What we mean by this is that even with regard to a future understood in merely 'this worldly' terms man is never related to this as though it were already present, planned down to the last detail, and requiring only that a specific interval should elapse before it was an achieved reality. Not merely the absolute future which is God himself in his inconceivability, but the 'this worldly' future too is an open one. It too is always unknown, a future which, when it arrives, takes us by surprise. And it is *precisely for this reason* that it can also be the medium leading to the absolute future.

Why is this the case? First it must of course be stated that man can and must plan, project, and control the future. Our thesis, therefore, in no sense involves any denial of the fact that at least today, in the age of rational technology and of the exact sciences, of cybernetics and futurology, there is such a thing as a planning of the future; that by comparison with earlier ages the element of the planned in the future has increased to an extent which was formerly inconceivable; that modern man has achieved an almost qualitatively different relationship to his future, and that too both because of the possibility of planning the changes which his environment is to undergo, and also in virtue of the fact that man can plan how to manipulate himself at the individual and collective levels. All this is obvious, and is here taken as given,[8] even though it in turn should be

[7] A full and detailed presentation of the position that to recognize God as the future of this world also implies an active responsibility for the world and for the transformation of the world on the part of the Christian is provided in K. Rahner, 'On the Theological Problems Entailed in the Idea of the "New Earth" ', *Theological Investigations* X (London and New York, 1973), pp. 260–272.

[8] This problem is investigated in fuller detail in K. Rahner, *Theological Investigation* X (London and New York, 1972) in the articles entitled 'The Experiment with Man' and 'The Problem of Genetic Manipulation', pp. 205–252.

thought out in greater detail in its own right. But all this does not alter the fact that even the questions of the 'this worldly' future is in principle such that we can never arrive at any comprehensive answer to it.

In order to perceive the validity of this second thesis we may concentrate on *three* considerations in particular, which are of course interconnected, while passing over certain others.

First, when it is the future that is planned and brought into being by man himself that is being treated of it must be borne in mind that the achievement of a future that is planned proceeds from certain prior conditions which man finds already in existence and the full significance of which he does not perceive. Today the harvest that man gathers does not consist solely of the fruits of nature which present themselves to him spontaneously to sustain his life. On the contrary he himself alters his environment. He creates new materials for himself. He does not merely domesticate plants and animals, but alters them as well according to plans of his own, and by a process of self-manipulation gradually arrives at a state where he is actually the *faber sui*. But however true it may be that we cannot already in the present determine how much or how little will show itself to be possible along these lines, this does nothing to alter the fact that in this creative activity of his man proceeds, and must proceed, from certain specific prior conditions. These prior conditions are subject to a twofold limitation: first they have a specific content, a determinate state of being 'so and not otherwise' which imposes certain definite and predetermined limitations on what can be made of them. Second, to the extent that they make it possible to introduce changes, they always require a certain period of time until these changes can emerge as the outcome of them, a period which again and again exceeds the personal life-span of any one individual.

This situation in which the point of departure is pre-determined in respect of its content and the time needed for the development to take place might at first sight lead us to suppose that because of it it was possible precisely to calculate accurately beforehand how the future would turn out, as in fact all such predictions of the future are based upon a knowledge of the conditions governing this point of departure and the intervals of time involved, which at least in macro-physical terms are accurately calculable. At the same time, however, a point that must not be overlooked is that we do not have and cannot have any comprehensive knowledge of all these prior conditions. Yet in order to make an exact prognosis possible the causes governing such concrete futures must be known not merely in their *general* structures, but also in their quite specific and unique dispositions in relation to one another.[9] Now this is impossible. For within the system governing the one world every element in this world depends upon every other, and at the same time all depend upon each. Any comprehensive determination, therefore, would only be possible if we had a comprehensive knowledge of the totality of this cosmic system. Yet in so far as such knowledge can be aimed at at all by man it can only be aimed at in virtue of an overall mastery of the system itself, and this would itself bring about and presuppose an alteration of this system in itself, even though it itself cannot in its turn be observed in this process since it itself constitutes an element in the observer. A further point over and above this is that it is impossible to achieve any point of observation which is absolutely separate from the world. And in view of this any comprehensive formula for the world on the part of one individual element within this world called human knowledge cannot be established. But this means that the future even of an individual element within this total system cannot be determined beforehand with complete accuracy on the basis of the knowledge of the history and the situation of this element at any given moment, for this element and its future in itself always remain subject to partial determination by all the other alterations of the system as a whole and, in accordance with what has been said above, this can precisely not be perceived and comprehended as a whole,[10] unless by an intelligence which stood outside this system, in the concrete, therefore, only by a divine intelligence, since in the light of the unity between spirit and matter any finite intelligences existing absolutely outside the world are surely quite inconceivable.

In this consideration we have taken the world considered as a human environment and as humanity itself merely as a physical system, and we have considered man's ability to prognosticate on the basis of his knowledge merely at the level of physics and natural science. The openness of the future to man's knowledge which is already inherent in this is radically

[9] Here we may recall the fiction of the 'Demon of Laplace' constructed within the framework of a mechanistic conception of the world. This had the power of using its knowledge of all the factors prevailing at a given point in time in the cosmic order, whether momentary situations or developing processes, and so of calculating comprehensively the course of the world's history both backwards and forwards. The findings of modern physics have shown that this fiction is no longer meaningful even in the sphere of physical knowledge today. *A fortiori* it is no longer meaningful when we take into account in our cosmic system the factor of human awareness. This is something which will appear from the considerations which follow.

[10] Without any exaggeration this state of affairs might be called the factor which brings an element of obscurity into any prognostication.

broadened still further when we reflect upon the fact that this world, the future of which we are looking to, is far from being a merely physical and biological world. However true it may be that it is based upon this physical and bio-physical reality or contains this within itself, it is at the same time a world of the psychological, the social, and not least of freedom. We have no need whatever to enter in detail into all the radical unknown factors which this entails, factors which prevent us from achieving any totally comprehensive prognosis of the future. We need only to point out the difficulty which has already revealed itself in the task of forseeing the development of the purely physical world and which now recurs in a fresh and radical form, for man as cognitive is himself an element in the psychological and sociological system which he is seeking to know, and he himself alters this by his own knowledge. For instance anyone who proclaims some form of determinism as an existing psychological and social factor himself modifies the social and psychological situation into which he emits this proclamation of his. In its prior assumption this knowledge itself is dependent upon that which it seeks to encompass and alters what it has to recognize.[11] In order to achieve an accurate knowledge of itself it would have to have reflected comprehensively upon the conditions which make it itself possible. In order to establish its findings beyond all doubt it would have to avoid itself altering its own subject-matter in the very process of the act of cognition itself. For the reasons that have been set forth such knowledge as this remains constantly in process of development and is never completed. Rather it projects itself into a future that is proper to it and unknown to it.

In all that we have said we have still not even begun to reflect on the freedom of man, which itself as an ultimate and original factor is incapable of reflecting in any adequate sense on the fact that its own point of departure is subject to prior conditions. Moreover as genuinely creative this factor of human freedom presupposes the unknown as a sphere which will be filled with a future that is known only through the creative freedom as an act which is not prior to any knowledge, for it is this that is unequivocally presupposed to it as its guide. This is a point of which we shall have to treat more fully at a later stage.

The *second* point to be considered for an understanding of this openness to the 'this worldly' future is the circumstance that in the contemporary situation in which man's creative freedom to shape his own future has become actual the *number* of possibilities available to this freedom is grow-

---

[11] A penetrating investigation of these areas has been carried out by J. Habermas in *Erkenntnis und Interesse* (Frankfurt, 1968).

ing, and precisely in virtue of this the question is becoming more open of which of these possibilities which have become so numerous will in fact be realized. From this point of view we shall only be in a position to answer this question when, out of all the many possibilities, one specific future has been turned into the present by a free and undeducible decision. It must be borne in mind that today the number of concrete possibilities for man to exercise his freedom has become greater than in earlier times. Two further factors are, however, first that not all possibilities can simultaneously be realized at one blow, and second that the realization of any one specific possibility renders the realization of the other possibilities which are given, and which up to that point have remained open, impossible. But these are points which in view of the linear development of history in time do not need to be expounded at any length. Admittedly it has been said that the age of a true liberation of man from his social self-alienation can, will and should be ushered in only at that point at which the most divers possibilities for self-realization available to the individual in society are offered to him as *simultaneously* realizable so that he is not confined merely to one specific possibility chosen by an authoritarian decision on the part of one individual, or in a democratic manner by the majority.

But however desirable it may be that the development of society should lead to the sort of situation in which each individual can determine his own personal self-realization, and has the means necessary for this realization made available to him by society without the different form of self-realization aimed at by another being thereby prevented, still there cannot be any doubt that at least in part the fact that all are confined to a single dimension of space and time, as well as the finitude of the means available in the concrete, sets certain quite notable limits which can never wholly be overcome to the simultaneous realization of alternative forms of self-realization which man may propose for himself. A further point which cannot be questioned is that because of the finitude of man's life-span the *specific* mode of self-realization of an individual always implies a renunciation of another possibility of self-realization subsequently being taken up, even though precisely today such a possibility would be present, at least as offered, to a greater extent than in former times. By a man's free decision to opt for a specific mode of self-realization, however, this possibility is ruled out, whether as present or as future. Which one among all such manifold possibilities which cannot be realized at the same time is in fact the one to be realized remains in principle obscure and undecided so long as the possibility opted for has not yet been realized.

To deny this statement would by implication be to deny the fact that several real possibilities of a future actively to be shaped by man himself do indeed lie open before him. The increase in the number of such possibilities, however, is precisely the characteristic feature of the situation of modern man by comparison with former times. And again it is precisely this increase in the possible ways of shaping some concrete future that makes it difficult to discern which of the possible futures will be the real one. In fact all the prognoses even of futurology point again and again to this indeterminate element, because no-one can really foretell the manner in which men will react to these future situations that are prognosticated. In all cases it is merely particular features of a future world of man that are predicted, and never a whole system in which some world of tomorrow can so be summed up that the reaction of future humanity to its presence can itself be taken into the calculations.[12]

In order to make clear the indeterminacy even of the 'this worldly' future there is a *third* point to which we can only barely refer, even though it is only when we have recognized this that we have arrived at the true and ultimate reason for this indeterminacy: it is the factor of freedom.

Once the forms in which freedom is objectified can already be taken as given, once they are in existence, they are, in principle, always capable of being explained and made intelligible in terms of causal or functional determinism from a consideration of the factors leading up to them. At the same time, however, there is a further factor, namely the free exercise of choice, which differs from that which is subject to these laws, and which can be explained in terms of them once it is an existing fact, in that this further factor cannot in its turn be explained in terms of any pre-existing conditions outside itself. It is this which most properly impells realities of this sort to emerge into existence as the outcome of the exercise of freedom, autonomously selecting and positing one specific possibility out of the wider range available to it. It is not possible here to demonstrate the existence of such freedom as the original positing factor by any transcendental deduction, a freedom which does not rule out the *a posteriori* explanation of what is already present as the outcome of certain laws, but

---

[12] The plans of H. Ozbekhan are to be estimated as an effort on the part of a futurologist to eliminate this uncertainty. Ozbekhan seeks to construct model futures by anticipation of such a kind that the variations in these models enable us to arrive at a conclusion as to what are the desirable reactions in the present in order to achieve these 'ideal' futures. Cf. H. Ozbekhan, 'Skizze einer "Look-out-Institution" ', *Atomzeitalter*, Vol. 4 (1967), p. 187.

at the same time cannot itself be accounted for, much less predicted, by any explanation of this kind.[13]

Here we must confine ourselves to pointing out that anyone who denies the existence of this kind of freedom, in which the subject becomes the ultimate source of action, is thereby failing to recognize the phenomenon of genuinely personal historicity and the nature of history itself, and *a fortiori* of the real future. Thereby he falsifies and distorts the nature of personal history (which in its very existence is orientated towards the real future) in that his conception of it is governed by a purely mechanistic image of evolution in which later developments are already unequivocally present in hidden form in earlier ones, and the beginning is master of the end. It may be conceded that genuine freedom is never manifested in isolation from the other factors prevailing in any given case, and that it always appears merely as a secret repudiation of the necessary concealing itself in the forms in which it is properly objectified so that it appears to be merely the outcome of causal factors, and explicable in terms of these. But however true this may be, if there is such a thing as genuine freedom at all, then there is a 'this worldly' future which is indeterminate and obscure, one which, so far as the historical subject himself is concerned, is in principle only brought to light in the very act in which it is posited and so rendered present. Up to this point it has been hidden in the limitless breadth of the possible, especially since this broader sphere of the possible is of course not to be thought of as comprising a definite number of separate projects and plans which have already been worked out, and each of which is thoroughly understood in its own right, so that the only question still unresolved is which of them will in fact be put into execution. The interdependence of such possible projects, the infinite possible variations (which are inexhaustible so far as our conscious thought is concerned) of such projects and plans, prevent us from distinguishing the one obscure possibility within a definite and comprehensive number of separate individual possibilities, and so to rationalize it in any adequate sense. To the extent that it is possible clearly to delineate certain distinctly defined possibilities for the future, what these constitute (even abstracting from what has been said at an earlier stage) is not a comprehensive articulation of the possible in general, but merely, in their multiplicity, indications of the one obscure possible course which freedom grasps at, only throwing light upon those points in them which it itself really brings into being by the decision in which it is exercised. If freedom is brought again and again to

[13] For a more detailed treatment of this point cf. K. Rahner, *Gnade als Freiheit* (Freiburg, 1968), pp. 31–89.

the dividing of the ways, this precisely does not mean that it can first trace all these ways to their respective ends at the conceptual level as on a complete map, and then decide which way it will embark upon. It is only the way that is actually trodden that reveals its real nature. All those which are recognized as possible but not followed remain behind as the unknown ones which lead into what is unresolved and obscure. In all plans even the 'this worldly' future remains that which is unresolved and obscure.

v

In conclusion a *third thesis* may perhaps be adduced with regard to the question of the future: in the very nature of his function the theologian is the guardian of this *docta ignorantia futuri*.[14] This thesis should not be regarded as presumptuous. For it is obvious first that the theologian is, in this sense, a counsel for the defence of the openness of the absolute and the 'this worldly' future only to the extent that he takes as his starting-point the gospel which is addressed to all, and returns to it; that he makes this the subject of his consideration and finds in it the *docta ignorantia*. Second, in order that the third thesis shall not be misinterpreted as pre-sumptuousness on the part of the theologian it must be realized that the Christian and the theologian can perfectly well concede that even one who does not consider himself a Christian in any explicit sense may, in his concrete personal living, be realizing what Christianity itself proclaims as its own interpretation of the significance of human life. In other words, for instance, even this wise recognition that we do not know the future, this determined submission of oneself to that which is unplanned, repre-sents not an unhappy survival of irrationalism which will gradually be eliminated, but rather an abiding existential modality and an intrinsic ele-ment in the dignity of human freedom.

On this basis, and in the light of the mutually conditioning relationship to be found between man's attitude towards his 'this worldly' future and his attitude towards his absolute future, we will perhaps be in a position to understand that element which in a positive sense can be called the 'utopian' in human existence, something which constitutes a prior condi-tion for every change that takes place in personal history, and so too at the social level. The utopian is the expression of the mutuality of this condi-tioning relationship. Anyone who, in moving towards the absolute future

---

[14] On this cf. also J. B. Metz, 'Gott vor uns', *Ernst Bloch zu Ehren* (Frankfurt, 1965), pp. 227–241; *idem, Zur Theologie der Welt* (Mainz – Munich, 1968), pp. 88 f.

encounters the concrete data of personal history, may experience in this concrete data the relativity of it as given in the here and now. And yet at the same time he neither can nor should let go of that which belongs to the particular categories of history as the medium of the movement towards the absolute future. In this position he must exercise his creative powers in order to construct for himself a 'this worldly' future goal, and it is precisely this which can, in a positive sense, be called the 'utopian' factor. For that which at any point is given in the here and now is real, and its historical modality does not rest merely upon rational criticisms or the assigning of a relative status to it in human thought. This point can be recognized so long as it is not viewed merely as belonging to the infinite perspectives of the absolute future, for it is only as viewed from these perspectives that it could still constantly and uncritically be maintained that its status as historical was due to these subjective factors. But its objective state as historically real is revealed when it is called in question by means of another factor belonging to history, and precisely to the future, in other words by the utopian factor which constitutes the point of reference for, and the representative of, the absolute future. This means that the utopian factor in history belongs essentially to the achievement of the fulness of Christian life as realized in man's assent to the absolute future and to absolute hope. This utopian factor is willed precisely because, and to the extent that, it is not yet achieved, and also not merely the foreseeable outcome of the present in a mechanistic or evolutionary sense. Christianity, therefore, should involve a genuine commitment to the world and an assent to the absolute future both in one, and in such a way that each attitude mutually conditions the other. And where this is the case its creative force gives birth to the utopian factor which becomes a standard by which to criticize the present and to impel it forwards to a new historical future. This is the medium of this mutually conditioning relationship, and obviously it always constitutes at the same time that which provides the critique of, and calls in question, the social situation actually prevailing. To put it quite simply: anyone who as a Christian sought simply and uncritically to identify himself with his existing social situation would have to ask himself whether in that case he believed in the absolute future in a really effective sense and in the real practice of his own living, instead of merely at the theoretical level and in some private and interior dimension. He should put the question to himself of how in that case he has any sincere realization of the fact that the present is that which is merely provisional, seeing that he does not critically measure it against some other 'this worldly' future, albeit one which in its turn always remains provisional. Thus it is precisely our hope in the absolute future which we do not create that demands that we shall keep our eyes upon the historical utopia which introduces an element of criticism and disquiet into history, and impels it forward, and, moreover, brings it into the social dimension.

Precisely in the light of these axioms, however, it must be stated that Christianity and, as the servant of this, theology, are and must be the guardians of the *docta ignorantia futuri*. In fulfilling this function they are contributing to man in his role as the free subject of creative activity. For if a point were ever arrived at at which the future were really understood as something which could be comprehensively prognosticated, and that was able to be calculated in all its aspects, at that point the future would, basically speaking, be eliminated in favour of a continually abiding present. For at that point it would in principle no longer be possible to avoid a position in which the present was explained as the already inaugurated realization of *that* future which as outlined in rationalist planning would be the only legitimate one. Only the *docta ignorantia futuri* provides a basic position for exercising a sustained critique of a present which is at all times only too ready to assert itself as the only right state of affairs.[15] Only an open future, which in principle is assented to as such, can stand up to the objection which every establishment raises against revolutionary critics of the present, namely that while they are ready to criticize, they themselves have no unequivocally clear and positive alternative to offer for the future. Of course we must agree with Paul in saying that man is not meant to launch himself blindly into the void. The critique of the present should as far as possible be combined with positively formulated projects for shaping the future. But anyone who demands that projects for the future shall be just as far-sighted and perceptive as is allegedly the case with the actual present, anyone who seeks in principle to rule out the possibility that the will to achieve a future also involves a commitment to the unknown, anyone who seeks radically to eliminate the factors of freedom and personal history, is adopting a rationalist and determinist attitude of radical hostility towards the *docta ignorantia futuri*. He is rejecting that medium of his hope in the absolute future which is indefinable, the medium, namely, which consists in a hopeful engagement of himself in

[15] The position that at least up to the present futurology itself has actually promoted this tendency instead of overcoming it, and indeed that it constitutes an 'ideological confirmation of an order which draws the veil over what is new in order to leave everything as it was before' (C. Koch, *Kritik der Futurologie*, Frankfurt, 1968 – Kursbuch 14, 2) is a point which C. Koch attempts to demonstrate.

the daily commitment to a 'this worldly' future which is open. Anyone who rejects the *docta ignorantia futuri* in this way is properly speaking no longer a Christian, even though this rejection is posited in a sphere which, since it is apparently wholly secular in character, seems to have nothing further whatever to do with Christianity and theology.[16]

The controversy between Christians, therefore, in their attitude towards the 'this worldly' future can only be concerned with arriving at reasonable and responsible measures of planning on the one hand and commitment to the openness and obscurity of the future on the other. But even though a controversy precisely of this sort does demand rational and objective discussion, ultimately speaking it is precisely incapable of ever being totally eliminated solely by means of such discussion. For in fact if a discussion of this kind is to be engaged in among Christians at all, it must constantly take into account and recognize the element of the unknown in the future that has to be planned for. Moreover both sides to the discussion must take this into account as an element which is not merely something to be put up with only at that point at which it is absolutely impossible to avoid it any longer, but one which is positively sought for and welcomed by the Christian. When we consider this point it must truly be a matter of surprise that the Christianity of today has fallen under the suspicion (and not without reason) of being a conservative force which favours the present rather than the future. Of course in inculcating a hope in the absolute future Christianity does also liberate man from a hysterical quest for that which is new at the 'this worldly' level, and which tends to be sought for merely because it is different. But as constituting a cure in this sense of this kind of disease Christianity is merely credible and healing when it itself avoids uncritically defending the existing state of affairs, and thereby itself tacitly denying hope in the absolute future. For this hope, whether consciously or unconsciously, constitutes the motive force and the critique for all strivings which are directed towards a 'this worldly' future, and it is this striving which constitutes the medium in which the hope for the absolute future is maintained.

[16] In this sense it cannot be objected even to the political theology of J. B. Metz that it undervalues the autonomy of the political sphere when it makes the attempt to show that the absolute future as understood eschatologically is critically mediated by the abidingly open ('this wordly') future of human society. The autonomy of the political sphere can in fact never be interpreted in Christian and theological terms as though the political future of mankind could be brought to a future capable of being totally worked out in rational terms and comprehensively planned for by technology On this cf. also J. B. Metz, 'Der zukünftige Mensch und der kommende Gott', H. J. Schultz ed., *Wer ist das eigentlich – Gott?* (Munich, 1969), pp. 260–275.

I I

PERSPECTIVES FOR
THE FUTURE OF THE CHURCH

I am of course no prophet, and hence I do not know what will become of the Church of Christ in the next few centuries. The fact that we do not know this is indeed an intrinsic part of our Christian faith, for otherwise it would be quite impossible for the command to be laid upon us that we should place all our hopes solely in the Lord of history and of the future. This would be impossible if a futurologist with his computer already knew what was to come. Properly speaking, therefore, the only certain point is that the word of the Lord will proceed on its course through the ages, that the gates of hell will not prevail over the community of those who believe in Jesus Christ as their Lord, but also that a point will never arise in this world's time at which the Church will achieve, on the basis of this, a total victory such as can be made manifest in terms which this world can recognize. The only certain point is that the nearer we draw to the day of Christ the more fiercely the Church will be assailed by the threat of Antichrist. But the concrete form of the abiding Church (concrete in respect of the numbers of her members, her life, the value that is attached to her, and her weakness in secular society) and the concrete form of the abiding assaults upon her – these we do not know. For all the foresight and planning which there is and which in fact there must be to an increasing extent, we Christians make pilgrimage into the unknown future. And so far as Christian living is concerned this unknown is not a regrettable survival which continues unresolved despite our planning, but an essential element which is necessary and expected in that hope and that patience which is set before the Christian as his task, and bestowed upon him as grace. Everything which has to be said here is subject to this proviso, which must never be forgotten.

Yet precisely in the light of this the Christian must consider the 'this worldly' future, however true it may be that that which is really awaited, hoped for, and prayed for is not the Church but the kingdom of God. For it is only the planner who has something which he can freely and silently leave to the sole Lord of history to decide, and it is only in this way that

202

hope is really hope instead of being a mere apathetic sinking into the obviousness of the present. What is it that can be foreseen in this way, concretely awaited and planned for? I will attempt only a *few* brief answers. Whether they are the most important ones or the right ones – this is something which I do not know. Bur for the patient and submissive in the spirit of ἐλπίς and ὑπομονή, who have as their only God the absolute future, this is something which is important and yet at the same time easy. My readers will not be irritated if they notice that here and there I formulate my answers on the basis of a *Catholic* understanding of Christian living and the Church, perhaps without myself clearly adverting to it. Nor is it so important to draw a precise distinction between the following two factors: first that which is simply destined to come because it is either in conformity with the omnipotent will of God to bestow grace in Christ, or else is a 'must' of saving history such that through it (albeit brought about through man's sin) God achieves his gracious purpose, and secondly that which man himself as Christian desires and can or should strive for on behalf of the Church without exactly knowing whether this desire of his will be fulfilled, a desire which God permits or even enjoins upon us for the age of this world without guaranteeing that it will be fulfilled within this world.

1. The Church is destined to be the 'little flock'. This is not merely because only God knows those who are his own, whom he has chosen, while we never know it, but only hope on our own behalf (as also on behalf of all others) that we are destined to overcome all our sins and attain to the final consummation of love and to the eternal peace of God. The Church of the future will also be the little flock at the empirical level of social living. In asserting this the Christian is brought into a situation which can rightly be described only with difficulty. For on the one hand he must have the missionary will for the gospel to be preached to all peoples, and so to all social groups in the world, that all shall be baptized and that the eschatological hope (to adopt the parlance of the Second Vatican Council) shall be imprinted upon all social orders, that the name of Christ shall be recognized by the 'kings' of this earth too, that Christianity shall be not merely an affair of the private conscience or of a few, but also a factor in public life, in society, in the world, and moreover among all. We recognize the duty to will this, and no definable limits can ever be imposed upon this will. We are never allowed to say: 'At this point there is enough of the Church in the world and its public life'. But while recognizing all this, the Christian can and must know that saving history and Church history are *de facto* never to be identified in the age of

this present world, that the gospel will always be contradicted, that the Church will remain the little flock that is assailed. And the recognition of this has nothing to do with the sectarian pride of the 'righteous remnant' which regards itself alone as the elect. In fact the Christian of today can wholeheartedly recognize that from the point of view of her position in society the Church of the future will be, to an even greater extent than hitherto, stamped with the character of the 'little flock' in all its harshness. Indeed he should allow the recognition of this fact already by anticipation to have its due and right influence upon his missionary aims and, since he can foresee that those aims will in practice be restricted in their effect, he should allow this to play its part in determining the manner in which he puts those aims into practice.

In other words: Christians cannot expect that any homogeneous society will once more emerge which as such can simply be called Christian. Those factors in civilization and society which once produced and sustained a society of this sort, which was in some 'mediaeval' sense homogeneously Christian, will never return. They were in any case not specifically Christian factors but rather secular, and they produced similar effects in constituting a society characterized by homogeneity in religious matters even outside the Christian sphere. In so far as it might ever be possible to aim at producing a homogeneously Christian society in the future the only way in which this goal could be pursued would be by using the means of a system which in social, political and ideological terms was totalitarian. And this is something which the Christian, precisely on principles of freedom of conscience and faith itself, must radically and unconditionally reject. The Church can only be the Church of the free believers, and in view of this must actually champion the cause of freedom for unbelief as well. Moreover in the future – different in this from earlier times – there will no longer be any point of departure for finding a homogeneously Christian society (except possibly through forced indoctrination of a totalitarian kind). And because of these two factors the future position of the Church from the social point of view will be one in which she exists side by side with a state of unbelief which will likewise be manifest at the social level. She will be the little flock, that is to say at best, and in the most peaceful circumstances, one element in a pluralistic society, a local community Church of believers more than a national Church with a social code of behaviour of its own, even though both these entities represent extremes of abstract thought such as will never be realized in a form that is 'chemically pure'. The important point is, however, that the Church must uncompromisingly take this point into account in considering her missionary plans for the future, even though this must not be allowed to lead to an attitude of defeatism in missionary work or a withdrawal into the sacristy or into a merely interior life, something which in any case a pluralistic society cannot of its very nature demand of any one individual group within it.

In the concrete this implies that the Church must not necessarily hold fast to those positions of power in society which in former times she came legitimately to acquire, and which perhaps even today cannot be proved to have become unjustified in the contemporary scene. But above all this also implies that there is something which the Church must not do for the sake of still continuing to be a Church of the people and the masses in the widest possible sense: she must not tolerate without condemnation every corruption of the pure gospel within her united social body or retain within it all those who seek to uphold heresies in the Church[1] yet do not quit the Church of their own accord. Certainly full freedom of conscience is to be accorded to every individual, but the Church would cease to be the Church of *one* faith, one creed, of the gospel, and of the right administration of the sacraments, if she had to grant any and every individual the right to do what the freedom of his own conscience dictated to him *within* the Church. In a pluralistic society in which failure to belong to the Church no longer has any social consequences, or is gradually ceasing to have such, the Church can and under certain circumstances must also have the courage to pronounce a sentence of excommunication even when thereby she is even more reduced to the status of the little flock. The sphere of freedom of conscience and the sphere of the Church are not identical, though it is true that precisely on this account the Church herself must uphold this wider sphere of freedom even in those cases in which on any human estimation she is acting against her own interests in doing so.

This small group within a broad pluralistic society will gradually overcome the temptation to an inferiority complex which can emerge through tension between the claim of Christendom to offer salvation to all on the one hand, and the very restricted degree of success which it achieves at any visible level in society on the other. This little flock will not overcome this temptation by falling into an attitude of over-compensating pride and anxiety, and so a sectarian attitude in which she regards herself as the community which alone is elected for eternal life. She will overcome this temptation by recognizing that she is the recipient of the grace and the

[1] On this cf. 'Heresies in the Church Today?' and 'Schism in the Catholic Church?' in this volume, pp. 98–141.

burden alike of being the sacrament of salvation for the *world*,[2] of being the manifestation of God's will to bestow grace at the social level, that divine will which causes grace and justification to take effect in an 'anonymous Christianity' in the depths of the human conscience and in much which belongs objectively speaking to the sphere of the human spirit, even though all this may have failed to achieve any conscious expression of itself to the point at which it is recognized and objectified in social forms for what it is: the grace of Christ which has its abiding presence in the world in the Church.

2. The Christian community of the future will have a quite different sociological structure from that which she now has both in the Churches and also in the sects.[3] For me as a Catholic this cannot mean that the theological essence of the Church as constituted as a society will be altered. But even in terms of a strictly orthodox Catholic ecclesiology this essence is so broad and elastic, is capable of being realized in so many different concrete social forms, that it must not be supposed that anything like the sociological image which the Church and the local Church communities present today has always to remain the same, or even that this image is in all circumstances worth striving for. This change will, I believe, imply, amongst other things, the following:

a) The community (whether at the level of a local Church, a diocese or the Church in the absolute) will be a Church of brethren. Certainly the present-day Christian Churches differ from one another very notably in respect of their doctrinal interpretation of their own juridical constitution to the point where the differences of opinion involved lead to a separation of the Churches. But abstracting from the Christian sects and admitting the fluid transitions between these and Churches in the true sense, we can say that all Christian Churches, viewed from the sociological rather than the doctrinal point of view, have been or are 'clergy' Churches. That is to say, viewed in their sociological aspects they exist *prior to* the free unity of their members as constituted by faith, hope, and charity. Not only in its nature but also in its effective mode of existence the juridical structure is a reality which is prior to the community of faith as such. Only on this

---

[2] On this characterization of the Church at the Council see 'Lumen Gentium' Nos. 1, 9, 48; 'Gaudium et Spes', Nos. 43, 45; K. Rahner, 'Konziliare Lehre der Kirche und künftige Wirklichkeit christlichen Lebens', *Schriften zur Theologie* VI (Einsiedeln, 2nd ed., 1968), pp. 479–498; E. Schillebeeckx, 'De Ecclesia ut Sacramento Mundi', *Acta Congressus Internationalis de Theologia Concilii Vaticani* II (Rome, 1968), pp. 48–53.

[3] cf. 'On the Structure of the People of the Church Today' in this volume, pp. 218–228.

showing in fact, abstracting from all other considerations, is it conceivable that the Churches can and do number almost the entire population of central Europe as members of themselves, applying very obvious criteria for this purpose, even though only a fragment of that population either feels itself to be, or can regard itself as genuinely Christian in a theological sense. Because after all it is obvious that to be a Christian is not simply identical with having been baptized in infancy.

In the future, however, this situation will no longer continue, even though, perhaps, it is far from being desirable that the change in events shall take the form of a spectacular revolution. The Churches will be Churches of brethren. They will exist because, and in virtue of the fact that men unite themselves with the community of Christ through faith and love. And everything which exists and must exist in the Church in the way of order, official authority, and constitution will be sustained in its real existence and effective force by this believing love and be virtually nothing else besides. (I say *virtually* because obviously it is again and again the case that those social realities which achieve objective status as a result of the exercise of freedom also achieve, and should achieve a value in their own right). Moreover, however true it may be that in the future too the officially constituted authority in the Church must be understood as an authority deriving from Christ and his mission, still the individual member of the Church will experience the one vested with official authority as he who, in his official activities, is sustained not by any social power or prestige in society such as is prior to the effective faith and loyalty of the members of the Church, but rather owes his position to the free faith, willingness to obey, and brotherly love of all men within the Church because every believer will rejoice and thank God when the grace of God makes it possible for one individual to take the burden of official position in his Church upon himself, a burden which brings with it no earthly honour and no worldly advantage. While a certain tension is inevitable in every 'society in which the work is distributed', I hope that apart from this there will no longer be any place in the Church of the future for any additional attitudes of anticlericalism or antilaicism. For in the diaspora situation then prevailing, since all will be believers as the outcome of their own free and most personal decision, and all will be seeking for the unity of love, they will also experience the Church as too intimately *their own* most personal concern for it to be possible in practice for the official authorities in the Church to be regarded as anything but identified with 'the Church' either by themselves or by the laity.

b) The individual communities (and on this basis the Church as such) will have to create their own social unity for themselves, and in fact to a certain extent as the outcome of their own planning. Hitherto it may have appeared as though the social unity of the community were constituted simply and exclusively by the common creed and the common liturgy (together with that which is the prior condition precisely for *this*). It was possible for this apparent situation to exist and this impression to be given because the ecclesiastical community was able to assume as already existing a *sufficiently integrated* secular society (for instance that of the village or the small town), and to raise it in its already integrated form to the level of a confessing and worshipping community, and again because even from the point of view of civil administration it had an undisputed social status and so to a certain extent was held together from without. Now that the society of the masses has to a large extent been disintegrated in the large cities these prior conditions for an integrated Church community are no longer present, and the unity of creed and cult are not sufficient in themselves to sustain the unity of the Church community in any concrete or effective sense. In order to exist and live the Church community needs an integration which it can no longer *assume* to be already existing in sufficient measure. Instead it itself has to create this state of integration. The rock which must at all costs be avoided in this course is the danger that in busying itself to achieve a state of integration between individuals in this way we may reduce the community to the status of a sect, a ghetto of insignificant people who seek in the Church community that cosy state of concealment which is so attractive to those who have proved inadequate in the public dimension of life, and which they cannot find in the pluralistic deserts of society in the broader sense. Again – and this is something that applies precisely to the Church community of the future – we absolutely *must not* seek to be self-sufficient in human terms, or seek to provide everything which a man needs in order to be a man in the way of human intercourse, culture, security, neighbourliness etc. Again the Church community of the future must be open to the outside world, must be ready to be shaped by individuals who obviously and whole-heartedly engage themselves in the life of the pluralistic society in general, in its struggles, in the self-commitment which it requires, in the pluralism of 'movements', interests, parties. The Church community must not identify itself with any specific formal or informal group in secular society, and yet it cannot achieve its own intrinsic integration through the 'merely' religious factor in the narrowest sense. In its spirit of brotherhood it must provide neighbourliness. It must be capable of providing a basis for Christianity to become engaged in the tasks of the world in the sphere which is proper to them. Here surely tasks are to be found which are as yet hardly recognized, still less fulfilled. The social structures of the Church community of the future have not yet been worked out.

c) At this point a more specialized consideration should perhaps be added, one which, as it seems to me, is of concern to all Churches, even though there may be some differences in the way in which the practical consequences of it are worked out according to the particular character of the individual Churches involved. It seems to me conceivable for all Churches (including the Catholic Church) that these fraternal communities of the future may in many cases – not always or in every case – differ from the Churches on the grand scale of the past in that the official positions in the Church will be vested in individuals who undertake them only at a mature age and who emerge from integrated communities of this kind having belonged to them in the fullest possible sense. Why indeed should it not be so? Must every preacher of the gospel, every dispenser of the sacraments and everyone who presides at the Eucharistic sacrifice also be a 'specialist theologian' who has undergone a course of academic studies in his youth, one whose career is like that of a civil servant, holding a series of 'posts' in due succession in a large-scale ecclesiastical administration, being transferred to other posts, promoted, etc.? Without prejudice to the mission and (sacramental) ordination conferred by the universal Church, why should not a fraternal community of the kind we have in mind appoint an elder from its own 'elders'? Provided such a one has the theological and cultural formation and experience, and the experiential knowledge necessary in *this* sphere and for *this* community (all requirements which cannot be fulfilled merely by following the course prescribed for the academic formation of a professional ecclesiastical functionary) why should he not serve this specific community as its 'presbyter'? In this way, it will be remarked in passing, the charismatic and institutional factors in the Church would once more achieve a clearer unity, and after all there is nothing in the constitution of the Church as required by the nature of the faith which would exclude such a measure *a limine*. Certainly we do not need to underestimate the value of theological study in its academic form. And in the future too it may be indispensable for many of the Church's officials. But at the same time I do not believe that in the future the type of the 'civil administrator' equipped with a special academic formation will continue in all circumstances to provide the standard for the kind of presbyter to be appointed over the community in the concrete. In the future the lack of priests (pastors) will be too great for this, and the significance of the 'charismatic'-religious personality will be too important.

It will be also clearly possible for older men who are still vigorous and in good health to be 'officially' appointed for fresh tasks after they have retired from their secular callings. (It may be remarked only in passing that on this basis the question of celibacy for secular priests in the Catholic Church may be raised once more in the future in a quite different form from hitherto.) Initiatives tending in this direction are in fact present everywhere. But we should have the boldness gradually to develop them, and that too not merely with a view to exceptional and particular cases, but in order that a new type of 'presbyter' may emerge as normal in the Church, one who is in principle on an equal footing with the professional administrator. In this task the Protestant Churches, with their principle of the universal priesthood, could find it easier and quicker to devize practical ways of achieving this, which could then, with relatively minor modifications, become practicable in the Catholic Church as well. A further point is that in the last analysis it would be wrong to misunderstand the efforts to restore the diaconate in the Latin Catholic Church as an emergency measure to make up for the lack of priests.

3. The creed and the preaching of the gospel will find new ways of making themselves felt in the Church of the future. Precisely in order that 'no other gospel' may be proclaimed or believed than that which is ever ancient and ever new, the interpretation of it must be presented in a different form from what was formerly the case. For in a world governed by different perspectives of thought and living it would inevitably become different in a bad sense if we sought to 'interpret' and present the preaching of the gospel in the future simply in the same way as it has been interpreted and presented hitherto. The only possible way for ensuring that it shall really remain the same is to introduce the right kind of changes. What this will mean in the concrete is difficult to predict. Perhaps amongst other things we can say this much:

a) What is signified by, and so badly formulated as the programme of 'demythologizing' and the 'existential interpretation' will, once it is both boldly and rightly carried through, become obvious. We will gradually learn in our reading of the scripture and the ancient creeds so to 'translate' them that we no longer notice at all that we are 'translating'. Instead the ancient truth contained in them will spontaneously find expression in terms which correspond to our own perspectives of thought. This does not imply that the kind of 'translation' arrived at by the school of demythologizing up to the present is correct, or that it does justice to the abiding gospel. We must recognize that an intrinsic element in that part of man's understanding of his own significance that endures is his commitment to real history (and not merely to speaking about historicity at the formal level). From our contemporary perspectives of thought we do not merely criticize those to be found in the scripture, but use the perspectives found there, and still more the actual statements contained in it, to criticize our own viewpoints. In other words we must allow them to spring up ever afresh, and to be transformed. We must not be too hasty to bring our considerations to an end. We must not be too hasty in refusing to advance beyond the point where we recognize a pluralism of theologies in scripture (though this is certainly present there). Instead we must take upon ourselves the task which this involves of achieving a synthesis (however imperfect this may be). And if we do all this then I cannot see why the basic task and the methods characterized by the sinister term 'demythologizing' will not be able to lead in the future to a new kind of theology, a theology which, while it will certainly lead man into the mystery of God, and not into the realm of a flat rationalistic humanism, will nevertheless also eliminate many difficulties of interpretation which modern man labours under with regard to the Christian message, and which we should not regard as of no account. And in all this this will still continue to be a wholly 'orthodox' theology of the ancient gospel, or alternatively it will preserve such a theology. Of course this is primarily a general programme, an overall vision for the future. But at the same time it is also a firm Christian hope. Let us attempt to treat of this point a little more in detail.

b) It seems to me that Christian theology, the moment it solves to some extent the general task that is laid upon it in view of the contemporary climate of ideas, should and could arrive at a quite new and *simple* statement of the Christian message. The simple statement that contains the whole is always the most difficult; not the most facile, slipped in with a seeming show of plausibility by the worst kind of over-simplification, but rather the prize won by putting forth our utmost efforts of thought. At least this is the case today, and will be so tomorrow. Yet we should achieve a position in which we are able to say to a modern educated unbeliever within the space of at most half an hour what we Christians really believe,[4] and that too in such a way that this does not strike him simply as incomprehensible and beyond his powers of assimilation, as though it were like an exposition of Tibetan medicine. Do we really manage this? Are we already in a position to do it today? The recitation of the Apostles' Creed

[4] For an orientation on the efforts which have been made to arrive at a brief formula of the faith cf. 'Reflections on the Problems Involved in Devizing a Short Formula of the Faith', *Theological Investigations* XI (London, 1973), pp. 230–244 (with bibliog.).

is unsuitable for this purpose, even though it still constitutes an authentic confession of what is our faith even today. Again a 'penny catechism' of the common sort cannot be used for this purpose, quite apart from the fact that it is unsuitable for children as such. In arriving at such a basic statement of our faith we are no longer, for instance, in a position to assume from the outset that everyone knows what is meant by the word 'God'. We must not formulate the doctrine of the Incarnation of the divine Logos in such a way that it sounds like sheer mythology\ to our contemporaries. We could uncompromisingly *begin* at that point at which the christology *prior* to Paul and John began, namely with the man Jesus of Nazareth. For instance in speaking his Resurrection we should from the outset present it in such a way that while continuing to be the miracle *par excellence* it is interpreted initially as a manifestation of the assertion of our own selfhood, grace-given and absolute, and in doing this we should ensure that it is not *a limine* misunderstood as a miraculous return of a dead man into our sphere of existence. I nourish the hope (to express the matter somewhat paradoxically for the moment) that a new *symbolum apostolicum* will have to be composed for the Church of the future, though this is not to say that the old one will be done away with.

c) The future theology cannot surrender anything which belongs to the genuine content of the ancient faith. Yet surely in all realism we must recognize the fact that in the case of most men the catechism of real Christian living in its fulness, and the learned catechism of theology are not identical; that there simply is, and can be, a blending of *fides explicita* and *fides implicita* and moreover one that varies. And if we do recognize this then there is no objection in principle to the idea that the real catechism of the heart in future Christianity will be organized on quite different lines from the ones which prevail today; that in it what are points of departure today will be points of arrival tomorrow; that themes concerned with a particular area of theology which seem difficult today will constitute the initial and almost obvious axioms of tomorrow, etc. Thus for instance it may be the case (to take only a random example) that the conviction of the universal will to save on God's part will be one of the starting-points in a history of grace and revelation which is co-extensive with the history of human thought for a consideration of why despite this fact there should be a special history of revelation extending from Moses to Jesus, or why the idea of 'Church' should continue to be meaningful. Today, on the contary, we are still toiling to find a starting-point in this particular history of salvation and revelation, and only timidly seeking to discover the universal will of God to save as it works throughout the whole history of mankind. In view of the historical vicissitudes to which human knowledge is subject we should not for one moment expect that all elements in the Christian faith will be equally explicit at all times, that the points of access and points of departure, the basic concepts accepted *hic et nunc* as needing no further explanation will always remain the same. The question, 'how can I discover a gracious God?' will always remain a decisive theme for Christian living and Christian doctrine. But this is still far from saying that it will remain the point of departure and the essential heart and centre in the preaching of the Church of tomorrow. Certainly we must not transform Christian doctrine into a formal hermeneutics of language about God, and so empty it of its real significance. But at the same time there is no need on this account to exclude the possibility that one who has stated in appropriate and acceptable terms what language about God is really intended to convey may not *ipso facto* have expressed the content of, or at least the point of departure attainable by us of today and tomorrow for this understanding of the God of grace in his fathomless compassion. Truly we cannot reduce Christianity to a shallow humanistic love of neighbour. But again this is not to say that in the future love of neighbour may not be the key term, or one of the key terms, which, interpreted in all its radical immeasurability, leads us on into all the mysteries of Christianity. We not merely may, we should arrive at such shifts of perspective in our preaching for the future. We should arrive at a theology which from the outset takes as its starting-point man's experience of himself, and which can do this because even prior to our preaching this theology falls under God's grace. We should arrive at a theology which from the outset has its place within an evolutive and historical '*Weltanschauung*', however true it may be that the theology must provide a standard of criticism for the *Weltanschauung* in that it imparts a radical dimension to it. We must arrive at a 'political theology', one which does not reduce Christianity from the outset to the private and interior sphere. We must arrive at a theology in which God, while infinitely transcending all other beings, still does not properly speaking move the world 'from without', but rather, overcoming the dilemma of transcendence and immanence, constitutes the innermost grace-given mystery of the world. We must arrive at a theology which does not seek to contain the mystery of God within its own system of co-ordinates, but rather launches man into these unnameable depths which constitute the incomprehensibility of love.

d) One further point should be noticed, namely that a theology of this kind, which really speaks to the man of today and tomorrow, is surely too the most 'ecumenical' theology of all. The theologies of the separated

Churches will achieve the most fruitful encounter and understanding if all of them, each from the point of departure given to it by its own historical background, transform themselves into the theology of the future Church, and discover that 'hierarchy of truths' which corresponds to the situation prevailing for the time being in the future.

4. What will be the attitude of the separated Churches towards one another in the future? This is a question which can be answered only with difficulty. But perhaps a few points can hopefully be raised[5].

a) All the Churches in a pluralistic society, if and in so far as they still remain as separate, will everywhere and in all countries have the status of diaspora Churches. They will count themselves fortunate if in order to avoid total disintegration and death, this society does not find refuge in a totalitarian state dominated by a forced ideology. Such an ideology would certainly not be Christian. On the contrary in its irreconcilability with Christianity it would be forced at the social level to declare Christianity to be the enemy of society and the state in a quite new manner and, from the point of view of this society, this would represent the mere instinct for self-survival. In any case, however, these separated Churches will spontaneously be drawn closer together in the one diaspora situation applying to them all. Without prejudice to the question of truth many of the controversies dividing the Churches will inevitably lose something of their force in the actual circumstances prevailing. If God becomes the one radical question for all Christians instead of merely being the assumption which they all hold in common, it will simply be impossible for them any longer to feel so separated by the question of the Pope as was the case between the sixteenth and nineteenth centuries. And there will be no lack of tasks and decisions in relation to the secularized world in which the Churches, provided they live with one another and not merely side by side with one another, can bear witness in common to the gospel of the liberating grace of God and of eternal life leading to the absolute future of God, taking these as enduring standards by which to evaluate all 'this worldly' ideologies in both theory and practice. Much that is involved in this common witness could also achieve a common institutional basis, and in addition the situation appears to be such that God will bestow the same or corresponding charismata on the different Churches. Admittedly a necessary prior condition for the Churches drawing together in this way in the diaspora situation prevailing in the world of today and tomorrow will be that we avoid falsely playing down the difference of opinion that

[5] On this point cf. also the fuller presentation, 'On the Theology of the Ecumenical Discussion', *Theological Investigations* XI (London, 1973), pp. 24–67.

still separate the Churches and that still have to be taken seriously in such a way that we assume the position, whether implicitly or explicitly, that the Churches have arrived at a common basic credal formulation of the gospel in the eyes of the world, one that already causes them to exhibit a real and genuine unity in relation to the world, and again we must not arrive at a false formula of unification such as is quite incapable of providing a basis for a common decision as to the task of the Churches for the world.

b) All the Churches, including the Roman Catholic one, will have to reckon in the future with a greater degree of pluralism among the theologies upheld within each Church. For our present purposes we may take it that the validity of this statement is recognized without any further explanation or justifying arguments.[6] But it does not merely imply a more difficult situation than formerly for each of the individual Churches taken separately with regard to the need to preserve substantially the same creed within each individual Church. It also implies a greater opportunity for the separated Churches to arrive at a better theological understanding among themselves. Already even now it is recognized that today very vital theological positions cut clean across the boundaries dividing the Churches. Indeed theological controversies within the Churches are no longer identical with the traditional controversies which separated them in the past. Admittedly, though it is hardly possible to dispute this finding, a further point should be added to it, even though it may sound hard to many ears and must not be misinterpreted as an attitude of presumptuousness on the part of the *beati possidentes*. The Protestant Christian and theologian who seeks to maintain the *credo* of the fathers of his Church must nevertheless ask himself today how and why he can maintain a state of association in Church matters and in worship with Christians whose interpretation of Christianity differs from his own far more radically and fundamentally than from the Catholic creed. I know that the question is not easy. I know that it is open to such a Christian and theologian to say that for the sake of freedom of conscience and doctrine he can *tolerate* such more radical forms of heresy within his Church because in fact they form no part of the creed of his Church. Doctrines in the Roman Church on the other hand which, so far as he is concerned impose a separation between the Churches, are regarded as intrinsically belonging to official Catholic dogma. This reply, in itself understandable, could admittedly lead on to the further question of whether there is not a certain way of tolerating

---

[6] On this cf. 'Pluralism in Theology and the Unity of the Creed in the Church', *Theological Investigations* XI (London, 1973), pp. 3–23.

specific and radical 'heresies' which is equivalent to recognizing them as equally justified as the tenets of his own Church, whereas logically speaking this is impossible. However this may be, the only real point which I would make is this: the growing pluralism among the theologies practised within the individual Churches including the Catholic Church opens up, although perhaps only gradually, a possibility for the future of being in a better position to decide what really belongs to the creed in which a Church must be at one, and what constitutes mere theological interpretation of this one creed on the part of particular schools. For at this level there is no need whatever for all the members of a given Church to be at one in order to be able to live within her single fold. If the difference between creed and theology, not merely in individual points of material content but at the essential and formal level were then made still clearer, and if it were shown that despite its essential content, with its orientation to history creed is precisely not simply 'doctrine', then this situation of a pluralism in theology which prevails in the Churches today and will prevail tomorrow would lead us to expect a greater possibility of the Churches no longer having to be disunited and separated from one another in the creed.[7]

I have made only a few points with regard to the future of the Church. Properly speaking one could and should say much more, especially with regard to the positive opportunities open to Christianity. And precisely on this point there would be much to say. For however much Christianity may be threatened by an explicitly formulated atheism or by the kind of atheism which has to a large extent ceased to pose any kind of religious question at all, still this situation has a positive significance for Christianity as well – not merely that of 'purifying' the concept of God in itself of which even the Second Vatican Council speaks, but also the significance that in a situation of this kind no new religions emerge. Yet so long as

---

[7] With regard to the question of what form the relationship between the Christian Churches will probably assume in the future we must view this question from yet another and quite different standpoint. The ecumenical efforts and dialogues proceed, whether tacitly or explicitly, from the assumption that the Churches involved are, regarded each in itself, homogeneous (ideologically determined) major groups, each with a firm body of doctrine (called 'creed'). It is assumed that so far as this is concerned the only disunity is between Church and Church, and therefore that they can precisely not be united. This assumption may be theologically correct, but from the point of view of the *sociology of religion* it is a figment of the imagination which, so far as the ecumenical question is concerned, is made a substitute for looking into the future. For further details on this point cf. the article, 'On the Theology of the Ecumenical Discussion', *Theological Investigations* XI (London, 1973), pp. 24–67.

religion remains – and it will remain, because man will again and again raise the question of the meaning of the totality of his existence, then the religion that does remain and is not constructed anew will be precisely that of Christianity. In a world civilization that has become one and homogeneous the different religions can no longer in the long run exist without mutual influence upon, and 'interpenetration of' one another. But in this mutual exchange Christianity will be the determining factor, because even from the empirical point of view it is the most comprehensive religion, the one that allows for most variations and is least of all attached to a specific cultural milieu.

For the Christian who is not merely a philosopher or a sociologist of culture and religion there is however one final point to be made in conclusion, and it is the most important and the crucial one: the future does not simply come in the course of a natural unfolding or as a blind fate. Rather it is wrought out in the solitary decision of the heart. In the last analysis our task is not to orientate ourselves to a future which we have already worked out beforehand, but rather to create it in a spirit of unreserved commitment and hope, fashioning it by our own decision. And this means that our glance into the future of Christianity and the Church has one message for us and only one: If you believe, if you commit yourself by hoping against all hope as the Apostle says Abraham did, then this position of faith, with the total and unreserved commitment which it involves, will of itself usher in the future which God has promised to those who believe in Jesus Christ and to his Church.

12

ON THE STRUCTURE OF
THE PEOPLE OF THE CHURCH TODAY

THE Church is neither an idea, nor a principle, nor a postulate. Nor is she simply or merely identical with that which she believes as having been promised to her by God and, moreover, ever destined in its essence to be kept alive by the power of God's predestinating grace, such that in its essentials the content of her belief will never simply cease to be a concrete reality. She is a 'visible' Church, the 'people of God' in the concrete, a social entity, a formal group, an institution in the world with all that that entails, and that too not merely in virtue of her 'nature' as instituted by God, but also in virtue of all that is in her and pertaining to her. This is because and to the extent that she is an institutionalized group of individuals who bring into this institution something different from, and more than merely that which is recognized as belonging to the Church by an ecclesiology treating of the Church's nature. If therefore the Church is to act aright, and in a manner appropriate to the particular situation prevailing at any given time (and this is something that pastoral theology has to enquire into), then she must be aware of what she *is* in *this particular* quite concrete sense. It is the constant temptation of the Church to conceive of herself *merely* in terms of her own nature ('juris divini'), and to conceal from herself her real concrete reality by hiding it behind this portrayal of her nature, in other words behind that which she should be. And this is all the more possible because at the same time she always is that which she must be, and this bold confession that of her nature she is what she ought to be itself belongs to this nature of hers as constantly maintained in existence by the grace of God. But in order to be able to act in a manner appropriate to the situation she must not overlook her historical and social reality, which is not simply identical with her nature. On this basis the question of the 'structure of the people of the Church' constitutes a serious question for pastoral theology. Merely on the basis of her nature there would be nothing to say with regard to this structure (or at least this seems to be the case) further than what is laid down in 'Lumen Gentium' with regard to the essential structures of the people of God which is the Church. Certainly this is of fundamental importance, but it is not all, because it does not describe the concrete form which the Church assumes here and now. This is all the more true because 'people of God' and 'people of the Church' are not identical concepts. 'People of God' is to be understood as equivalent to 'Church', 'people of the Church' as equivalent to the laity. It is true that much has been said at the theological level concerning the laity in the Church at the Second Vatican Council. But hardly anything has been said which directly concerns the sociological structure which belong to the position of laymen. The people of the Church as constituted by the laity is described merely in terms of the Church's nature, or at most quite general characteristics (such as sex, age, education, professional life) have been introduced into this picture.

Now there certainly are structures of the people of the Church which are present within the Church simply because she is made up of men who are subject to natural conditions. An ecclesiological monophysitism has no place in a Catholic ecclesiology or pastoral theology. This human factor in the Church is not merely something inevitable that has to be put up with, or an irreducible remnant in a Church which properly speaking should be the invisible Church of the predestined. The human factor, including, therefore, the social life of man (with all that should be the case and all that is so merely *de facto*) is – 'undivided and unmixed' – an intrinsic element in the Church herself. In the light of this it is in itself permissible, indeed obligatory, to enter into a description of the 'structures of the people of the Church', using for the purpose secular sociological categories and models. In itself this is a point of which we have always in principle been aware. The old key phrase, 'societas perfecta' as used in ecclesiology still has a good sense even today, although we of today recognize more clearly that on this basis alone the hidden reality of the Church (which is accessible only to faith and hope) cannot be arrived at. When secular sociology of religion seeks to describe the Church we must not be over-sensitive in our reaction to it. It describes the human factors and (in the Church of sinners) the inhuman ones too which exist and will exist even in the Church, which is the historico-sacramental manifestation of the grace of God. For it is quite impossible for it to be this manifestation, this basic sacramental sign of grace, otherwise than through the medium of this human factor within her, which also falls within the purview of the secular sociologist in his study of human life.

But surely it is also permissible for a theologian as such, and on the basis of his own data and principles, to attempt to arrive at a description of those structures of the people of the Church which are hardly ever discussed, if at all, in the usual presentations of ecclesiology. In doing this he is not disputing the right of the specialist in sociology in the true sense to evaluate the people of the Church by his own standards, and to classify those belonging to that people according to his own categories, producing a variegated and vivid picture different from the usual pallid portrayal of the people of the laity in the Church by viewing them as they are and not merely (as for instance in 'Lumen Gentium') as they ought to be. But it will appear that the theologian himself also has the right to use such data and such principles (of a Christian anthropology) which can help him too to arrive at a far more variegated portrayal of the people of the Church than is commonly supposed. And if from this certain conclusions have to be arrived at which are important for pastoral theology, and which emerge spontaneously in the process – so much the better. Nor is it matter for regret that the considerations proceeding from such principles often encounter structures which *should be* present instead of actually *being* so in any clear sense. In this way we can learn to recognize structures which are present in rudimentary form but are overlooked, and which, once we have become more clearly aware of them, turn out to be capable of and to require further development.

1. Man is an individual and, as endowed with freedom, every individual is unique. Certainly this is a datum of theological anthropology. But the Church's attitude towards this datum is different from that of any other society. For a secular society has to cater for what is common to all men, and merely to ensure that man's uniqueness is accorded the necessary scope. The Church, however, as the mediatrix of salvation, has as her goal that in the existence of a free being which is wholly unique in each particular case, namely his salvation. Certainly we should not overlook the radical difference between the mediating of salvation and the achievement of salvation. And in the Church too this distinction leaves the individual free in his inalienable responsibility before, and immediacy to God. The salvation of the individual neither can nor should be controlled in a totalitarian sense. It must be remembered, however, that the Church is not merely the mediatrix of salvation, but something more than this as well. As the *visible* community of those who genuinely believe, hope, and love, she is the historical manifestation of the event of salvation as effectively achieved and victoriously imposing itself (DS 3014; the question of how this is possible is difficult. How can that factor which is at once the most individual of all and at the same time the most total of all in human existence, namely its final and definitive value in God's eyes, or even merely

the promise of this and the process by which it is being achieved, be made available to empirical 'experience' in such a way that the Church becomes the great witness for the working of God's grace in the world? This, however, is a question which cannot be discussed here. The *fact that* the Church can achieve a visibility precisely of *this* sort is something which we simply presuppose, referring for our authority in this to DS 3014, and we shall merely draw from this the conclusions which are relevant to our present interests). But because the Church is a *visible* community in this sense, the personal history of the individual as uniquely vested with freedom belongs intrinsically to her. It must at least be made manifest in her, and must be capable of revealing itself for what it is. In other words the Church must make a permanent place within her for a manifestation of this sort. The biography of a 'great man' is out of place in the history of the state or of its institutions. But the life of a saint surely does have a place in the history of the Church precisely as *such*. The Church as such, therefore, has the duty of recognizing the great Christian personalities, the 'enthusiasts', and she must not do this only when they are dead. She must do it precisely if, and in virtue of the fact that, they are not simply the happy product of the merely institutional factors within her, but rather of the charismatic grace that moves freely within her. The official authorities in the Church are false to their own nature if they fail to respect such individuals and to make them visible in the Church. A 'pilgrimage' of the Church's officials to such 'men of God' is just as reasonable as the converse. (In former times such pilgrimages were known. Today such a thing is difficult to discover.) It would be perfectly reasonable for a certain spiritual kind of 'aristocracy' to appear in the Church even as a phenomenon in her social life, and the recognition of such an 'aristocracy' is not identical with respect for the official hierarchy. If we seek to level out this 'structure' or dimension, then we are responding to the humility of such 'men of God' in an unworthy way. A further point that will be intelligible in the light of the basic datum referred to above is that certain formal groups must emerge as the upholders of and the social manifestation of individual charisms of this kind. They must emerge in the Church *as such*, and as part of her manifest social image. Moreover these groups must 'emerge from below' and not as manipulated by techniques or controls from above. Thus for instance orders or members of orders are not *ipso facto* or of their very nature (in spite of the necessity for official recognition of them) functionaries organized to fulfil the task of the officially constituted authority in the Church. (This is at most a secondary and quite 'consequential' function). Rather they are the social manifestation of the individual charisms and callings of individuals as such. And this remains true even though the 'disciples' may be shaping their lives according to an exemplary 'productive pattern established by their founder'. It is precisely as the social manifestation of individual charisms and callings in this sense that the orders and their individual members belong essentially to the Church. Now if, on this showing, exemplary Christians of this kind belong not only to the Church but also, and necessarily to her public manifestation, and if it is certainly not the case that they are *a priori* to be identified with those holding office in the Church, then there is or should be in the Church a movement in which the people of the Church group themselves round such charismatic personalities. And this 'structure' would not simply be identical with the grouping of the worshipping community about its official leader. We should have the courage to make room for such groups. Churches belonging to religious orders could fill this role, so long as they are not designed too much with 'normal pastoral activities' in view.

Despite all the factors of a 'mass society' to be found in her the people of the Church has become more 'individualistic', and that too not merely in the 'secular' order but in the ecclesiastical one as well. And this is in conformity with the intrinsic tendency of a community which is based, in the last analysis, on the free decision of the individual to believe. The uniform and homogeneous people of the Church of former ages, to which the hierarchy could adopt a fatherly and paternalist attitude, is becoming ever smaller in number. It its place there is an increase within this people in the number of those individuals who are vividly alive to the legitimate distinction which exists between the universal commitment of faith (as represented by the hierarchy) and the individual commitment of faith, together with the personal history of this in each individual's life. There is an increasing number of individuals in the Church who are no longer willing simply to fulfil the (passive) role of the taught, the mere recipients of directives from the hierarchy responding blindly to the 'information' supplied to them from above. Instead they seek to be selective in their acceptance of this, and wish not merely to hear but also to be heard. They demand a 'dialogue' with the hierarchy. Since salvation always takes place at the individual level (for all the institutional factors through which it is mediated), and since this individual salvation is an element in the Church as such, and even in the form of her historical manifestation, the process of 'individualization' taking place within the people of the Church is not merely a regrettable situation to which the Church is forced to reconcile herself as inevitable, but on the contrary a radical goal for the Church in the achievement of her own fulness. How much still remains to be done at the institutional level in order that this process of individualization of the people of the Church may achieve its beneficial effects for the Church! It might perhaps be pointed out that 'sects' constitute (in their initial intention and origins) the socially institutionalized protest against a Church of the masses, tending to reduce all to the same level. But in reply to this we would have to say: 'In order to be equal to the situation in which she actually finds herself at the present the Church of today should integrate the 'sects' within herself and, while upholding the unity of the creed and of her leadership, she should maintain sufficient scope for them to operate within her. Nor should it be regarded as a criterion of whether such individualist movements are capable of integration that there shall be a total absence of *friction* in the process by which such individualizing movements, whether of isolated persons or of groups, are incorporated into the 'apparatus' of the Church. It is at this point that the work of the sociologist properly so called should be brought to bear. He it is who, with his own special methods, should teach us to recognize more clearly and in a more concrete form, factors which have so far precisely not been recognized from a theological standpoint.

2. Man is constantly threatened by sin and unbelief as an *internal* as well as an external element in his personal life. Certainly traditional ecclesiology (rightly) states on the one hand that everyone who is baptized, at least publicly professes his allegiance to the Catholic faith, and submits to the hierarchy and the unity of believers, belongs to the Church, while on the other hand there is a difference in the mode of belonging to the Church between those who belong to the holy Church '*corpore*' (as sinners) but not '*corde*', and those who stand under God's grace as justified. At the same time, however, as a characterization of the differences which exist between the members of the people of the Church this is still inadequate – inadequate as a description even of those differences which can be recognized from the data of theology. As applied to the various modes of belonging to the Church the norms mentioned above serve rather to reduce all to a single uniform level, instead of enabling us to recognize the differences within the people of the Church. For the difference between the sinner and the justified in their respective ways of belonging to the Church is not a sociological difference, since the basis for it (the possession of, or loss of, grace) is at least in a direct sense, and for all practical purposes, not an empirical datum, and the concept of the 'public sinner' hardly takes us any further, at any rate today. The question already appears in a somewhat different light the moment we take the abstract concept of

'communio', which is one of the factors constitutive of Church membership, and seek to fill it with concrete content and to ask at what point a
sufficient degree of 'communio' ceases to be present. The internal assaults
through sin and unbelief manifest themselves (as in a chain process) in a
state of alienation and withdrawal from the Church's life in innumerable
ways and degrees, and the instance that is most evident to the sociologist
is that of the 'non-practising' Catholics. The points of obscurity and controversy concerning the precise point at which such a state of alienation
from the Church's life, and such a refusal to take part in it constitute an
actual state of separation from the Church are well-known. The point of
primary importance here is that not every refusal to participate in the
Church's life *ipso facto* involves a loss of membership of the Church. The
directly opposite thesis would materially speaking lead to the position
that sinners do not belong to the Church. Now there are very weighty
theological grounds for holding that this thesis is untenable. This has a
bearing on that grey throng made up of the weary, the indifferent, and the
uninterested, and of those who, from the ideological point of view, are
characterized by other and non-Christian opinions more than by faith in
the Church. So long as this lack of Christianity on the part of the baptized
Christian does not solidify into a clear and decisive negation of the
Christian faith, such as can be recognized even at the public level, this grey
throng does belong to the people of the Church, in other words to the
Church herself and not merely to the objects of the solicitude of the
Church (that is, of her official institutions!). Since in her explicit ecclesiology the Church regards the 'border-line Catholics' as belonging to her,
she must not adopt an attitude of latent and unexplicitated Novationism
by acting as though despite this it was only the 'attendants at Sunday Mass'
who really belonged to her, while the rest merely had to be patiently put
up with as 'bad Catholics'. However true it may be that the situation of
the 'so-called border-line Catholics' also constitutes the objective manifestation of the 'sin of the world' and its unbelief, still this relationship which
the 'border-line Catholics' have to the Church cannot *ipso facto* be diag-
nosed with any certainty as their personal and subjective sin. It cannot
ipso facto be judged to be this even when this state has been preceded by a
zealous participation in Church life during their childhood. In principle
they can just as well be regarded as '*still* half Catholics and Christians' as
'*already* half Catholics', provided the 'still' and 'already' here refer not to
a practice of the faith belonging to their childhood and to a large extent to
a stage when their personality had not yet developed, but to the history
of a developing personal faith and life as at least possible in principle.

Viewed in this light it is far from being *ipso facto* justifiable either objec-tively or as a matter of pastoral policy for us to suggest through the attitude of the clergy to those who do not regularly attend Sunday Mass that they themselves should regard themselves as centrifugal border-line Catholics. We can also adopt that attitude of Evangelical patience in which we allow them to grow in hope, and so regard them as border-line Catholics who are centripetal, as the kind of Catholics who, in the circum-stances, are doing all that is appropriate here and now to *their particular* phase of religious development, all the more so when we consider that so long as we divide the people of the Church into those who fulfil their Sunday and Easter duties and those who do not we are, in a strange way, deciding whether individuals shall be accounted as Catholics or not not according to whether they fulfil a divine commandment but according to whether they fulfil a precept of the *juris ecclesiastici*. A point which we should recognize clearly once and for all is that at least from the theo-logical point of view this distinction is a very secondary one. An adulterer or an unscrupulous and power-hungry politician is more truly a 'border-line Catholic' even when he is seen at Church on Sundays, than certain non-attenders at Sunday Mass who have not yet come to terms with this parti-cular commandment of the Church, something which from the Christian point of view is more easily understandable and more tolerable than violat-ing the divine commandments. The social prestige of such border-line Catholics in the Church varies very greatly according to the particular country to which they belong. An Italian intellectual who has temporarily given up practising does not feel himself so alienated from the Church *on these grounds alone* as a German or Englishman in the same position. In any case there is no dogmatic reason for attaching any special importance to the Church-going prestige of such Catholics. In this connection it would already be a considerable achievement if the people of the Church had a clearer awareness of the fact that the commandments of the Church have a status which is certainly relative, a fact which has been recognized by the Church herself. It can hardly be feared that even today a recognition of this would still have greater negative consequences for the zeal with which individuals practised their religion. The status of the 'border-line Catho-lics' in terms of the sociology of the Church carries within itself as an intrinsic element its own interpretation on the part of the official Church. In the light of this alone it is a variable entity. From this point of view it could be very much altered even though to all appearances nothing is altered in the 'objective facts'. These 'border-line Catholics' cease to some extent to be 'border-line' when they are viewed from a different point of view, namely as Christians who have not yet developed the course of their Christianity to that point at which an individual achieves a positive relationship to the Church and her life, something which under normal conditions is both attainable and desirable, and to be striven for as a concrete goal by those engaged in pastoral work. If the position of the 'border-line Catholics' were interpreted in this sense by public opinion in the Church, they themselves would also be more ready to understand their own position in this sense, and this (by a kind of reaction) could strengthen that development which we assume to be taking place in them in the desired direction. Hence the effects of sinfulness and assaults on the faith in the individual are also to be numbered among the structures of the people of the Church.

But even in addition to this, or abstracting from it, it would be naïve to picture the 'practising Catholics' to oneself as a crowd of uniform individuals with absolutely the same convictions in an 'ideological' sense. The fact is that faith inevitably has an individual *history* and development of its own, and further that there is a justifiable no less than an unjustifiable way of distinguishing between the collective commitment of faith of the Church and the individual commitment of faith of the individual. (We may, for instance, distinguish between the degrees of implicit and explicit awareness of what is contained in the faith, and between the varying degrees in which that which is conceptually believed is appropriated at the 'existential' level. Again that which is believed in theory has varying degrees of effectiveness in practical life, and these differences may be so great as to lead to 'heresies in the Church'). Now these facts give rise to the most manifold structural subdivisions within the people of the Church. The printed catechism and the unprinted catechism in the head, and above all in the heart, are not identical. Merely by way of example it may be pointed out that without any official difference of faith groups do exist within the people of the Church in whose religious life indulgences or devotion to our Lady play a significant part, and others in which for all practical purposes these factors do not exist; groups in which specific moral requirements carry a quite different weight and influence as characterizing their way of life. Precisely in those cases in which it is the effectiveness of Christianity as a force in social politics that is in question very great differences arise in the real structures of the people of the Church, but even from a theological point of view the fact that the history of the faith is ultimately not ours to shape or control should lead us to expect this. There are groups of Church Christians who live their Christianity as a basis for their social status (this must all too often be the case), and others who take the message of the gospel as a critique of the social order and as a stimulus to action to bring about changes in society. There are so many ways of forming groups within the people of the Church which are ultimately based on the distinction between the commitment of faith of the Church as a whole and the personal commitment of faith of the individual considered in his own personal history.

But because this situation is precisely that of the Church herself, and because she is the Church of sinners, it is also possible to conceive of structures entering into the people of the Church which tend in a contrary direction (and it may be hoped that such structures will always be present in sufficient measure in her). There must be individuals and groups within the Church who are the representatives of a protest against the sinfulness and latent unbelief in the Church, and the Church on her side must maintain sufficient scope within herself for 'non-conformists' and 'protestants' in this sense. It is in fact simply not the case that in the points they emphasize and in their efforts to meet the demands of the particular hour and the particular age the official representatives of the Church's teaching and pastoral work are the representatives of Christianity in the absolute, pure and unalloyed in such a way that it would be impossible for any non-conformist 'protest' on the part of individuals or groups within the people of God in the Church to be directed against the officials in the Church. The worker priest movement constituted a protest group of this kind against the bourgeois tendencies developing within the Church. Were they given sufficient scope, and was their voice heard with sufficient humility?

3. *Gratia supponit naturam.* This is an ancient principle, although theologically speaking it is only with difficulty that we can interpret it precisely and correctly. But let us apply it to our present question. This will yield the following conclusion: the society of the Church as such is constituted not merely by that which belongs specifically to the Church's nature (Spirit, word, sacrament, official institutions). Rather it presupposes and implies the 'natural' structures of an integrated society. If we did apply this principle it would emerge that whereas in earlier times these structures both could be and were presupposed by the Church in working out the organization of her own membership, today, because of the disintegration of society, they have to a large extent to be discovered afresh and in part created afresh by the Church herself. The parish priest with his local place of worship can no longer base himself on an already integrated village society such as existed in earlier times. But since it is no longer the case that this society is already present for him to work upon, a worshipping

community has a strangely ideological effect. Yet taken by themselves the common creed and cult upheld by the community are quite incapable of constituting this worshipping community as it ought to be. Anyone who holds this to be the case is running counter to the principle, *gratia supponit naturam*, i.e. as applied in the present instance, the social factors in the Church presuppose the social factors at the human level. If these natural structures cannot be presupposed (neighbourliness, mutual acquaintance, a readiness to help one another in the secular sphere, and the necessary conditions for all this, a common language, similar problems to face, a level of education which is to some extent homogeneous etc.) they must be created by the Church. She must constantly be looking for such structures when they are present in still rudimentary form. She must promote new initiatives in this sphere, discover and bring forward those actively engaged in promoting such structures. In our need to work out a sociology of the people of the Church we still know far too little of these structures and those who promote them: the 'natural' spokesmen of a society which aims at becoming a worshipping community, the 'trend-setters' who have a selective influence in determining which elements of the official pronouncements really shall become an effective force among the people of the Church, etc. From this aspect too there is a need for any dogmatic ecclesiology to include within its purview the researches of 'secular' sociology in order to achieve a correct view of the real structures of the people of the Church and to pay due regard to them.

13

THE FUNCTION OF
THE CHURCH AS A CRITIC OF SOCIETY

THE subject, 'the function of the Church as a critic of society' certainly has the utmost relevance to the contemporary situation. Everywhere in the world, and on both sides of all so-called 'curtains' the students are in revolt against the ideologies and institutions of a society that has become established and 'frozen'. When they are Christian and Catholic they demand that the Church shall take part with them in their struggle. One of the extremely wide variety of theological key-words developed today is that of 'political theology'. It has emerged in the Protestant theology of Germany and America (for instance in the works of Altizer, Cox, Marsch, Moltmann, Sauter, Shaull),[1] and also to an increasing extent in Catholic theology, chiefly in the works of J. B. Metz.[2] This political theology is already being sharpened (above all in South America) to a theology of revolution and force.[3] The Churches too

[1] Cf. especially the following studies: J. Moltmann, *Theologie der Hoffnung* (Munich, 1964); G. Sauter, *Zukunft und Verheissung* (Stuttgart and Zurich, 1965); Th. J. J. Altizer, *The Gospel of Christian Atheism* (Philadelphia, 1966); *Diskussion über die 'Theologie der Hoffnung'* edited by W. D. Marsch (Munich, 1967); W. D. Marsch, *Die Freiheit erlernen*, Beiträge politischer Theologie (Freiburg, 1967); R. Shaull, *Containment and Change* (New York, 1967); *idem*, 'A Theological Perspective on Human Liberation', *New Blackfriars*, Vol. 49, No. 578 (1968), pp. 509–517; H. Cox, *Der Christ als Rebell* (Kassel, 2nd ed., 1968); *idem*, *Stirb nicht im Warteraum der Zukunft* (Stuttgart, 1968).

[2] Cf. J. B. Metz, *Zur Theologie der Welt* (Mainz, Munich, 1968); *idem*, 'The Church's Social Function in the Light of "Political Theology"', *Concilium* 6/4 (1968, Church and World), pp. 3–11; *idem*, *Reform und Gegenreformation heute* (Mainz and Munich, 1969); *idem*, 'Political Theology', *Sacramentum Mundi* 5 (New York and London, 1969), pp. 34–38. As a *prise de position* on political theology cf. the articles in the compendium volume entitled *Diskussion zur politischen Theologie* edited by H. Peukert (Munich, 1969).

[3] Material information and judgements on this are supplied by C. Jaime Snoek, 'The Third World Revolution and Christianity', *Concilium* 5/2 (1966, Moral Theology), pp. 18–27; J. B. Metz, 'Religion und Revolution', *Neues Forum* XIV (1967), pp. 460–464; 'Theologie der Revolution', *Evangelische Theologie* Vol 12 11967); T. Rendtorff and H. E. Tödt edd., *Theologie der Revolution* (Frankfurt,

229

are already taking an official interest in the subject of political theology. In the case of the Second Vatican Council even though the actual concept of political theology has not been invoked it has ratified a long Pastoral Constitution on the Church in the World of Today. Several of the ency-clicals of John XXIII and Paul VI are concerned with sociological issues and with a critique of society. On the Protestant side the same concerns are in evidence in discussions which have taken place within the frame-work of the World Council of Churches at Geneva and Uppsala.[4] In brief the task of the Church or of the Churches as providing a critique of society is a theme that is actual and relevant today.

It is self-evident that within the restricted scope of our present study we can put forward only a few very fragmentary observations on a theme that is so novel, so comprehensive and so difficult, and furthermore that we can have no intention of exploring all the heights and depths of a political theology of this kind.

I. A Critique of the Church is Implicitly Involved in the Church's Under-standing of Her Own Nature.

Before attempting to say something of the sociological function of the Church with regard to secular society, it will be useful, by way of pre-liminary, to offer a few remarks with regard to the possibility of, and the necessity for a sociological and political critique of the Church herself. For practical purposes and in the concrete a critique of the Church herself of this kind is the necessary prior condition enabling her to fulfil her function as providing a sociological critique of society, something which is demanded of her today, and that too on the assumption and with the impression that she is not *de facto* fulfilling this function to a sufficient extent, and is herself insufficiently equipped for the fulfilling of it. These

---

(968); on the situation in South America cf. also the bibliography supplied in the same volume, pp. 164–165, and also J. C. Bennet (ed.), *Christian Ethics in a Changing World* (New York and London, 1966). For a general orientation cf. E. Feil and R. Weth edd., *Diskussion zur Theologie der Revolution* (Munich, 1969).

[4] Cf. the official documentation in *Appell an die Kirchen der Welt. Dokumente der Weltkonferenz für Kirche und Gesellschaft* edited by the Ecumenical Council of Churches (Stuttgart, 1967), and also *Uppsala 68 spricht*, edited by N. Goodall (Geneva, 1968). On the conference at Uppsala cf. *Ökumene zwischen Routine und Erneuerung. Ein Uppsala-Report*, Evangelische Kommentare 1 (1968), pp. 428–435; 'Die Vollversammlung des Weltkirchenrates in Uppsala', *Herder Korrespondenz* 22 (1968), pp. 383–388.

facts in themselves are sufficient to justify the approach we are taking here. The Church is a social entity. She is this even as embodied in the different Churches, and even though at the theoretical level these Churches have a very different theological understanding of their own nature, and that too precisely with regard to their sociological constitution. All Churches are institutionally constituted. They have social structures and institutions, and even though they may not wish to do so, they do in fact exercise an authority which is prior to the free decision and assent of the individuals within them. They do this not merely with regard to society in general, but also with regard to the individual and the smaller groups belonging to these Churches themselves. The Church and the Churches are themselves social entities. In the light of this it is obvious that they are inevitably exposed to the dangers which threaten every process of social institutionalization, namely that these institutions do not adapt themselves swiftly enough to the changes in the historical situation, that they are made an end in themselves, that they become merely conservative forces which lose living contact with other social realities. From this point of view alone it is clear that with regard to the concrete forms of social institutionalization which she has undergone the Church is open ever anew to criticism, and stands in need of criticism even while that understanding of her nature which dervies from the Church's own faith credits her with an ultimately abiding identity persisting throughout history and in accordance with the will of her founder. If, as the Second Vatican Council says, the Church always remains an *ecclesia semper reformanda*, then there can be no doubt that this applies not merely to her 'moral' situation, and does not merely imply that as a sinful Church of sinners[5] she must take refuge again and again from her own sinfulness in the grace of God in Christ. It also implies that she stands again and again in need of reform in respect of her forms of institutionalism. Applying this to the Catholic Church, it means, for instance, that the relationship between clergy and the people of the Church, the relationship between centralization in the Church and autonomy on the part of the subdivisions of the Church, the introduction of democratic structures, and much else besides, constitute subject-matter for an ever-fresh enquiry, and are subject to historical change even though, on a Catholic understanding of the Church certain specific structures belong to the *jus divinum* of the Church and are abiding. For our present purposes, however, it will not be the individual material details of a

[5] On this cf. K. Rahner, 'The Church of Sinners' and 'The Sinful Church in the Decrees of Vatican II', *Theological Investigations* VI (London and Baltimore, 1969), pp. 253–269 and 270–294.

critique of the sociological aspects of the Church of this kind that we shall be considering, because this would lead us too far from what is our real theme.

Let us confine ourselves to adding one further observation with regard to the sociological and political criticism of the Church herself. Only a Church with a clear and unambiguous creed and dogma can be subjected to this critique. The dogma is itself the necessary prior condition for a critique.[6] This statement may sound surprising. Nevertheless it seems to me to be valid. Obviously it is possible to apply negative criticisms to a social institution from a standpoint which it itself does not share. But in that case all that we can do is precisely to apply negative criticisms to it. We can only transform an institution by criticizing it precisely if we can appeal in this criticism of ours to its own understanding of its nature, if we can demonstrate to it that the actual concrete form it has come to assume is, at least in part, in contradiction to that which it recognizes as its own true nature, as the law governing its initial emergence, and which it itself seeks to approximate to ever anew, albeit as an asymptotic ideal. But in the nature of the case this means that when we develop a critique of the Church we do so on the basis of her own theological understanding of her own nature, in other words, of her own dogma. Thus this critique can constitute an intrinsic element in herself. It is not a critique *ab externo* which either fails to affect her or else destroys her. Rather it is a critique from within, based on the intrinsic tension within her between that which she herself seeks to be and that which she *de facto* is. This interior critique as an element in the Church herself does not cease to be interior to her merely because this critique always at the same time takes occasion of an external historical situation in which the Church is involved at the secular level, and needs to take occasion of this in order to emerge and to become articulate. Opposition, criticism, protest, belong to the very life of the Church herself because she recognizes her own nature as the pilgrim Church, the Church of justice, of respect for the dignity of man, of love etc., and of its very nature such criticism provides weapons to be used in the war against her own inadequacies. Any sociological critique of the Church herself is itself an element in the Church precisely at those points at which in the name of the Church herself it protests against such inade-

---

[6] Dogma, considered as the Christian Church's articulation of her awareness of her own nature, constitutes on the one hand the basis from which the Church (in contrast to other forces of criticism) is able to criticize the world and society from her own standpoint, and on the other the standard by which to determine more precisely the goal of such criticism.

quacies, where the critique as such is based upon a committed faith in her. However, a critique of the Church in the name of the Church is always possible because her own understanding of her own nature is always wider, freer, and more exalted than that which is *de facto* realized in the form which she assumes in history, and is in fact wider in scope than that which we have already formulated to ourselves about her at the level of speculation and theory. To understand the significance of a critique of the Church conducted from within the Church herself in this way does not mean that the critical dialogue with the official Church which we conduct must always take the form simply of a peaceful and friendly discussion between two bodies who are at basis totally at one from the first. We can already see in the controversy between Peter and Paul that this critical dialogue can also take the form of a face-to-face confrontation, a genuine struggle as to the shape of a future which neither of the disputants can plan beforehand in any adequate sense.

II. The Self-Critical Church as an Authoritative Critic of Society

This brings us to our real theme, namely the function of this Church as a critic of society when she is herself in turn subject to criticism, and changes in response to it. First let us put forward considerations with regard to why a function of criticizing society of this kind is to be ascribed to the Church on the basis of her own understanding of her own nature.

1. The Distinction Between Criticism of Society on the Church's Part and Political Action.

In order to avoid from the outset certain misunderstandings which it is very easy to fall into it must first be emphasized that the thesis concerning the function of the Church as a critic of society is not intended to conjure up the idea of a Church actively engaged in politics. It is obvious that the Church cannot deprive secular society and the institutions belonging to it of its political decision making, and also that it has no intention of doing this; that the Church cannot act as a higher authority to manipulate or control this autonomous secular society.[7] Perhaps it is true that in the course of history she often has done this, sometimes for good reasons and sometimes for bad. But she should not do it, and moreover she has

[7] On this cf. K. Rahner, 'On the Theological Problems Entailed in a "Pastoral Constitution"', *Theological Investigations* X (London and Freiburg, 1973), pp. 293–317; *idem*, 'Theological Reflections on the Problem of Secularization', *ibid.*, pp. 318–348; *idem*, *Gnade als Freiheit* (Freiburg, 1968), esp. pp. 64–67, 80–82.

basically and explicitly committed herself to this principle in ever clearer measure. Culture, history, society, state and the economy are all matters which the Church neither can nor should in any direct sense control, guide, or manipulate. Nor is it possible to justify such a course on her part by invoking the so-called natural law, even though the Church considers herself to be the guardian and interpreter of this. For even this natural law, considered as the sum total of those demands which have a permanent claim to be recognized as valid by man in his decisions has itself a history and, what is more important still, it does not in itself yield any absolutely unreserved and concrete imperatives such as would deprive man and society of the power to commit themselves to historical decisions, and such as could be arrived at deductively by the Church herself. The function of the Church as a critic of society, therefore, does not imply that the Church herself should engage in politics either explicitly or behind the scenes. Obviously in her position as one social group within a pluralistic society[8] she both can and should defend and maintain the position that her members, even as constituted in free social groupings, have the right to exercise an influence on society as a whole in legitimate ways, and has the same rights in this respect as any group in a society of this kind. The Church can proclaim and put forward those moral maxims which she regards as norms defining the limits within which every moral decision, and so too every political decision, must fall. And she can do this without exercising any illegitimate compulsion upon others. Again with regard to power, even though this may be engaged on the side either of sin or of the kingdom of God in the world, the Church can develop a theology of power[9] through which she can, under certain circumstances, communicate to those actively engaged in politics a more or less impartial attitude towards power. But presumably this is still far from being sufficient to enable us to achieve a clear view of the true function of the Church as a critic of society, a function which in no sense consists in political activity on the part of the Church herself. It is not easy to define in the abstract what this function of the Church as a critic of society is, having due regard to these

[8] Cf. K. Rahner, 'Reflections on Dialogue Within a Pluralistic Society', *Theological Investigations* VI (London and Baltimore, 1969), pp. 31–42; idem, *Handbuch der Pastoraltheologie* II/1 (Freiburg, 1966), pp. 208–214.

[9] For an introduction to the problems involved cf. R. Hauser, 'Macht', *Handbuch theologische Grundbegriffe* II (Munich, 1963), pp. 98–111 (bibliog.). In addition to this cf. esp. K. Rahner, 'The Theology of Power', *Theological Investigations* IV (London and Baltimore, 1966), pp. 391–409; idem, *Handbuch der Pastoraltheolgie* II/2 (Freiburg, 1966), pp. 358 ff., 362 ff., 365 ff. (bibliog. pp. 337–341).

factors. Indeed if the function of criticizing society is intended precisely to be a critique of existing practical activities with a view to further practical activities – in other words a stimulus designed to bring about a real alteration in society, and not merely a theory of what social activity ought to be – it is in principle quite impossible to obtain an idea of it by means of a mere theoretical and general statement of its nature, just as it is quite impossible in any adequate sense to reduce will to intellect, hope to faith, practice to theory, orthodox practice to orthodox thought. With this proviso, which in spite of its decisive importance cannot be thought out any more fully at this point, we may attempt to make the following statement with regard to the nature of the function of the Church as critic of society: It consists in opening up ever anew a perspective which transcends the concrete social reality such that within this perspective the social reality concerned appears in its relative value, and so as capable of alteration. To the recognition of this relative value and alterability of the social reality as it *de facto* exists it adds a further factor. For it provides the opportunity and the power to introduce practical changes into this reality even though it does not supply with this any concrete formula or any absolute imperative for a quite specific new social reality to be introduced by the use of creative forces in history. It cannot supply any such concrete formula and does not seek to do so. In other words this function of the Church as critic of society does not *ipso facto* or in itself constitute any absolute political decision.

2. The Origins of the Perspective Provided by the Church as Critic of Society as Found in the Gospel Itself.

This critical perspective as applied to social realities and changes in social politics can, to the extent that it is opened up by the Church, only be the gospel which the Church preaches and lives by,[10] though of course this is not to deny, but rather to maintain, that the Church herself needs to be brought back ever anew by her own Spirit to this gospel as providing the perspective for social criticism. She needs to be brought back to it by her own history, to which the history of the world itself belongs. The task to which we must now apply ourselves, therefore, is first to throw light in somewhat greater detail on the question of why and how the

[10] If the Church seeks adequately to reproduce in her own life that impulse which she must of necessity receive from any critical theory of society, her way of achieving this should not be through any excessive application of theological concepts or through the mere further exploitation of a borrowed conceptual apparatus. Instead she must achieve it by seeking the answer she needs from the gospel, critically enquiring into it and submitting herself to the message it yields.

gospel of the Church has the significance of providing a perspective of
this kind, opening up possibilities for social criticism.

The first point to be considered is concerned with the difference and
the separation that has grown up today between the Church and secular
society[11]. This is something which more clearly than in former times makes
it possible and requisite for the Church to adopt a critical position with
regard to society. And it is a factor which ultimately corresponds to the
nature of the Church herself, albeit only in her later historical development.
Let us consider the process by which the world has been de-numinized.
From a position in which it and man himself constituted a static reality
controlled by God and representing him directly, and immutably prior to
the exercise of man's own freedom, it has come to be material for man
himself to control by the free exercise of his critical faculties. This therefore is the process of secularization,[12] and despite the danger of a sinful
and atheistic interpretation inherent in it it is a process which, ultimately
speaking, has been demanded and initiated by Christianity's own understanding of God, of the world, of man, of history, and of the nature of the
Church herself. This remains true even though the Church as she exists
in the concrete has very often sought in matters of detail to close herself
to this development and to act against her own ultimate understanding of
her own nature. This means that the development which leads away from
the state Church and the ecclesiastical state towards a secularized world,
and so too to a manifest separation between Church and secular society
is legitimate, even though the concrete form which this separation has
assumed has in practice always been subject to sinful corruption for which
both parties are responsible.

Yet it is precisely through this separation, and only through it, that it
has become more clearly possible for the Church to exercise her function
as a critic of society. Certainly it is true that the Church herself is consti-

[11] For basic information on this complex cf. *Handbuch der Pastoraltheologie* I
(Freiburg, 1964), pp. 415–448; II/1, pp. 222–233; II/2, pp. 109–267. In particular in
the context of our present enquiry cf. W. D. Marsch, *Gegenwart Christi in der Gesellschaft* (Munich, 1965).

[12] On the principles governing the relationship between the Church and the
world cf. K. Rahner, 'Kirche und Welt', *Zehn Jahre katholische Akademie in Bayern*
edited by the same (Würzburg, 1967), pp. 9–27; *idem*, 'Theological Reflections on the
Problems of Secularization', *Theological Investigations* X (London and New York,
1973), pp. 318–348; From the comprehensive literature on this subject the following
studies in particular may be mentioned: H. Cox, *Stadt ohne Gott* (Stuttgart, 3rd ed.,
1967); F. Gogarten, *Verhängnis und Hoffnung der Neuzeit* (Stuttgart, 2nd ed., 1958);
H. Lübbe, *Säkularisierung* (Freiburg and Munich, 1965); H. Blumenberg, *Die
Legitimität der Neuzeit* (Frankfurt, 1966).

tuted as a society. At the same time she has an abiding place in the world, and this means that she herself is justifiably exposed to contradiction arising from criticisms of her as a society. The reason for this is that even in this state of separation it is quite impossible for her to avoid participating in the social life of the environment in which she exists at any given time together with the short-comings inherent in it. But for all this the position in which she stands today – and moreover it is a position which she has accepted and willed – is one of greater separation from secular society and the institutions belonging to it which have critically to be called in question. The age of Constantine with the imperial Church and the bond between throne and altar is at an end, even though this stage must not be short-sightedly condemned as the age of a Church that has been made worldly, a base surrender of the gospel to a sinful world. On the contrary it can equally well be interpreted as a commitment of the Church to the world, albeit one which in the specific historical form which it assumed, was transient, and this commitment of the Church to the world is something which is precisely demanded of the Church today, albeit in a quite different form. It is also true that many remnants of this Constantinian age, with its naïve symbiosis between Church and society, gospel and world, still survive today in the most divers forms among the so-called Christian nations. Such survivals would only be qualified as reprehensible from the outset if we were to adopt the position that every social commitment in which the Church seeks to impress her Spirit upon concrete social realities as well is from the outset reprehensible.

The secularization of the present-day world, then, is something which derives historically from the spirit and intention of Christianity itself. And it is a primary condition enabling the Church to exercise a critical function with regard to society.

The Church seeks to be the mediatrix of salvation to the individual man in God's sight, working in God's power and towards him as her goal. But the Church has never interpreted this salvation in an individualistic sense as a matter of man's merely private and interior life.[13] It is true that as a result of the process by which the world has become more worldly the danger of misunderstanding Christianity, faith, religion, and salvation in this individualistic sense has become very great, and certainly it cannot be said that Christianity and the Churches have not in a measure succumbed to this temptation. The Churches can misunderstand the process of secularization by regarding it as a sign that they should withdraw into

[13] To the extent that political theology is directed against this tendency to restrict salvation to the private sphere it represents a genuine concern of the Church.

themselves, into the private interior lives of their individual members and by regarding the sphere of interior conscience and the individual quest for salvation as the sole sphere in which the Church can still exist in the present-day secularized world. But any such understanding of Christianity and Church would, after all, constitute a radical misunderstanding in which the Church would find herself in contradiction to her own true understanding of her own nature.

God's promise of himself to man is addressed not only to each individual in the freedom of his own unique personhood. From its very origins this promise is at the same time aimed at mankind as a unity, a unity which is always historically and socially constituted. It is aimed at history, society, the people of God..[14] As the subject to whom God's grace-bestowed will to save is addressed, the individual is always aimed at as the member of a community of mankind, and always and necessarily this also has a social manifestation. Original sin, saving history as a factor in the life of the community, the redemption of all through one, salvation through the mediation of the Church – these, and many other data of the Christian faith are in radical contradiction to a conception which would seek to confine Christianity exclusively to the sphere of the individual's private interior life. Salvation and grace are wrought out in that which constitutes the social basis for what is called saving history and the Church, and these are in themselves a historical and social embodiment in space and time. Now if this is true, then this reality necessarily comes into contact with other social realities, shares a common life with them in a single sphere of human existence in which there are no absolute rules of separation, and in view of this it must adopt a critical position towards, and call in question these other social realities which constitute its environment and modify them. As a reality which is constantly also achieving visible form at the social level, it is quite impossible in principle for salvation not to be concerned with the social realities within which it has to be realized and made manifest in history.

A further point is that the dimension of the explicitly sacral, of the cult and of the preaching of the gospel, is far from being identical with the dimension in which salvation is achieved.[15] This sphere in which salvation

[14] As an introduction to the problems involved cf. K. Rahner, 'History of the World and Salvation History', *Theological Investigations* V (London and Baltimore, 1966), pp. 97–114.

[15] On the question of desacralization cf. H. Schürmann, 'Neutestamentliche Marginalien zur Frage der "Entsakralisierung"', *Der Seelsorger* 38 (1968), pp. 38–48 and 89–104; *Handbuch der Pastoraltheologie* II/2, pp. 35–45; A. Th. van Leeuwen, *Christentum in der Weltgeschichte. Das Heil und die Säkularisation* (Stuttgart, 1967).

is achieved is identical with the sphere of human existence in general. As the mediatrix of salvation, therefore, it is quite impossible for the Church to adopt an attitude of indifference towards this total sphere of human existence which also always involves social structures. And this is just as true as it is true that she should not determine or manipulate this sphere in any direct sense. For in fact it is an intrinsic part of what is demanded of the Christian as such – precisely that he shall commit himself to the world while it still remains worldly as a matter of his own personal venture and decision.

The possibility of the Church exercising a critical function towards secular society can be made still clearer from a different aspect. Christianity is the proclamation of the absolute hope in the absolute future which is God himself,[16] God himself in his unassailable dominion, a dominion which cannot be established by man, himself wills to be the infinite future of man, infinitely transcending all that man could ever plan or fashion for himself. The movement towards this future is implanted in the world all along by the universal will of God to save through that which in Christian terms we call grace. God himself is the sustaining ground, the ultimate perspective and orientation for the total movement of man through history, whether he is explicitly aware of it or only experiences it at the unconscious level and without acknowledging it in the movement of the personal history of his own spirit as it develops in freedom. From this standpoint, therefore, an infinite perspective of this kind and an infinite entelecheia implanted in history in this sense serve as standpoints from which to criticize and estimate the relative value of all the individual goals which can be planned and set up on the part of historical man, and they impart to all these the character of the provisional, that which can be transcended, that which is merely transient and that which can be called in question. These finite, intermediate and individual goals and particular forms in which man realizes himself in his own history are not rendered insignificant or indifferent by this fact. On the contrary it is precisely in virtue of this alone that they achieve their radical importance and their inexorable seriousness. For it is only through them, and not in by-passing them, that man can realize his assent of faith and hope to his absolute future. But precisely as particular goals of this kind, and as being never

[16] On this cf. K. Rahner, 'Marxist Utopia and the Christian Future of Man', *Theological Investigations* VI (London and Baltimore, 1969), pp. 59–68; *idem*, 'The Church and the Parousia of Christ', *ibid*, pp. 295–312; *idem*, the articles grouped under the general heading 'Eschatology' in *Theological Investigations* X (London and New York, 1973), pp. 235–291.

more than provisional and capable of being transcended, they are subject
to critical evaluation from the standpoint of a higher goal. This is that
perspective of infinitude, that infinite point of orientation, which man has
come to terms with as such and in itself once he has been endowed with
grace. A further point is that this ultimate and infinite point of orientation
is something far more than merely that which enables man constantly to
set before him particular goals definable in terms of subordinate categories
of being. But the critical evaluation of these particular and 'this worldly'
goals from this standpoint is not merely a formal disclosure of their relative
status. As has already been said, a mutually conditioning relationship does
in fact exist between the experience and the acceptance in faith of the
absolute future of God on the one hand, and the realization of 'this
worldly' tasks and goals on the other.

The assent to the absolute future of God, and so the recognition of the
relative status of these 'this worldly' goals, is achieved in the affirmation
of these particular goals within history, and not in a mere attitude of dis-
carding them in a flight from the world. And the recognition of their
relative status, so far from diminishing their importance, actually increases
it.[17]

We can achieve a realization of how possible it is for the gospel and the
Church as representative of this gospel to exercise a critical function in
relation to society from yet another point of view, and one that is very well
known to Christians, namely from the Christian perception of the unity
between love of God and love of neighbour.[18] It is a basic conviction of
the gospel that love of God can be effectively realized in the transient state
only in the act of love of neighbour, and that love of neighbour achieves its
radical depths and its absolute significance only when either explicitly, or
at any rate in a state in which it has not been consciously formulated, it
itself constitutes love of God as the innermost reality of man. This is
something which we must plainly recognize, and in doing so we must
grasp the fact that love of neighbour is no mere matter of natural disposition, or of some private inclination of our own towards someone else. On
the contrary it is an act which has to permeate all the social dimensions of
human life, and which implies soberly and realistically giving others their
due and respecting their freedom in the social sphere as well. A further

[17] In this connection cf. K. Rahner, 'The Question of the Future' in this volume
pp. 131-201.
[18] Cf. K. Rahner, 'Reflections on the Unity of the Love of Neighbour and the
Love of God', *Theological Investigations* VI (London and Baltimore, 1969), pp.
231-249.

point which we must recognize is that this love of neighbour as understood here has to impose its influence in a world that is constantly sinful, a world of injustice and self-alienation on man's part. And once we recognize all this, then it becomes clear that this unity between love of God and love of neighbour implies an attitude of protest and criticism of society.

Finally attention may be drawn to one last aspect from which we can achieve a further insight into what is meant by saying that the Church has the function of criticizing society. The gospel is always and essentially a gospel of the Cross as well, of the acceptance of failure and death within this world in a spirit of faith and hope. Christian theology is always a theology of the Cross. Even the Cross should not be interpreted in a private sense. The death of Christ is certainly not the death of a social revolutionary who, in his activities merely as a critic of society and nothing more, is reduced to failure. At the same time, however, this death of his did take place in the social and public life of Israel, and in a hostile confrontation with the social forces and institutions then prevailing. It was no merely private fate which befell him but a public one, a political event, if we like to express it in these terms. If we cannot be Christians except by following our crucified Lord in the assent of faith and hope to all the futility of human existence, which at least in death achieves its most radical and palpable manifestation, if, furthermore, this act of faith and hope in accepting the futility of existence on the part of the Christian has to be posited not merely in purely cultic acts or in the private and interior sphere alone, but in the hard down-to-earth secular sphere of the Christian's worldly life, then it follows that from his Christian understanding of existence the Christian can find the understanding and the courage to venture upon that commitment which he has to take upon himself without any assurance of success and which has to be ventured upon in any really effective attempt at achieving social change in the struggle against all the forces in society that cling onto their own selfish interests.[19]

[19] Clearly we cannot treat of all the possibilities here, as for instance the question of whether a basis can be found for the function of the Church as critic of society in that problem of biblical criticism, the 'delay of the Parousia', or whether it can be arrived at through a discussion of the reproach that earlier presentations of eschatology have been lacking in any historical sense.

A further point to be considered as a counter to that reproach which is often too hastily raised, namely that Christianity has restricted itself to the 'private' sphere, is that even the most 'private' form of religion, provided only that it is genuine and vital in its practice, necessarily has extremely significant social effects. For instance it can bring man to the point of recognizing the evil elements in his existence as merely 'relative' and to experience them as such instead of according them an 'absolute'

3. The Upholders of the Function of Criticizing Society in the Church.

From the question of why and how the function of criticizing society is in principle to be attributed to the Church on the basis of the gospel we now turn to another question, that namely of who are the upholders of this function in the Church.

When we speak of the function of the Church as a critic of society, we are influenced by a certain concept of the Church which in practice still persists and has not wholly been overcome. This leads us to think primarily of the official Church and so of the hierarchy. In fact the protest of young Catholics of the present day, of the 'critical' movement in Catholicism, of the 'Kapo' etc., constantly involves a reproach levelled against the officially appointed authorities of the Church for their lack of commitment to social criticism. Indeed this protest goes so far as to accuse them of entering into an unChristian union with the social establishment.[20] This means that it is assumed, whether tacitly or explicitly, that it is precisely in her officially appointed authorities that the Church must discharge this function of hers of social criticism. Now certainly it is justifiable to say that a function of this kind also belongs to the officially appointed authorities in the Church as such. At the same time, however, we must recognize what this function precisely consists in and what limitations are imposed upon it to the extent that it has to be exercised precisely by the officially appointed authorities as such. The true nature of this function of criticizing society as exercised by the officially appointed authorities as such has hardly been thought out as yet at the theological level. For perhaps two hundred years we have been accustomed to distinguish the basic task of the hierarchy into three official functions, and it has been assumed that these three official functions are sufficient to define and to delineate the total area covered by the tasks proper to the hierarchy. This threefold division has been re-stated above all at the Second Vatican Council. Yet the Church's function as a critic of society can hardly be subsumed under any of these three official functions of the hierarchy. It is immediately

---

status. Any enquiry into a function of social criticism should not neglect this simple fact.

[20] 'Kapo' = 'Catholic Extraparliamentarian Opposition'. However it is not the opposition groups among Catholics who have initiated this reproach. Rather it has already been expressed in far sharper form in other works in which it is used to express the suspicion of those concerned that the Church is collaborating with the ruling powers. Such a work is that of P. Blanshad, *Communism, Democracy and Catholic Power* (London, 1952); R. Hernegger, *Macht ohne Auftrag* (Freiburg, 1963); K. H. Deschner, *Mit Gott und den Faschisten* (Stuttgart, 1965).

obvious that the task of the official authorities in the Church as critics of society cannot be subsumed under the heading of the teaching or priestly office, for on the one hand the task of the teaching office strictly as such is to preach the gospel in its abiding and permanent validity, even though, of course, under the direction of the teaching office this preaching has to be made relevant ever afresh and performed in a manner appropriate to the intellectual and social situation. A further reason why it is impossible to subsume the Church's function as critic of society under the teaching office is that obviously the more practical conclusions to be drawn from this gospel, to the extent that they can be arrived at by a process of deduction, are still not sufficient in themselves to represent the total contents and the real contents of that social criticism which we can expect from the Church and even from her official authorities. Again with regard to the pastoral office in practice at least we understand this as a task of guiding and instructing the faithful in the specifically religious sphere. And this means that it would be very difficult to subsume this function of the official Church as a critic of society under this heading of the pastoral office.

It can justifiably be said, therefore, that the function of the official authorities of the Church as critics of society has still not found any clear theological *topos* for itself. This is not very surprising in view of the fact that this theme is capable of emerging into clarity only when social change proceeds more rapidly, comes more clearly to be recognized as a fact and a necessity, and is recognized as something that has to be planned for by man and for which man himself has to take responsibility. We must realize, then, that this task of criticizing society which belongs to the official Church has still not achieved any theological definition, and so too any recognized position in theology. And once we do realize this fact we may perhaps characterize it as prophetic[21] instruction in social criticism. There are two points to be made about such instruction. First it is something different from mere theoretical teaching, with all the deductive (still, therefore remaining at the theoretical level) applications to a historical and social situation which this entails. On the other hand it implies a practical appeal to the freedom of Christians and of the world to take historical decisions, an appeal which leaves unimpaired in those to whom it is addressed the freedom to take historical decisions of their own and their personal creative responsibility. At the same time, however, it

---

[21] On the concept of 'prophetic instruction' cf. 'On the Theological Problems Involved in a "Pastoral Constitution" ', *Theological Investigations* X (London and New York, 1973), pp. 260–272.

does not withhold from them the offering of a concrete course of action which of their freedom they can, and actually should decide to adopt provided only that they experience this course of action that is recommended in its own right as well, as that which is prescribed and demanded by the circumstances of that particular moment in history, something which cannot ultimately be determined on any theoretical basis.

We could call this function of social criticism prophetic instruction because as instruction it is not simply a conclusion deduced from general Christian norms, and it can be called prophetic to the extent that it is the outcome of a conviction that it is sustained not merely by those 'this worldly' forces from which the future can be held to derive, but by the spirit of Christ.

A prophetic instruction of this kind, which must be distinguished from the teaching put forward by the teaching office and by the binding directives of the pastoral office, can surely be ascribed to the official authorities in the Church, since on the one hand the function of social criticism in the Church cannot be sustained merely by the individual Christian or by individual groups of Christians alone. A further point is that in practice the official bodies in the Church actually have really promulgated guidance in social criticism of this kind, recommending it to Christians and to the world in their historical freedom, at any rate in recent times. Let us consider, for example, two encyclicals of the recent popes, 'Mater et Magistra' and 'Populorum Progressio', and also the document of the Second Vatican Council entitled 'Gaudium et Spes'. It would surely be to deny the true nature of these documents if we sought to reduce the pronouncements contained in them to mere general norms at a merely theoretical level in the sphere of social politics, albeit concretized, to some extent. What they contain is something more concrete: proposals, imperatives, a utopian element, if we like to call it so, and this is presented not as doctrine or binding prescription, but as something that is recommended to the historically created freedom of man. This remains true even though the authors of these pronouncements may not have been consciously aware, in any strict sense, of the difference between orthodox teaching and the directives of the pastoral office on the one hand, and a recommendation to orthodox practice on the other. But from this point of view too we can understand the limits imposed upon the official bodies in the Church in exercising the function of social criticism in this way. It is not only that its pronouncements in this direction are for the most part an echo of, and a taking up of criticisms of society which have initially emerged as a charismatic movement from below. It is far from being the case that they can be demanded *ipso facto* as an exclusive initiative on the part of the official bodies. Such instructions in social criticism on the part of the official body are quite different from the doctrinal pronouncements of faith and the decisions of the pastoral office in their application to the free historical decision of the Christian and of the world, and of their very nature are (whether explicitly or implicitly) subject to criticism on the part of the faithful and of the world. In order to achieve a better understanding of what has been said by means of an example we need only for instance to think of the desire for a super-UNO, or of the concrete proposals for aid to developing countries.

But the main promoters of a function of social criticism of this kind in the Church are the Christians in general and their formal and informal groupings within the Church, in other words the so-called laity themselves. Precisely in this respect the Christians themselves are something more than mere recipients of directives from the official bodies. They have to develop an autonomous initiative of their own from which they alone are responsible. They can do this even when they are not specifically commissioned or particularly encouraged to do so by the official bodies in the Church. They can do this even when the *de facto* attitude of the Church's authorities is by contrast so much at variance with such initiatives as to appear to restrict them. Under certain circumstances they can and must do this in the name of the gospel and their own Christian moral responsibility even when on the one hand other Christians or Christian groups oppose them in it, while on the other an autonomous initiative of this kind, together with the antagonisms within the Church which it entails, must still preserve mutual love and the unity of the Church. This is explicitly stated in 'Gaudium et Spes' in the following pronouncement which this Constitution contains concerning the laity: 'Often precisely a Christian view of things will cause one particular solution to recommend itself to them in a given concrete situation. More frequently, however, and certainly legitimately, it is the case that other Christians, while exercising the same degree of conscientiousness and applying themselves to the same question, may arrive at a different judgement. In such cases it is very easy, even when it is contrary to the will of the parties involved, for either solution to be regarded by many others as clearly following from the message of the gospels. But a fact which should never be lost sight of is that in such cases no-one has the right to claim the authority of the Church exclusively on his own behalf and in defence of his own opinion. But they should constantly seek to help one another in an open dialogue in order to clarify the question involved. In doing this they should preserve mutual love, and above all bear in mind the common good'.[22]

We cannot interpret this text of the Council any more closely here. But it will be clear from it that even though specific individual groups of Christians cannot claim the authority of the official Church herself they can appeal to the authority of the gospel. In other words they are authorized by the Church herself to conceive of and attempt to carry through a social programme even in those cases in which their particular conception of society in the future is not that of another group within the Church. The function of specific members and groups within the Church in criticizing society extends further, therefore, than that of the official authorities within the Church as such.

III. The Problems Entailed in a Theology of Revolution

Today the question of the function of the Church as a critic of society (taking 'Church' here to include the several different sense of the term distinguished above) is sharpening into the question of a theology of revolution and force.[23] And in view of this an attempt must be made to say something further on this point within the extremely brief compass available. First it must be pointed out that the concepts of revolution and force are extremely abstract and ambiguous, so that from this point of view alone the question of any Christian justification of revolution and force becomes complex and ambiguous in the extreme. The border-lines between evolution and revolution in social relationships is extremely difficult to determine. And even if we say that revolution is the introduction of change into social relationships by means of force, whereas a social evolution takes place without force, still this way of drawing the border-line between the two is not really clear. For this is merely to shift the terms of the question so that it becomes a question of what constitutes force. If we define force (and from the existential and ontological aspect it would be perfectly reasonable to do so) as the bringing about of change

[22] Quoted according to the version of K. Rahner and H. Vorgrimler, *Kleines Konzilskompendium* (Freiburg, 1967), p. 492.
[23] For the sake of comparison see nn. 3 and 4, as well as the compendium volume edited by H. E. Bahr, *Weltfrieden und Revolution* (Reinbek bei Hamburg, 1968). On the flood of studies on the theology of revolution currently appearing it must be observed by way of criticism that in their essentials they no longer have any new patterns to present, but for the most part constitute discussions of old principles with a mere change of emphasis in the direction of revolutionary pathos.

in that situation in which another is freely placed prior to any freely given approval on his part to this change, then it becomes clear that unless we allow an element of force as understood here to enter in it is absolutely impossible for men to live together at all. For by our activities, with the autonomy and spontaneity inherent in them, we are constantly altering the situation freely belonging to others without any prior assent on their part, whether we wish it or not. On this showing then it is clear that every evolution also includes an element of revolution in the sense defined below, so that any distinction between social evolution and revolution becomes a question of the proportion between the two elements of evolution and revolution present in any concrete social change. But this question in turn leads on to the further one of striking the right balance in a mixture of this kind, a decision which can no longer be arrived at by means of the speculative reason alone, but is a matter for the practical reason, for freedom, for social decision, and so once more in turn a question of the power which is in fact involved and applied.

But to extricate ourselves from all these existential and ontological lines of enquiry, if we want to say that in all these questions what is being treated of is not power in a metaphysical sense but that particular kind of power which is effectively felt by the average man as an incursion upon his freedom in a concrete historical situation which is never the same – in other words of 'bloody force' – then the whole problem is certainly set on a somewhat more concrete and manageable plane, but is not rendered much easier to solve thereby, for even then it still remains an open question what such 'bloody' force, assumed to be unjust, means in the concrete. For instance those who uphold an absolute rejection of (bloody) force in bringing about changes in society certainly do not confine their objecttions merely to manslaughter and similar brutal measures against humanity. The border-line between justifiable and unavoidable force and the kind of force that is condemned as bloody and reprehensible remains obscure in the extreme.[24] With these provisos all that we can assert is surely the following: On the basis of the Sermon on the Mount the Christian will always argue in favour of the least possible use of power in bringing about changes in society, though admittedly with the proviso that a principle of this kind, which he accepts with absolute sincerity, does not condemn him to immobility, and that it is not used as a means for consolidating the kinds of social relationships which are unjust and amount

[24] An enlightening discussion of these questions is provided by W. Benjamin, *Kritik der Gewalt* (Frankfurt, 1965), and also by B. Moore, *Zur Geschichte der politischen Gewalt* (Frankfurt, 1967).

to an oppression of humanity.[25] The Christian will stand firm in the conviction that we are still far from having sufficiently thought out, formulated in practical terms, distinguished, or applied, the possibilities and methods of producing non-violent change in social conditions. At the same time, however, he will be aware of the fact that concupiscence is an abiding factor in the human situation, and one which constantly prevents man from achieving an absolute transformation of the world solely on the basis of the single and central idea of love. And in view of this the Christian will not commit himself to the declaration that any application of force, or even one which may lead to human killing, is immoral and unChristian in any possible situation in society.[26] According to Pius XI[27] situations may arise in which the social order not merely institutionalizes particular kinds of injustice but actually threatens the ultimate basis of human living and human rights. And in such cases even a revolutionary struggle in the true sense and including the use of force in the concrete sense of the term is permitted and, in certain circumstances, actually prescribed. Of course the question of where to draw the boundary line between institutions that are unjust in either the first or the second sense is, once more, a question of degree, and one surely to which no one univocal solution can be found even by Churchmen who seek to draw their inspiration from the gospel and the Sermon on the Mount. Here then we find in its most extreme form the case envisaged in the text of the Council, a case of dissent between Christians in which both sides appeal to the gospel in support of their position.

Although at basis our remarks have been only very fragmentary, we

25 For a general treatment of the problems concerned here cf. R. Schnackenburg 'Bergpredigt', *LTK* II (2nd ed. 1958), 223–227 (bibliog.); U. Luck, *Die Vollkommenheitsforderung der Bergpredigt* (Munich, 1968) (bibliog.), and P. Pokorny, *Der Kern der Bergpredigt* (Hamburg, 1969).

26 Cf. K. Rahner, 'Peace on Earth', *Theological Investigations* VII (London and Baltimore, 1971), pp. 132–135; idem, 'The Peace of God and the Peace of the World', *Theological Investigations* X (London, 1970), pp. 371–388 (bibliog.); also, in order to refer to the most recent manifestations, cf. the articles by H. Marcuse, H. Morgenthau, F. M. Schmölz in *Neues Forum* XV (1968), pp. 702–713, and H. Schmidt, *Frieden* (Stuttgart, 1969); A. Mitscherlich, *Die Idee des Friedens und die menschliche Aggressivität* (Frankfurt, 1969).

27 Cf. Pius XI, *Ep. encycl.* '*Firmissimam constantiam*' ad episcopos foederatarum Mexici civitatum (*18th March, 1937*), AAS 29 (1937), 189–199; for further information on the pronouncements of the official teaching authorities on this question cf. also R. Coste, Le problème du droit de guerre dans la pensée de Pie XII (Paris, 1962), and also the positions adopted by John XXIII in 'Pacem in terris', *AAS* 53 (1961), 401–464, and Paul VI in 'Populorum Progressio', *AAS* 59 (1967), 257–299.

have spoken at length concerning the possibility and the duty of the Church exercising a function of criticism of society. All that we have said has remained at the level of abstract theory. For the question still remains: Is such a function of criticizing society in fact being fulfilled in the Church of the present day? Is it being exercised in the degree that is necessary and adequate? Is the Church – that is, are Christians and groups within the Church – such that, overcoming their own egoism, in a spirit of self-criticism and selflessness, they recognize and seek to change the institutionalized injustices in society which derogate from man and his dignity? Surely we shall have to answer this urgent question as follows: A function of social criticism of this kind does exist in the Church and is carried on by groups and individuals within her. But it is still very far indeed from being exercised in that measure which is demanded by the hour or by the historical circumstances now prevailing. The younger clergy in Spain or South America may already be alive to the necessity for seriously bending themselves to this task in the Church. Much of what the Popes have said in the last few years may represent a contribution to this task in so far as it is a task of the official authorities in the Church, though admittedly it has not met with any really effective response in the Church as a whole. But by and large the Church considered as the people of God has not yet bent itself to this task of social criticism, and not yet responded by any effective action. Where the Church herself is not directly threatened in any palpable sense by the institutions of society and the state, and where the leaders of thought in the Church (by this we refer to officials and laity alike) do not feel themselves directly injured by institutionalized injustice, there in all such cases the task of the Church as critic of society is still to a large extent neglected and remains unfulfilled. It is true that at the Second Vatican Council the Church has laid down more clearly than in former times that she exists to serve the world, that she is there on behalf of mankind and stands for a life worthy of mankind. But she is still far from having fulfilled in sufficient measure what she herself declares to be her mission. If we have understood what the Church is, namely ourselves and the whole people of God rather than merely the hierarchy, if it is clear what has been said up to this point with regard to the true upholders of the Church's function as critic of society, then we have pronounced judgement upon ourselves in saying that the Church is not yet that which the present and the future require her to be, and that she has not fulfilled her task in the political sphere, her task as critic of society. For when we say that this task belongs to the Church we have pointed to ourselves, called our own position in question, and probably accused ourselves too.

LIST OF SOURCES

THE TEACHING OFFICE OF THE CHURCH IN THE PRESENT-DAY
   CRISIS OF AUTHORITY
Lecture delivered at the 30th Conference of the Ecumenical Study
Circle of Protestant and Catholic Theologians at the Priory of Harde-
hausen from the 24th to the 28th of March 1969 on the theme 'Authority
in Crisis', and to the KSG Würzburg on the 27th June 1969.
W. Anz, G. Friedrich, H. Fries, K. Rahner, *Autorität in der Krise*
(Regensburg-Göttingen, 1970), pp. 79–111.

THE POINT OF DEPARTURE IN THEOLOGY FOR DETERMINING THE
   NATURE OF THE PRIESTLY OFFICE
First published in *Concilium* (1969), pp. 194–197.

THEOLOGICAL REFLECTIONS ON THE PRIESTLY IMAGE OF TODAY
   AND TOMORROW
Delivered as a lecture at a Conference of the Catholic Academy in
Bavaria on the 28th to the 29th June 1968 in Munich; on the 1st April 1969
to the theologians attending the Pastoral Course at Prague. First published in *Weltpriester nach dem Konzil* = Münchener Akademie-Schriften
46 (Munich, 1969), pp. 90–118.

ON THE DIACONATE
Delivered as a lecture on the 7th December 1968 at a conference on
Questions Concerning the Diaconate at Freiburg, held by the *International
Informationszentrum für Fragen des Diakonats*.
Published in the Reports of the Conference.

OBSERVATIONS ON THE FACTOR OF THE CHARISMATIC IN THE
   CHURCH
First published in *Geist und Leben* 42 (1969), pp. 251–262.

SCHISM IN THE CATHOLIC CHURCH?
First published in *Stimmen der Zeit* 184 (1969), pp. 20–34; *Schisme dans
l'eglise* (Paris, 1969).

HERESIES IN THE CHURCH TODAY?
Lecture delivered in the context of a discussion of the 'Theological Academy' at Essen (18th December 1967), Frankfurt (10th January 1968), Cologne (18th January 1968), Koblenz (19th January 1968), and to the Movement for Catholic Education at Graz on the 1st March 1968. Published in the following: *Theologische Akademie* V (edited by K. Rahner and O. Semmelroth) (Frankfurt, 1968), pp. 60–87; *Au Service de la Parole de Dieu.* (*Mélanges offerts à Monseigneur André-Marie Charue*) (Gembloux, 1969), pp. 407–430.

CONCERNING OUR ASSENT TO THE CHURCH AS SHE EXISTS IN THE CONCRETE
Delivered as a lecture in the course of discussing the theme of the 'Theological Academy' at Frankfurt (the 15th October 1968), Cologne (the 22nd October 1968), Essen (the 5th November 1968) and Koblenz (the 15th November 1968). Published in *Theologische Akademie* VI, edited by K. Rahner and O. Semmelroth (Frankfurt, 1969), pp. 9–28.

ANONYMOUS CHRISTIANITY AND THE MISSIONARY TASK OF THE CHURCH
Hitherto unpublished.

THE QUESTION OF THE FUTURE
Lecture delivered to the KHG Cologne on the 20th June 1969. Published in revized form as a contribution to the symposium volume, *Diskussion zur 'Politischen Theologie'*, edited by H. Peukert (Mainz, 1969), pp. 247–266.

PERSPECTIVES FOR THE FUTURE OF THE CHURCH
Lecture given at a conference of the Protestant *Michaelsbruderschaft* on the 6th October 1967 at Bochum, as a public lecture at Prague on the 2nd March 1969 as one of the series of lectures entitled 'Living Theology'. Published in various forms under the following titles: 'Kirche der Zukunft zwischen Planen Hoffen', *Kirche zwischen Planen und Hoffen*, edited by the Protestant *Michaelsbruderschaft* (Kassel, 1968), pp. 33–47 and *Wort in Welt* (*Festgabe für Viktor Schurr*, edited by K. Rahner and B. Häring, (Bergen-Enkheim 1968), pp. 369–382.

ON THE STRUCTURE OF THE PEOPLE OF THE CHURCH TODAY
Unpublished hitherto

THE FUNCTION OF THE CHURCH AS A CRITIC OF SOCIETY
Lecture delivered to the Society for Socialist Studies Unna-Soest
(Westphalia) (the 8th November 1968), and to the Thomas More Study
Group at Gütersloh (the 28th October 1968); also at the Ecumenical
Seminary at Prague on the 1st April 1969. Published in the following:
Communio Viatorum. Theological Quarterly XII (Prague, 1969), Nos. 1–2,
pp. 7–22; *Krestanskárevue* 36 (Prague, 1969), No 7, pp. 150–156, No. 8,
pp. 172–175. Further: *Ulisse – La Chiesa post-conciliare* 10 (1969), pp.
156–170.

In the above list of sources not all the publications in German have been
recorded. Radio broadcasts are adduced only if the article concerned was
specially written for such broadcasts. Only the publication in which they
initially appeared is adduced, whether this was in German or in a foreign
language.

INDEX OF PERSONS

Adam, K. 6 n.
Alfaro, J. 82 n.
von Allmen, J. J. 7 n.
Altizer, Th. J. J. 229 n.
Ambrose 166
Arnold, K. 82 n., 170 n.
Aubert, R. 11 n., 123 n.

Bahr, H. E. 246 n.
von Balthasar, H. U. 32 n., 82 n.
Bánez 123 n.
Baraúna, G. 82 n., 88 n.
Barth, M. 166 n.
Baum, G. 12 n.
Baümer, R. 15 n., 82 n.
Beasley-Murray, G. 166 n.
Benjamin, W. 247 n.
Bennet, J. C. 230 n.
Benz, E. 88 n.
Berger, K. 172 n.
Bettencourt, E. 82 n.
Blanshad, P. 242 n.
Blumenberg, H. 236 n.
Böckle, F. 118 n.
Böhm, A. 117 n.
Bottee, B. 6 n.
Brechter, S. 161 n.
Brosch, J. 83 n., 117 n., 126 n.
Breuning, W. 33 n.

Congar, Y. 6 n., 9 n., 11 n., 17 n., 36 n.,
    82 n., 169 n.
Cornelius 171
Cox, H. 182 n., 229 n., 236 n.

Darlap, A. 172 n.
David, J. 118 n.
Deschner, K. H. 242 n.
Dhanis, E. 169 n.
Dolch, H. 15 n., 82 n.

Ebeling, G. 189 n.

Feeney, Leonard 167
Feil, E. 230 n.

Flatten, H. 126 n.
Flechtheim, O. K. 182 n.
Fransen, A. 19 n.
Freyer, H. 121 n.
Fries, H. 7 n., 15 n.

Goddard Clarke, C. 167 n.
Gogarten, F. 236 n.
Goodall, N. 130 n.
Görres, J. 82 n.
Gregory XVI 123 n.
Greinacher, N. 121 n.
Grillmeier, A. 32 n., 166 n.
Grundmann, H. 88 n.
Le Guillou, M. J. 161
Guitton, J. 9 n.

Habermas, J. 194 n.
Hampe, J. 169 n.
Harent, S. 167 n.
Häring, B. 118 n.
Hasenhüttl, G. 82 n.
Hauser, R. 234 n.
Hegel 164
Hohlbein, H. 3 n.

Innocent VIII 123 n.

John XXIII 92 n., 248 n.
Jüngel, E. 189 n.

Käsemann, E. 88 n.
Kasper, W. 33 n.
Knox, R. A. 88 n.
Koch, C. 200 n.
Küng, H. 82 n.

La Bonnardière, A. M. 6 n.
Landgraf, A. M. 166 n.
v. Leeuwen, A. Th. 238 n.
v. Leeuwen, B. 82 n.
Lehmann, K. 21 n., 33 n., 36 n.
Leuba, J. L. 24 n.
Linder, R. 121 n.
Lods, M. 6 n.

Löhrer, M. 8 n., 124 n.
de Lubac, H. 162 n.
Lübbe, H. 236 n.
Luck, U. 248 n.
Ludwig, G. 6 n.

McDonagh, E. 118 n.
Mácha, K. 121 n.
Malmberg, F. 82 n.
Marot, H. 6 n.
Marcuse, H. 248 n.
Marsch, W. D. 183 n., 229 n., 236 n.
Maurer, W. 3 n.
Metz, J. B. 124 n., 183 n., 198 n., 201 n., 229n.
Meyer, S. H. 91 n.
Mitscherlich, A. 248 n.
Möhler, J. A. 82 n.
Molina 123 n.
Moltmann, J. 182 n., 183 n., 229 n.
Moore, B. 247 n.
Morgenthau, H. 248 n.
Mühlen, H. 24 n., 82 n.
Müller, A. 95 n.

Nédoncelle, M. 11 n.
Newman, J. 9 n, 82 n., 150
Niermann, E. 33 n.
Noonan, J. T. 124 n.

O'Hanlon, D. 82 n.
Ott, L. 36 n.
Ott, L. 36 n.
Ottaviani, Cardinal 118 n.
Overhage, P. 187 n.
Ozbekhan, H. 196 n.

Pannenberg, W. 182 n.
Paul, St. 171, 200
Paul VI 98 n., 118 n., 248 n.
Perrone, J. 82 n.
Peter 171
Peukert, H. 229 n.
van Peursen, C. A. 189 n.
Philipp, W. 117 n.
Pilgrim, F. 82 n.
Pius IX 123 n.
Pius XII 123 n., 248 n.

Pokorny, P. 248 n.
Ranke-Heinemann, U. 117 n.
Ratzinger, J. 7 n., 32 n., 90 n., 169n.
Rendtorff, G. 229 n.
Reuss, J. M. 18 n.
Riesenhuber, K. 161 n.
Roberts, T. 118 n.
Rousseau, O. 7 n.

Sanders, J. O. 117 n.
Sauter, G. 229 n.
Scheeben, M. J. 82 n.
Schillebeeckx, E. 166 n., 206 n.
Schmidt, H. 248 n.
Schmied, A. 162 n.
Schmölz, F. M. 248 n.
Schnackenburg, R. 248 n.
Schönmetzer, A. 169 n.
Schoonenberg, P. 24 n.
Schrader, C. 82 n.
Schultz, H. J. 201 n.
Schüller, B. 135 n.
Schürmann, H. 88 n., 238 n.
Schütte, J. 161 n., 169 n.
Semmelroth, O. 13 n., 33 n., 82 n., 83 n.
Shaull, R. 229 n.
Snoek, C. J. 229 n.
Spitalen, A. 83 n.
Steck, H. G. 88 n.
Stirnimann, H. 24 n.
Suarez 170
Suenens, Cardinal 82 n., 98 n.

Thomas Aquinas 170, 172
Todd, J. M. 11 n.
Tödt, H. E. 229 n.
Trütsch, J. 17 n.

Valeske, U. 24 n.
Vorgrimler, H. 33 n., 61 n., 69 n., 246 n.

Weth, R. 230 n.
Willems, B. A. 161 n.
Wulff, F. 118 n.

Zimmermann, H. 19 n.
Zwetsloot, H. J. 123 n.

INDEX OF SUBJECTS

aggiornamento 145
Alienation from the Church 223 ff.
Anamnesis, sacramental 36, 51
Anathema 136
Anointing of the sick 46, 51
Anonymous Christianity 161 ff.
Anthropology, theological 220
Antichrist 202
Apostasy 118
Apostles 55
Apostles' Creed 211 f.
Assent to the Church 142 ff.
Atheism 120, 166, 167, 216, 236
Authority in the Church 3 ff., 9 f., 25 ff.,
    54 ff., 90 f., 95, 103 f., 107, 111, 125,
    143 f., 157, 207, 221
Autonomy of subordinate Churches 105,
    155

Baptism 55, 72, 79, 163, 165, 166, 176,
    207
Basic Sacrament of Salvation 44, 46, 219
Bible 33, 43, 53, 58, 154, 157–158
Bishops 4, 5, 16, 17, 33, 34, 36, 57, 90 f.,
    99 f., 108
'Borderline' Catholics 224 ff.

Catechetics 135
Catechism 125, 212, 226
Celibacy 58–59, 118
Character, sacramental 37, 78
Charism 8, 11, 63, 78, 81 ff., 111, 209,
    214, 222
Christ 9, 24, 30, 33, 36, 50, 59, 79, 126,
    127, 140 f., 152, 157 f., 171, 175, 182,
    189, 202, 212
'*Christentum*' 162
Church:
    as Body of Christ 13, 33, 83
    as Church of sinners 227, 231 ff.
    as mediatrix of salvation 220 f., 237,
        239
    as open system 89 f., 94 f.
    as people of God on pilgrimage 93,
        202, 221, 232

as sacrament of divine self-bestowal
    33 f., 87, 219
as society 10, 16, 31 ff., 45, 50, 51,
    71 f., 81 f., 100, 163, 218 ff., 231 ff.
human factors in 11, 52 f., 145 ff.,
    156 f., 158 f.
Condemnation of heresy 132 f.

Deacon 61 ff.
Decree on the Eastern Churches 67 n.
Decree on Ecumenism 123 n., 168 n.
Decree on the Missions 67 n., 85, 169 n.,
    176
Defintions of doctrine 132 f.
Dei Verbum 8
Democracy 7, 13, 15, 16, 20 f., 110
Demythologizing 210
Diaconate 33, 34, 47, 61 ff.
Diaspora 57, 207, 214
Discerning of spirits 116
Docta ignorantia futuri 181, 182, 198,
    200, 201
Doctrinal Letter of the German Bishops
    117 ff., 123, 133 ff.
Dogma:
    Development of 29, 144, 155 f., 175 f.
    History of 33, 64, 65, 66
Dogmatic Constitution on the Church
    See *Lumen Gentium*
Donatist 86
Doubts concerning the Church 149 ff.
Dutch Catholics 98, 117 f.

Easter Duties 224 f.
Ecclesiology 13, 50, 52, 81 f., 85 f., 142,
    206, 218 ff., 223 ff., 228
Ecumenism 213 f.
Education:
    of children 55, 56, 76 f., 178
    of priests 56
Entelecheia 239
Episcopate 51, 65 f., 67, 72 f.
Error, doctrinal 133 ff.
Eschatology 9, 45, 50, 83, 86, 107, 182,
    184

Eucharist 32, 35, 36, 45, 48, 50, 62, 67, 209
ex cathedra 14 f.
Excommunication 104, 205
Existential interpretation 210
Explicit Christianity 177

Faith 7, 8, 26, 27, 28, 48, 51, 55, 56, 83, 119 f., 123, 130, 169, 204, 212
First Vatican Council 7, 14 n.
Force, justified use of 247 f.
Future 68, 181 ff., 202 ff., 213 f., 239 ff.
Futurology 59, 93, 181, 184 ff., 191

Gaudium et Spes 244, 245
Ghetto 208
Gospel 27, 36, 48, 49, 64, 168, 171, 174, 175, 176, 177, 202, 205, 209, 235 ff., 241
Groups within the Church 110 ff.

Heresy 99 f., 117, 205, 215 f.
Hermeneutics 213
Hierarchy:
of Order 49, 59, 62 ff., 65, 69, 71 f., 222, 242 f.
of truths 24
History 159, 163, 175, 188 f., 193 f., 196 f., 211 f., 233
Holiness, note of 81
Holy Office 167
Holy Spirit 20, 49, 77 f., 80, 86 f., 97, 141, 145, 166, 171

Incarnation 188, 212
Incomplete identification with the Church 112 ff.
Indefectibility 86
Individualism 122 f., 124, 127
'Individualization', the process of 222 ff.
Infallibility 9, 10, 11, 66
Infralapsarian 166, 175

Justification 176

Laity 7, 32 f., 44 f., 47, 52 ff., 65 ff., 69, 71, 85, 90, 165, 206 n., 218 ff.
'Little Flock' 203 ff.
Liturgy 62, 208
Local Church 57, 67, 96, 105 ff., 206, 209, 230 f.
Logos 175, 183, 188 f., 212

Lumen Gentium 5 n., 7, 11, 50, 61 n., 67 n., 84 n., 90, 218 f., 220

Magisterium 3 f., 119, 136 ff. See also Teaching Office
Man as *faber sui* 192 ff., 194, 202 f.
Mass society 222
Mater et Magistra 244
Matrimony 86
Mediation 33, 72
Membership of the Church 223 ff.
Missionary task 37, 161 ff., 168, 174 f., 209
Missions 55, 176
Modern man, condition of 121 f.
Molinist 170
Monophysitism 219
Montanism 84
Moral law 175
Mystici Corporis 84

National Church 54 ff., 56
Natural Law 186, 234
Nestorianism 82
New Testament 34, 43, 62 f., 67, 82 f., 166, 168, 177

Obedience to the Church 95 f., 101 f., 115, 157
Office, ecclesiastical 34, 36, 43, 46, 48 ff., 50, 52, 54 ff., 58, 61 ff., 66 f., 68, 70, 73, 75, 78, 83 f., 85, 101 f., 113, 118, 145, 207, 209 f., 242 f.
Order, sacramental 32, 34 f., 47 f., 51, 57, 58, 64 ff., 69 f., 86, 209
Original sin, 164, 175, 238
Orthodox Churches 99
Our Lady, devotion to 226

Papalism 89
Parents 55, 56, 125, 178
Parish 57, 227
Pastoral Constitution 230
Pastoral Epistles 63
Pastoral Office 21, 137
Pauline Doctrine 140, 171, 200
Penance, sacrament of 32, 46, 48, 49, 51, 173
Pentecost 168
Political Theology 181, 184 f., 229 ff.
Pope 7, 14 f., 16, 90 f., 98, 99 f., 117, 125, 214, 249
Populorum Progressio 244

Preaching 44, 47, 49, 56, 135, 137 ff., 169, 170, 171, 174, 188, 209
Presbyter 57, 209 f.
Priesthood 31 ff., 36, 39 ff., 61 ff., 67 f., 72 ff.
  as 'part-time' occupation 57 f., 64 f., 77
  as profession 41 ff., 46, 47, 52 ff., 64
  image of 39 ff.
  indelible character of 37
  leadership functions of 35
  subdivisions in 34, 52 f., 69 ff.
  teaching functions of 35
Prophet, prophecy 4, 40, 51, 243 f.
Protestant 3, 129, 215, 227, 230

Redemption 238
Relationship of the individual to the Church 142 ff.
Religious orders 222
Repentance, perfect and imperfect 172
Resurrection, the 6, 36, 50, 118, 136, 212
Revelation 175
Revolution, theology of 246 f.

Sacraments 32, 35, 48, 51, 58, 64 ff., 69, 78 f., 83, 171, 183, 205
Saving History 173
Scepticism 151 f.
Schism 98 ff.
Scholasticism 108
Science 157, 193
Second Vatican Council 4, 5, 8, 11, 14 f., 24, 36, 47, 49, 50, 61, 65, 69, 81, 84 f., 87, 90, 99, 105, 119 f., 123, 128, 136, 145, 165, 166, 176, 202, 216, 230 f., 244, 249
Secular Institutes 64
Sects 223
Self-bestowal, the divine 9, 10, 33, 35, 44, 141, 185, 188
Seminary theology 23, 47

Separated Churches, the 213 f.
Sermon on the Mount 248
Society:
  Church as critic of 229 ff., 253 ff.
  Changing aspects of 40, 41 f., 120 f., 144, 146 f.
Sociology 219 f., 224, 228, 230, 232
Specialization 58
Structure of the Church 24, 33, 37, 45, 49, 206, 218 ff.
Sunday Mass attendance 224
Synagogue 85, 173 f.

Teaching Office 3 ff., 35, 109
Theology 183
  biblical 43, 62 f., 88
  dogmatic 34, 35, 37, 39, 64, 170, 182
  fundamental 27
Thomism 169, 170, 172, 173
Transcendence and immanence 213
Translating the Church's message 210 f.

Universal will to save 175, 212 f.
Universal priesthood 45, 71
Unity of Church 106
Unity of the creed 114, 205
UNO 245
Ursakrament 172
Utopia 183, 187, 190, 198 f., 244

Vocation 52, 56, 162
Voting 15 f., 17 f.
Votum baptismi 166

Weltanschauung 213
Witness 52, 64, 87
Word of God 44, 49, 50, 51, 52, 53, 138, 174, 183
Worker Priest movement 227
World as secularized 44, 46, 52, 53 ff., 59, 64, 68, 74, 96, 119, 176, 202, 217, 233 ff.
World Council of Churches 230